RUTHERFORD COUNTY, TENNESSEE

BIBLE AND FAMILY RECORDS

With
TOMBSTONE INSCRIPTIONS
and
MISCELLANEOUS RECORDS

Originally Prepared By:

The Historical Records Project
Transcription Unit
Division of Women's and Professional Projects
Works Progress Administration (WPA)

With New Index Added

Nashville, Tennessee
1938

> *Notice*
>
> This book has been reproduced from carbon-copies of the original transcriptions of court records by the Works Progress Administration (WPA) in 1930s. In many instances, the resulting text is light, the documents are physically flawed, and foxing (or discoloration) occurs. The pages of this reprint have been digitally enhanced and, where possible, the flaws and markings eliminated in order to provide clarity of content and a pleasant reading experience.

Rutherford County, Tennessee, Bible and Family Records
With Tombstone Inscriptions and Miscellaneous Records

Originally transcribed by:
The Works Progress Administration (WPA)
1938

New Added Index
Copyright © 2005, Samuel Sistler

Reprinted by:

Janaway Publishing, Inc.
732 Kelsey Ct.
Santa Maria, CA 93454
(805) 925-1038
www.JanawayGenealogy.com

2006, 2012

ISBN: 978-1-59641-031-2

Made in the United States of America

TENNESSEE

RUTHERFORD COUNTY

BIBLE AND FAMILY RECORDS

TOMBSTONE INSCRIPTIONS

MISCELLANEOUS RECORDS

HISTORICAL RECORDS PROJECT
Official Project No. 465-44-3-115

COPIED UNDER WORKS PROGRESS ADMINISTRATION

MRS. JOHN TROTWOOD MOORE
STATE LIBRARIAN & ARCHIVIST SPONSOR

MRS. ELIZABETH D. COPPEDGE
DIRECTOR OF WOMEN'S & PROFESSIONAL PROJECTS

MRS. PENELOPE JOHNSON ALLEN
STATE SUPERVISOR

MISS MATILDA A. PORTER
DISTRICT SUPERVISOR

Copied
by

MISS ANNIE CAMPBELL
MISS MABEL DuBOIS
MRS. SADIE McLAURINE

RUTHERFORD COUNTY

BIBLE & FAMILY RECORDS

CONTENTS

Baird 1,2
Bass 3,6
Binford 7,8
Blanche 9
Buchanan 10,11
Butler 12,13

Campbell 14,15
Carlton 16,17
Carlton-Yeargan 18,19
Cimmons 20,21
Collier 22

Dement 23

Eagleton 24,25
Eagleton 26
Edwards 27,29
Elam 30

Fathera 31
Fergusson 32

Goodwin-Morton-Quayle 33,36

Haynes 37,38
Henderson 39
Hunt 40,41

Jackson 42

Locke 43,45
Lowe 46

McAdoo 47,48
McClanahan 49,51
McFadden 52
Meriwether 53
Mitchell 54,55
Moore 56,57

Murfree 58,59
  Brickle 60,62
  Murfree 63,64
  Dickinson 65
  Hair-Dickinson 66,67
  Maney-Baker 68,69

Newsom 70,71
Nugent 72,74

Patterson 75,76

Reeves-Shaw 77,78
Rucker 79

Searcy 80,81
Short 82,83
Sims 84,88
Spain 89,90

Travers 91
Trousdale 92
Tatum 93,94
Taylor 95,97

Walton 98,106
Ward 107,109
Williamson 110

v

RUTHERFORD COUNTY

MISCELLANEOUS RECORDS

Letters: Josiah Philips to David Philips, 1793-1799   pages 158,160

Civil War Records

Letter: Josiah G. Duke to Mrs. Rebecca Phillips (n.d.)   Page 162,163
Letters: O. R. Hight to Mary C. Hight, July 11, 1861   164,165
           O. R. Hight to Mary C. Hight, Aug. 16, 1861   166
           O. R. Hight to Mary C. Hight, Sept. 22, 1861   167
           O. R. Hight to Mary C. Hight, Jan. 18, 1862   168
           O. R. Hight to Mary C. Hight, Feb. 3, 1862   169
Letter: Gen. Joseph E. Johnston to James D. Markham, May 2, 1865,170,171
Murfree Collection: Page 172,187
           Preface
           W. B. Avent, Surg. Gen.C.S.A. to Dr. James B. Murfree, Aug. 1, 1861
           E. D. Hancock to Dr. James B. Murfree, Feb. 22, 1862
           Hardy Murfree to Dr. James B. Murfree, May 12, 1862
           Order for Leave - Dr. James B. Murfree, Aug. 1, 1862
           "L.P.Y." to Dr. James B. Murfree, May 5, 1863
           Diary of Dr. James B. Murfree, Sept. 7 - Oct. 13, 1863
           S. Moore, Surg. Gen. C.S.A. to Dr. James B. Murfree, Oct. 18, 1864
           Gen'l Robert E. Lee - General Order No. 9, April 10, 1865
           Wm. Morrow to Gen'l Stoneman, July 15, 1865
           Gen'l Morrow to Dr. James B. Murfree, July 28, 1865
Letter: Robert M. Rucker to Mrs. Samuel R. Rucker, Mar. 13, 1865,188,189
           Robert M. Rucker to Mrs. Samuel R. Rucker, April 4, 1865,191,192
Letters: R. H. Taylor to Nora Taylor, Preface   193
           R. H. Taylor to Nora Taylor, June 30, 1861   194
           R. H. Taylor to Nora Taylor, (n.d.)   195
           R. H. Taylor to Nora Taylor, (n.d.)   196

Burial place of Col. C. D. Venable   197,198

RUTHERFORD COUNTY

BAIRD BIBLE RECORD

Copied from the Baird family Bible, owned by Miss Kate Leatherman, 1027 East Main Street, Murfreesboro, Tennessee.
The Baird family came to Tennessee in 1805 from Lincoln County, North Carolina.
Copied by Miss Mabel B. DuBois, Murfreesboro, Tenn., March 6, 1938.

William Dinwiddie Baird & Abigal Martin were joined in Matrimony, Sept. 13th, 1803.

Lemuel P. Baird and Elener White Kirk Joined in Matrimony 9 Aug. 1833

Josiah M. Baird and Elizabeth Eliza Henderson joined in Matrimony October 29th, 1835

Mary R. Baird and John D. Alexander Joined in Matrimony 16th November 1837

William D. Baird Born 4th of March 1780

    Abigail Martin Born 28th of March 1784
    United in Matrimony 13th of September 1803

    Lemuel Moore Baird, Born 19th September 1804

    Fanny Henderson Baird Born 20th of March 1807

    James Pinkney Baird, Born 9th of August 1808

    Josiah Martin Baird, Born 5th of May 1811

    Mary Robeena Baird, Born 12th of January 1815

    William D. Franklin Baird, Born 7th of August 1821.

      Candaces Children

    Harriette Born Nov. 10th, 1821
    Lucinda & Eliza Born August 5th, 1824
    Levi Born Augt. 5th, 1827
    Anthony & Julia Born Oct. 20, 1829
    Mary, Born Augt. 5th, 1831
    Sarah, Born April 12th, 1833
    Matilda, Born July 1837

Fanny Henderson Baird departed this life 1807, 21st of March Aged 23 hours.

RUTHERFORD COUNTY

(Baird Bible Record p. 2)

William D. Franklin Baird
Departed this Life 1825, 18th
of March - aged 3 years 7 months
  "Suffer Little Children to Come
  unto Me for of such is the
  Kingdon of Heaven."
  "Those who sleep in Jesus will
  god living with him."

    Died on the 17th day of April
       Wm. D. Baird
       Aged 63 years
1 Month 13 Days 1843 Tuesday

Mary R. Alexander
Died Saturday the 26th of April 1851
Aged 35 years 3 months 11 days

Lemuel M. Baird
Died Tuesday the 7th of October 1851
Aged 47 years 18 Days

Abigal Baird
Died Monday 2 of April 1855
Aged 71 years & 4 days.

Jane A. Ward
Died the 27th July 1856
Aged 21 years $7\frac{1}{2}$ months.
J. P. Baird's Daughter.

Wm. D. Baird
Son of L. M. Baird
Died on Wednesday
21 of November 1860.

Josiah Martin Baird
Died 24 of December
1887 Aged 76 years 7 months 19 days
Saturday.

James Pinkny Baird
died on 17 of February 1900

Amanda Virginia Baird
Born Aug. 7, 1851

William Dinwiddie Baird Jr.,
Born May 24, 1854

Violet Henderson Baird
Born March 24, 1856

Chas. Beady Baird
Born July 25, 1858.

RUTHERFORD COUNTY

FAMILY RECORD OF BENJAMIN BASS

INDEX

A
Avant, Nancy, 2

B
Barfield, Road, 1
Bass, Ambrose, 1, 2
Bass Andrew, 1,2
Bass Ann, 1, 2
Bass Benjamin, 1
Bass, Ben Jordon, 1
Bass, Eliza, 1, 2
Bass, Frances, 1, 2
Bass, Fred, 1
Bass, George, 1
Bass, Hartwell, 1
Bass Hartwell Jordon 2
Bass Hartwell Polk, 2
Bass, Henry, 1
Bass, John James, 1, 2
Bass, Lida Howse, 2
Bass, Martha, 1
Bass, Martha Sarah Hix, 1
Bass, Mary, 1-2
Bass, Mary Ann 2
Bass, Mary Yeargan, 2
Bass, Nancy, 1
Bass, Nathan, 1
Bass, Robert, 1,2
Bass. Sarah, 1,2
Bass, Temperance Jordon, 1
Bass, Thomas, 1-2
Bass, William, 1-2
Bass, Wyatt, 1
Batey, Martha, 1
Batey, William, 1
Blackman, 1
Blackman, Alfred W. 2
"Bun" 2
Burge (Mr) 1

C
Chattanooga, 2
Christian, Sarah, 2
Coutney, (Miss) 1

D
Davis, Ralph, 2
Davis, Ralph (Jr) 2
Dicon, Malinda, 2

E
F
Franklin, Tenn. 1
Frost, Ruth, 2

G
Giles County, 1

H
Hix (Mr) 1
Hix, Martha Sarah, 1
Holmes, Chas. Wade 2
Holmes, Virginia, M. 2
Holmes. William, Mims, 2
Howse, Eliza Catherine Ann, 1
Hyde, H.B. 1
Hyde, Hartwell, Blount, 2

J
Jordon, Temperance, 1

L
Lannier, (Miss)
Laughland, Samuel, 1
Louisianna, 2

M
Mary, 2
McMinnville, 1
Miles, Lida, 2
Mississippi, 2
Murfreesboro Tenn. 1,2

N
Nashville 2

P
Pocahontas, 1

R

Ransom, Bob (P.C.M.D.) 2
Ransom, Dick (M.D.) 2
Ransom, J.J. (D.D.) 2
Ransom, Richard, P. (D.D.) 2
Richardson, Mary, 1
Rolph, John, 1
Rucker, Ben, 1
Rutherford County, 1

S
Sims, Charlotte Amelia, 2
Sims, Sarah Jane Meriwether, 2
Smart (Mr) 1
Smith, Frances, 1
Smith, Payton Randolph, 1
Smith, Tom, 1

T
Texas, 2
Thomas, William, 1
Thompson, Eva, 2

V
Virginia, 1

Y
Yeargan, Rebecca, 2

RUTHERFORD COUNTY

FAMILY RECORD OF
BENJAMIN BASS

Property of Mrs. H. B. Hyde, Murfreesboro, Tennessee, Rt. # 1, about 5 miles from Murfreesboro, on Barfield Road,(4 miles on Murfreesboro & Eagleville road, & turn to left on Barfield Road)

This record copied by Miss Annie Campbell, Murfreesboro, Tennessee.

Miss Coutney, a lineal descendant of John Rolph & Pocahontas, married a Mr. Hix. They had one daughter named Martha Sarah Hix.
Benjamin Bass married Martha Sarah Hix.
(Benjamin Bass' mother was a Miss Lannier)
Children of Benjamin Bass and Martha Sarah Hix Bass.

(1) John James Bass, born 1761-died 1826
(2) Fred Bass (2nd son) never married, lived to be 90 yrs. old, died in 1863.
(3) Ann Bass married William Batey and came to Tennessee in 1808.
(4) Eliza Bass married William Thomas of Franklin, Tenn.
(5) Nathan Bass married Martha Batey and moved to Giles County, Tenn.
(6) Martha Bass married a Mr. Burge.
(7) Wyatt, (8) Henry & (Benjamin Bass lived and died in Virginia.

John James Bass was a Revolutionary soldier. He was given a land patent of 2500 acres of land in Rutherford Co. Tennessee around Blackman. The old Bass cemetery where John James Bass was buried is situated on this grant. The D. A. R. unveiled & dedicated a monument to his memory Oct. 27, 1934.

John James Bass married Temperance Jordan.

THEIR CHILDREN.

(1) Ben Jordan Bass Married Frances Smith
(2) Nancy Bass married Payton Randolph Smith, and lived to be 100 years old.
(3) Temperance Jordan Bass married, 1st Tom Smith, 2nd, Ben Rucker.
(4) Mary Bass married 1st Samuel Laughland, 2nd Mr. Smart of McMinnville,
(5) James Bass married Eliza Catherine ann Howse.
(6) Hartwell Bass married Mary Richardson.

James Bass and Eliza Catherine Ann Howse had 13 children.
(1) William, (2) Thomas, (3) Mary, (4) James,(5) Robert, (6) Ambrose, (7) Frances, (8) George, (9) Andrew, (10) Eliza, (11) Sarah,(12) Hartwell, (13) Mary Anna.

(Family Record of Benjamin Bass Page-2)

    William Bass died-never married
    Thomas Bass married Nancy Avant
    Mary Bass never married
    James Bass married Sarah Christian
    Robert Bass married Malinda Dicon, of Miss.
    Ambrose Bass married Rebecca Yeargan
    Frances Bass married Richard P. Ransom
    D.D., (Father of J. J. Ransom D. D. of Nashville,
    Dick, M.D. of Texas and "Bob" P.C. M.D.
    George Bass never married killed in Civil War.
    Andrew Bass, never married, killed in Civil War.
    Eliza Bass, born April 20, 1840, died March 21, 1901
    Sarah Bass, born May 18, 1842, died April 17, 1894
    Hartwell Polk Bass, married Sisters, 1st Charlotte Amelia Sims,
    2nd Sarah Jane Meriwether Sims, (see note)
    Mary Ann Bass married Alfred W. Blachman, born April 17, 1846, died Oct. 17, 1915.

    The above record was copied from papers loaned me by cousin Lida Miles, gathered from old family Bibles and much research work.

                            (Signed) Mrs. Mary B. Hyde,
                                    Oct. 16, 1934

(Note) Hartwell Polk Bass was a confederate soldier.

    Hartwell Polk Bass & Sarah Jane Meriwether Sims, family.
First child and last child died when infants.
    Mary Yeargan Bass married Hartwell Blount Hyde
    Lida Howse Bass married Chas. Wade Holmes
    Hartwell Jordan Bass married Ruth Frost of Chattanooga.

Mary and "Bun" have no children, Lida and Charles had 3, 1st a girl who died, when a few hours old.
(2) William Mimms Holmes, married Eva Thompson of La.
(3) Virginia M. Holmes married Ralph Davis of Murfreesboro.
They have one child, Ralph, Jr.

                                      END

BIBLE - RECORDS

RUTHERFORD COUNTY

Record from the Binford Bible.
Present owner: Mrs. W. M. Draper.
Residence: 619 East Lytle St., Murfreesboro, Tenn.
Copied by Miss Annie Campbell, Murfreesboro, Tenn.
January 25, 1937.

MARRIAGES:
Joseph Binford and
Nancy Legrand
Were married,
Feb. 28, 1801.

BIRTHS:
Joseph Binford,
Born Dec. 15, 1775.

Nancy S. Legrand,
Born Oct. 17, 1783.

THEIR CHILDREN:
Elizabeth K. Binford,
Born Feb. 16, 1802.

Nancy F. Binford,
Born Oct. 9, 1803.

J. M. L. Binford,
Born May 2, 1805.

Maria W. Binford,
Born Nov. 1, 1806.

Susan S.C. Binford,
Born June 20, 1808.

Lucy B. Binford,
Born Dec. 2, 1809.

Thos. A. Binford,
Born July 29, 1811.

John P. Binford,
Born Jan. 25, 1814.

Jas. W. Binford,
Born Nov. 2, 1815.

Baker L. Binford,
Born Aug. 31, 1818.

James H.L. Binford,
Born Aug. 13, 1820.

Henry L.S. Binford,
Born Aug. 28, 1823.

Peter E.T. Binford,
Born July 25, 1825.

Sarah A.E. Binford,
Born May 12, 1828.

DEATHS:
Joseph Binford,
Died March 2, 1842.

Nancy S. Legrand,
Died June 13, 1844.

Elizabeth K. Binford,
Died June 13, 1826.

Nancy F. Binford,
Died Oct. 20, 1830.

Maria W. Binford,
Died April 8, 1822.

Susan S.C. Binford,
Died July 20, 1848.

Lucy B. Binford,
Died Oct. 22, 1840.

Thos. A. Binford,
Died Aug. 30, 1840.

(Binford Bible Record p.2.)

John P. Binford,
Died Aug. 5, 1847.

James H.L.Binford,
Died Aug. 5, 1852.

RUTHERFORD COUNTY

BLANCHE BIBLE RECORD

Blanche Family of Virginia from paper belonging to Miss Margaret J. Book, 226 Walnut St., Murfreesboro, Tennessee
Copied by Miss Annie E. Campbell, July 1, 1938

Rev. Ezekiel Blanche, born in Brunswick County, Va., June 10, 1757
Lieutenant Colonel in Revolutionary War
His wife, (2nd) Mildred Cook Blanche, born Jan. 22, 1777.

>Samuel White Blanche Born Feb. 18, 1785
>John Blanche born Jan. 20, 1789
>Polly Blanche, born Mar. 1, 1790
>Sally White Blanche, born Nov. 16, 1795
>Nancy Taylor Blanche, born Aug. 20, 1800
>Lucy K. Blanche, born Mar. 8, 1803
>Rebecca M. Blanche, born _____
>James B. Blanche, born Feb. 9, 1807
>Elizabeth A. Blanche, born Nov. 20, 1809
>Margaret H. Blanche, born Sept. 12, 1810
>William H. Blanche, born May 27, 1812
>Caroline M. Blanche, born Feb. 12, 1816
>Alfred E. Blanche, born July 6, 1819

Marriages

Ezekiel Blanche to Mildred Cook, Dec. 25, 1801
Polly B. Blanche to Wm. Waltrop   July 2, 1812
Lucy K. Blanche to John E. Dromgoole, Dec. 18, 1828
Rebecca M. Blanche to John E. Dromgoole, July, 1839
W. H. Blanche to Mary C. Rogers Oct. 8, 1834
E. A. Blanche to Emily Fitts Jan. 24, 1840
Caroline M. Blanche to Dr. Amos Jones, Feb. 24, 1848
Margaret H. Blanche to Stephen A. Jordan Nov. 18, 1847
(In Rutherford County, Tennessee)
Samuel Blanche to Rebecca Goodman, Apr. 7, 1807
Will Allen Dromgoole, Author and Journalist, was the youngest daughter of John E. Dromgoole and Rebecca M. (Blanche) Dromgoole.

Margaret Caroline Jordan, only child of Stephen Jordan and Margaret (Blanche) Jordan, married Adam Book of Murfreesboro, Tenn. Their children are

>Margaret Jordan Book
>George Book
>John Book
>   all of Murfreesboro, Tennessee and
>Estelle Book (Mrs. M. LaDelle Smith)
>Los Angeles, Calif.

RUTHERFORD COUNTY

BUCHANAN FAMILY RECORD

These records are from the "Buchanan Family Tree" owned by
Mrs. Paul H. Hartman of Manson Pike, Murfreesboro, whose late husband
was a direct descendant of this Buchanan family.
Copied by Mrs. Sadie McLaurine and Miss Mabel B. DuBois, March 5th, 1938.

John Buchanan I, married Jane Trindell Russell. To this union 6 children
were born, viz: James Buchanan, John Buchanan, Alexander Buchanan,
        Sarah Buchanan, who married James Todd &
        Nancy B. Buchanan, who married James Mulherin.

James Buchanan married Elizabeth Spear in 1788, to whom eleven children
were born, the 2nd child being James Buchanan, the 15th President of the
United States, born Apr. 23, 1791, and died June 1st 1888, at Wheatland, Pa.

John Buchanan II, was later known as Major John Buchanan of Tennessee,
was born Jan. 12, 1759 and died Nov. 9, 1832. He was married first to
Margaret Kennedy and to this union one child was born, John Buchanan III,
whose son, John P. Buchanan was Governor of Tennessee from 1891 to 1893.

John Buchanan II, was married the second time to Sarah Ridley, who was
born Nov. 24, 1774 and died Nov. 23, 1831. To this union thirteen children
were born, viz:

	Born	Died	Married
George Buchanan	Oct. 11, 1792	Jan. 22, 1816	Not married
Alexander "	Mar. 22, 1794	Apr. 8, 1836	Mary Ridley
Elizabeth "	Dec. 29, 1795	Apr. __ 1874	Thos. H. Everett
Samuel "	Aug. 27, 1797	Feb. 20, 1836	Not married
William "	Jan. 12, 1800	No date	Jane Hogan
Jane R. T. "	Mar. 23, 1802	May 6, 1837	George Goodwin
James B. "	Mar. 10, 1804	July 6, 1862	Letty Roberts
Moses R. "	Apr. 4, 1806	No date	Sally Ridley
Sarah V. "	Dec. 31, 1807	Apr. 10, 1866	James B. Williams
Charley B. "	Oct. 28, 1809	Apr. 13, 1836	Not married
Richard G. "	Nov. 3, 1811	No date	Martha Murphy
Henry R. "	Nov. 8, 1814	No date	Not married
Nancy Mulherin Buchanan	July 31, 1818	July 18, 1873	(1. Jackson Smith (2. Henry Bridges

Alexander Buchanan was born Mar. 22, 1794, died Apr. 8, 1836 married
Mary Ridley. To this union Eight Children were born, viz:

	Born	Died	Married
Sarah B. Buchanan	Jan. 31, 1820	July 29, 1845	A. B. Joyce
John R. "	Apr. 2, 1822	No date	M. E. Hays
Jane T. "	Oct. 31, 1824	July 29, 1843	Thos. W. Haynes
Mary Ann "	Sept. 1, 1826	No date	A. M. Green

RUTHERFORD COUNTY

(Buchanan Family Record   p. 2)

Children of Alexander Buchanan and Mary Ridley Buchanan (Continued)

	Born	Died	Married
Elizabeth Buchanan	Feb. 28, 1829	No date	C. T. Love
George A. "	Apr. 2, 1831	July 1, 1913	Margaret Patterson
Alexander B. "	May 8, 1833	No date	T. A. Buchanan
Henrietta M. "	Aug. 12, 1835	No date	Thos. A. Shiloutt

George A. Buchanan was born April 2, 1831, died July 1, 1913, Married Margaret Patterson Nov. 21, 1855. To this union nine children were born, viz:

	Born	Died	Married	Date
Ida B. Buchanan	Nov. 4, 1856	Jan. 20, 1911	Jno. B. Hartman	Dec. 4, 1878
Louella M. "	Dec. 6, 1859	Sept. 24, 1880	Wm. P. Hartman	" 19, 1877
William Y. "	Jan. 26, 1862	Jan. 29, 1862		
Mary James "	Jan. 8, 1863	Oct. 5, 1918	Frank P. Brumbach	Feb. 28, 1883
Richard G. "	Nov. 20, 1865	Oct. 12, 1923	Edw. M. Fergus	Dec. 24, 1899
Henrietta E. "	May 3, 1868	Living	Wm. E. Akin	Jan. 14, 1889
John D. "	Mar. 19, 1870	no date	Lena B. Owen	Oct. 2, 1902
Margaret O. "	June 3, 1872	Living	Joe P. Hall	
Katie McKay "	July 21, 1875	Dead	(Emmet Mullins	Aug. 21, 1896
			(Jno. B. Hartman	Aug. 8, 1912

John B. Hartman, and Ida B. Buchanan were married Dec. 4, 1878. To this union seven children were born, viz:

	Born	Died	Married	Date
Alonzo Bascom Hartman,	Oct. 2, 1879	Living	Mai Johnston	May 16, 1915
Mary E. Hartman	July 16, 1881	Died in Infancy		
Maggie Maud Hartman	Aug. 24, 1883	Mar. 18, 1920	B. B. Taylor	Jan. 15, 1908
Ida Blanche Hartman	May 26, 1886	Living	J. B. Phillips	May 16, 1917
Jno. Buchanan	May 2, 1888	Living	Missie Haynes	Dec. 28, 1910
Hallie B. Hartman	Aug. 25, 1891	Nov., 1935	W. B. Harding	Aug. 24, 1922
Paul Hays Hartman	Dec. 28, 1894	Apr. 26, 1937	Florence Parmon,	Jan. 14, 1920

Paul Hays Hartman and Florence Parmon were married Jan. 14, 1920. To this union four children were born, viz:

	Born	
Helen Margaret Hartman	Oct. 23, 1920	Living
Catherine Bateman Hartman	June 24, 1922	Living
Amelia Claire Hartman	Nov. 18, 1923	Living
Paul Hays Hartman,	Aug. 6, 1934	Living

RUTHERFORD COUNTY

Bible Record

Copied from a Bible owned by Mrs. John Leiper,
Residence 510 20th Avenue, North, Nashville, Tenn.
Copied by Annie Campbell Dec 1, 1936

BIRTHS

William Smith Butler,	March 26, 1798,	Granville County, N. C.
Nancy E. Campbell,	February 15, 1812,	Rutherford County, Tenn.
John Samuel Butler,	March 13, 1832,	" " "
Dennis S. Butler,	August 6, 1833,	" " "
William Reuben Butler,	September 22, 1834,	" " "
Warner Lewis Butler,	December 17, 1835,	" " "
Thomas Overton Butler,	May 6, 1837,	" " "
Josiah Edmonson Butler,	February 9, 1839,	" " "
Isaac Watson Butler,	February 7, 1841,	" " "
Ann Laura Butler,	January 15, 1843,	" " "
Lucy Katherine Butler,	May 14, 1845,	" " "
James K. P. Butler,	1847	" " "
Henry Warren Butler,	January 29, 1850	" " "
Solomon Satterwhite Butler,	July 1, 1852	" " "
Bettie Olivia Butler,	January 16, 1855	" " "

MARRIAGES

W. S. Butler and Nancy E. Campbell,	June 30, 1831
William R. Butler and Isadora Smith,	November 1, 1859
John S. Butler and Mary Ann Sims,	
Robert J. Turner and Ann L. Butler,	
Solomon Satterwhite and Lucy K. Butler,	December 7, 1870
Jas. M. Knight and Bettie O. Butler,	December 29, 1880

Butler Bible Record (Continued)
P.2.

DEATHS

Dennis S. Butler,	January,	1834
Warner L. Butler,	May 7,	1837
Josiah E. Butler,	November 6,	1866
Isaac W. Butler,	November 27,	1863
James K. P. Butler,	February,	1848
Henry W. Butler,	August 25,	1870
Wm. Reuben Butler,	November 15,	1883
William S. Butler,	January 30,	1873
Nancy E. Butler,	October 22,	1888

RUTHERFORD COUNTY

BIBLE RECORD

Copied from a Bible owned by Mr. John A. Campbell
Residence 310 North Maple Street, Murfreesboro, Tenn.
Copied by Annie Campbell Dec. 1, 1936

BIRTHS

Samuel Campbell, Sr.,   January 15, 1769   (Campbell Co. Va.)

Nancy Mann Campbell,   1778   (Georgia)

Their Children

Name	Date	Place
Archibald Campbell,	October 15, 1798	
Elisabeth M. Campbell,	July 5, 1800	
Mary M. Campbell,	September 3, 1802	
Virginia B. Campbell,	October 11, 1804	(Rutherford Co. Tenn.)
Camilla T. Campbell,	October 25, 1807	" " "
Josiah Campbell,	December 25, 1809	" " "
Nancy Campbell,	February 15, 1812	" " "
Samuel Campbell, Jr.	January 9, 1815	" " "
Martha Campbell,	July 15, 1818	" " "

DEATHS

Nancy Mann Campbell,	August 28, 1841
Samuel Campbell, Sen.,	September 7, 1846
Margaret Cora Campbell,	November 9, 1850
Samuel Campbell, Jun.,	April 28, 1875
Elvira H. Campbell,	January 6, 1878
David S. Campbell,	February 7, 1879
Virginia B. C. Gentry,	September 28, 1889

Campbell Bible Record (Continued)
P. 2.

MARRIAGES

Samuel Campbell, Jun. and Elvira H. Eagleton, August 7, 1844
    (By the Rev. William Eagleton)

BIRTHS

Samuel Campbell, Jun.	January 9, 1816 --
Elvira H. Campbell,	July 27, 1821

Their children

William Eagleton Campbell,	June 30, 1845
David S. Campbell,	March 25, 1847
Margaret Cora Campbell,	December 19, 1848
George Ewing Campbell,	September 22, 1851
John A. Campbell,	October 25, 1853

BIBLE - RECORDS

CARLTON BIBLE
RUTHERFORD COUNTY

Record from the Carlton Family Bible.
Present owner: Mrs. Minos B. Carlton, Rockvale, Tenn.
Residence: 9 miles S.W. of Murfreesboro, Tenn., on the Murfreesboro & Eagleville Pikes.
This Bible was formerly owned by Blake and Mary Walker Carlton.
The home place, occupied by Mrs. Minos B. Carlton is part of the original tract bought by the father of Blake Carlton, -from the U.S. Government.
Copied by Miss Annie Campbell, Murfreesboro, Tenn.
June 1, 1937.

Blake Carlton &
Mary Walker,
Was married Oct. 22nd, 1835.

William J. Carlton &
Sarah J. Spence,
Was married August 30th, 1860.

Robert M. Smotherman and
Margaret E. Carlton,
Was married December 20th, 1866.

William J. Carlton and
Nanie V. Williams,
Was married December 19th, 1866.

Robert L. Whitus and
Julia A.F. Carlton,
Was married Dec. the 11th, 1867.

J. M. Carlton, and
Lizzie Drumwright,
Were married Dec. 21, 1868.

J. N. Carlton, and
S.A.R. Patterson,
Was married December the 22nd, 1868.

M. B. Carlton and
Tabitha Nance,
Were married July 26, 1883.

BIRTHS:
Blake Carlton,
Was born Jan. 11th, 1814.

Mary Carlton, Wife of
Blake Carlton,
Was born March 17th, 1818.

William J. Carlton, Son of
Blake & Mary Carlton,
Was born Oct. 18th, 1837.

James M. Carlton, son of
the above,
Was born Sep. 28th, 1839.

John N. Carlton,
Son of the above,
Was born Sep. 23rd, 1841.

Julia Ann F. Carlton,
Daughter of the above,
Was born Jan. 17th, 1844.

Margaret E. Carlton,
Daughter of the above,
Was born April the 23rd, 1846.

Mary Jane Carlton,
Was born July 30th, 1848.

(Carlton Bible Record p.2.)

Martha M. Carlton,
Was born Oct. the 16th, 1850.

Thomas F. Carlton,
Was born March 7th, 1853.

Minus B. Carlton,
Was born May 5th, 1855.

James F. Carlton, Son of
William & Sarah J. Carlton,
Was born May the 29th, 1861.

Richard W. Carlton, Son of
J.M. & S.A.R. Carlton,
Was born December the 18th, 1869.

M. B. Carlton,
Was born May 5, 1855.

Tabitha E. (Nance) Carlton,
Was born March 21, 1864.

Children of M.B. & T.E. Carlton:

Leila Estelle Carlton,
Born May 18, 1884.

Beula May Carlton,
Born April 18, 1886.

Ira Ernest Carlton,
Born April 7, 1888.

Irvin Lee Carlton,
Born March 21, 1892.

Nannie Vera Carlton,
Born July 5, 1897.
M. B. Carlton, Jr.
Born Aug. 23, 1904.

Mary Walker Carlton,
Born Sept. 23, 1907.

Kirby Gordon Carlton,
Born March 10, 1911.

DEATHS:
Blake Carlton,
Departed this life,
On the 17th day of
August, 1856. Aged 42 years
and seven months, & 6 days.
(Killed by the first horse-
-power thresher ever brought
to the community.)

Martha M. Lofton,
Departed this life,
July the 5th, 1894.
Age 43 years, 8 months,
and 19 days.

Mrs. Mary Carlton,
Departed this life,
May the 27th, 1898.
Age 80 yrs. 2 mos. 10 days,

Children of M.M. Carlton & wife.

Lula Estella Carlton,
Died Dec. 14, 1909.

Kirby Gordon Carlton,
Died April 10, 1911.
Age one month.

Nannie Carlton,
Died July the 30, 1919.
Age 22 yrs. and 20 days.

Minos B. Carlton, Sr.
Died January 4, 1930.
Age 74 yrs. and 8 months.

BIBLE - RECORDS

CARLTON-YEARGAN
RUTHERFORD COUNTY

Record from the Carlton-Yeargan Family Bible.
Present owner: Mrs. C.E. Yeargan, Rockvale, Tenn., 10 miles South-West of Murfreesboro, Tenn., on the Murfreesboro and Eagleville Pikes, on Highway # 51.
This Bible was formerly owned by Mrs. Bettie Carlton, (Minerva Elizabeth Taylor Carlton), mother of Mrs. C.E. Yeargan.
Copied by Miss Annie Campbell, Murfreesboro, Tennessee.
June 1, 1937.

BIRTHS:
Francis Marion Carlton, Son of
Kinion & Hannah(Walker)Carlton,
Was born June 14th, 1851.

Minerva Elizabeth Taylor, Daughter
of Benjamin B. and Minerva Ann Taylor,
Was born Aug. 3rd, 1852.

David Walker Carlto, Son of
Francis & Bettie Carlton,
Was born Sept. 13, 1878.

Frank Elam Carlton, Son of
F.M. & Bettie Carlton, (Minerva
Elizabeth Taylor),
Was born March 24th, 1881.

Samuel Herbert Carlton, Son of
F.M. & Bettie Carlton,
Was born Feb'y 29th, 1888.

Robert Taylor Carlton, Son of
F.M. & Bettie Carlton,
Was born Feb'y 9th, 1890.

Mary Anna Carlton, Daughter of
F.M. & Bettie Carlton,
Was born March 29th, 1892.

MARRIAGES:
Francis Elam Carlton(son of
F.M.& Bettie Carlton), and
Cora Jackson, were married
Dec. 4, 1902.

Clinton Edwin Yeargan, and
Mary Annah Carlton,
Were married September 24, 1913.

BIRTHS:
Clinton Edwin Yeargan, son of
Robert Andrew and Hattie Glenn
Arnold Yeargan,
Was born Aug. 26, 1891.

Mary Annah Carlton, daughter of
Francis M. and Minerva Elizabeth
Carlton,
Was born March 29, 1892.

Frank Carlton, Son of
Clinton & Mary Annah Yeargan,
Was born May 20, 1915.

Mary Elizabeth, Daughter of
Clinton & Mary Yeargan,
Was born April 1, 1919.

(Carlton-Yeargan Bible p.2.)

DEATHS:
David Walker Carlton,
Departed this life,
Aug. the 15th, 1879.
Aged eleven months,
and two days.

Samuel Herbert Carlton,
Departed this life,
Sept. 15th, 1889.

Robert Taylor Carlton,
Departed this life,
June 24th, 1890.

Frank Elam Carlton,
Departed this life,
July 4th, 1903.

F. M. Carlton,
Departed this life,
Sept. 20, 1906.

Mrs. Bettie Carlton,
Departed this life,
Feb. 5, 1927.

BIBLE - RECORDS

RUTHERFORD COUNTY

Record from the Cimmons Bible.
Present owner: Mr. Tom Brown.
Residence: One mile North*East of Murfreesboro on Halls Hill
Pike, Murfreesboro, Tennessee.
Copied by Miss Mabel DuBois, Murfreesboro, Tennessee.
January 27, 1937.

MARRIAGES:
John White and His Wife,
Mary, Was married,
March 27, 1897.

Christen Clyne & his Wife,
Katherine, Was married,
March 15th, 1814.

Edward Cimmons and
Nellie Cimmons, Was married,
the twenty-seventh day of
April, 1811.

BIRTHS:
William Kimmons,
Was born In August 26th, 1831.

Robert Cimmons Nenier,
Was born August 20th, 1754.

Bartlet Yansey,
Was born May 13, 1829.

E. Samuel Cimmons,
Was born the 25th Day
November, 1829.

Margaret Clyne,
Was born June the 13th, 1814.

Mary Clyne,
Was born January 15th, 1817.

Edward Cimmons,
Was born in March, 1790.

Thomis Cimmons,
Was born the 22 Day
of desember, 1811.

Robert Cimmons,
Was born the 1 Day
of Desember 1819.

Peggy Burney,
Was born 18 Sept. 1823.

Jas. Haway,
Was born the 21 Day
September 1800.

Nancy Sackwell,
Was born the
20 of September 1805.

thomas Sackwell,
Was born the
15 of October 1808.

frankey Sackwell,
Was born the
7 of Appril 1810.

Elzebth Sackwell,
Was born the
9th of June 1811.

(Cimmons Bible p.2.)

Robert Sackwell,
Was born the
17 of November 1814.

Pruciller Sackwell,
Was born the
20 of January 1816.

Elizabeth Carman,
Was born the
27 of June 1805.

Polly Carman,
Was Bourn the
12 of April 1807.

Hanner Carman,
Was born the
15 of July 1809.

Lanny Carman,
Was born the
6 of June 1811.

William Carman,
Was born the
27 of May 1816.

Edward Cimmons,
Was born March 12, 1790.

Nancy Cimmons,
Was born November 1794.

DEATHS:
Elender Cimmons,
Depart this life
September the 27, day, 1842.

Jane Cimmons,
Departed this life,
November the forth Day, 1816.

Prissy Cimmons,
Depart this life,
August the Eight Day 1817.

Sally Cimmons and her Sister
Nancy, departed this life,
Augst. the fifteenth 1817.

Iby Cimmons,
Departed this life,
September the twelth day 1817

John Cimmons,
Departed this life,
December the 21 day, 1807.

RUTHERFORD COUNTY

COLLIER BIBLE RECORD

From a Bible owned by Misses Anna and Sophia McFadden,
226 N. Walnut St., Murfreesboro, Tenn.
Formerly the property of Mrs. Eliza L. McFadden Collier.
Copied by Miss Annie E. Campbell, Sept. 6, 1937.

James M. Collier was born on the 19th of October, 1818

E. L. Collier (Eliza L. McFadden Collier)
was born on the 22nd day of January 1822

James M. & E. L. Collier was married on the
6th November 1845

James M. & E. L. Collier's first (Child) was born on
the 25th day of July 1847 and died on
the 7th day of October, 1847

James M. & E. L. Collier's Second (Child) was born on
the 8th July, 1849 and died same day.

BIBLE - RECORDS

RUTHERFORD COUNTY

Record from the Dement Bible.
Present owner: Mrs. Ben Jordan.
Residence: 9 miles North-East of Murfreesboro, Tenn., near Lascassas, Tenn.
Copied by Miss Mabel DuBois, Murfreesboro, Tennessee.
January 7, 1937.

MARRIAGES:
Lucinda Dement married,
----, Martin, Mar. 4, 1819.

David Dement married,
Elizabeth Jordan,
March 11, 1858.

BIRTHS AND DEATHS:
Elizabeth Martin,
Died Sept. 22, 1884.

Obiadiah Martin,
Died Jan. 9, 1822.

Artie Sullivan,
Died Apr. 8, 1887.

John Sullivan,
Died Mar. 2, 1838.

Mary Martin,
Born July 18, 1831.
Died Feb. 4, 1864.

John Dement,
Born Aug. 17, 1824.
Died May 14, 1906.

David Dement,
Born June 22, 1822.
Died Aug. 8, 1907.

Abner Dement,
Born Dec. 18, 1848.
Died Sept. 10, 1878.

Sallie Baker,
Born Mar. 8, 1848.
Died June 21, 1929.

John Dement,
Born November 14, 1854.

Clemmie Hill,
Born December ---, 1853.

David Dement, Jr.
Born Dec. 1, 1855.
Died Dec. 10, 1930.

Sallie Elizabeth Barton,
Born Aug. 23, 1866.
Died Sept. 23, 1929.

RUTHERFORD COUNTY

BIBLE RECORDS

Copied from a Bible Record owned by Mrs. G. C. Terry
Residence 1001 Audubon Parkway, Louisville, Kentucky
Copied by Annis Campbell Dec 1, 1936

David Eagleton of Scotland had two daughters, Isabella and Jean; also two sons - John and David. The last named, David Eagleton, came to America before the Revolutionary War. He married and settled in Blount County, Tennessee.

BIRTHS

David Eagleton was born March 16, 1748, and died May 17, 1828. He had the following eight sons and two daughters:

Mary Eagleton	born	December 1, 1783
John Eagleton	"	October 20, 1785
Alexander Eagleton	"	February 2, 1788
David Eagleton	"	April 15, 1791 (died early)
James Eagleton	"	June 20, 1794
Rev. William Eagleton	"	March 25, 1796
Robert Eagleton	"	December 16, 1798
Margaret Eagleton	"	March 24, 1800 (Tarbet)
Rev. Elijah Eagleton	"	February 2, 1802 (died Mar. 18, 1838
David Eagleton	"	December 31, 1803

BIRTHS

Rev. Wm. Eagleton, D. D.	Born	March 25, 1796 (Blount County, Tenn.)			
His wife					
Margaret Ewing Eagleton	"	August 4, 1795	"	"	"
Their children					
Margaret Angeline Eagleton	"	January 27, 1817	"	"	"
Samuel Ewing Eagleton	"	December 30, 1819	"	"	"
Elvira Hamilton Eagleton	"	July 27, 1831	"	"	"
Isaac Anderson Eagleton	"	May 7, 1823	"	"	"
William Clark Eagleton	"	August 30, 1825	"	"	"

24

Eagleton Family Record (Continued)
P. 2.

Eliza McEwen Eagleton   Born   May 14, 1830   (Rutherford Co. Tenn.)
George Ewing Eagleton   "   December 31, 1831   "   "   "
John Alexander Eagleton   "   December 11, 1838   "   "   "

MARRIAGES

Rev. William Eagleton and Margaret Ewing	April 2, 1816
Margaret Angeline Eagleton & Dr. E. D. Wheeler	August 7, 1844
Elvira Hamilton Eagleton & Samuel Campbell	August 7, 1844
Eliza McEwen Eagleton & Dr. L. W. Knight	May 20, 1851
William Clark Eagleton & Mary A. Green	July 20, 1853
Rev. George Ewing Eagleton & Mary Ethlinda Foute	January 23, 1856
John A. Eagleton & Mollie Bethel	December 17, 1856
Dr. James M. Eagleton & Mary A. Potts	April 24, 1862

DEATHS

Isaan Anderson Eagleton Died	March 18, 1824
Mrs. Margaret Ewing Eagleton,	July 7, 1864
Rev. Wm. Eagleton, D. D.	March 28, 1866
Elvira Eagleton Campbell	January 7, 1878
Samuel Ewing Eagleton	August 16, 1886
John Alexander Eagleton	October 21, 1886
Margaret Angeline Eagleton	August 18, 1895
George Ewing Eagleton	April 12, 1899
William Clark Eagleton	April 30, 1899
James M. Eagleton, M. D.	January 1, 1905
Eliza McEwen Eagleton Knight	November 13, 1906

RUTHERFORD COUNTY

EAGLETON FAMILY RECORD

Family Record of John Alexander Eagleton, son of Rev. William Eagleton, D.D.
and Margaret Ewing Eagleton.
Owned by Elvie Eagleton (Mrs. C. T.) Mathews,
1802 Acklen Ave., Nashville, Tennessee
Copied by Miss Annie E. Campbell, Feb. 8, 1938

John Alexander Eagleton
    born Dec. 19, 1835, Murfreesboro, Tenn.,
    died Oct. 21, 1886
    Married to Mary Ann Judson Bethel,
    daughter of Rev. Hall Bethel and
    Elizabeth Buchanan Bethel
    Dec. 17, 1856
From this union were born the following children:
    Mollie & Johnnie Eagleton
    Born Oct. 2, 1857, died Oct. 3 & 4, 1857
    Margaret Elizabeth Eagleton
    Born Sept. 6, 1858
    William Lemuel Eagleton
    Born Nov. 7, 1860; died July 16, 1926
    Newton Walker Eagleton
    Born April 4, 1862; died May 20, 1865
    Angeline Avondale Eagleton
    Born March 19, 1865
    Adele Eagleton
    Born July 25, 1867; died Oct. 26, 1898
    George Eagleton
    Born Dec. 29, 1869; died Oct. 7, 1871
    Elvira Eagleton
    Born May 20, 1874
    Bethel and Samuel Eagleton
    Born May 28, 1877
        Sam died June 1, 1877
        Bethel died July 1896

Marriages

Margaret Elizabeth Eagleton married Samuel S. Henderson (Marshall Co.)
Jan. 15, 1879
Wm. L. Eagleton married Mattie Sanders, West Tennessee 1899
Angeline Avondale Eagleton married Thomas J. Arrington July 16, 1885
Adele Eagleton married Wm. Rufus New, Jany. 8, 1890
Elvie Eagleton married Cephas T. Mathews, Jan. 20, 1898.

RUTHERFORD COUNTY

EDWARDS FAMILY RECORD

This record is owned by Miss Kathryn Quayle,
209 West Grundy St., Tullahoma, Tennessee
Copied by Mrs. Sadie McLaurine, September 1938

Will of Owen Edwards, dated Nov. 15, 1820,
County Court Clerk's Office, Murfreesboro, Tenn.

Name of great-grandfather, Owen Edwards, born about 1744, died about 1820.
Name of great-grandmother, Judith Morton, born _____, died _____.
They were married at Martinsville, Va., October 29, 1794.

	Their Children	Born	To Whom Married
(1)	Catherine W.,	Nov. 17, 1796	Thomas Lofton
(2)	Arthur M.,	Dec. 21, 1797	Nancy Harwell
(3)	Nancy T.,	Nov. 14, 1799	_____ Nelson
(4)	James A.	Dec. 25, 1801,	Susan Ann Goodwin

(My grandfather)

Their Children:	Born	Died
Jane M.,	Nov. 3, 1838	Mar. 30, 1846
George Marr,	Mar. 29, 1840	1866
Sallie Hickman,	Nov. 29, 1841	Dec. 27, 1874
Susan Marr,	Dec. 26, 1845	Mar. 1846

	Children	Born	Married
(5)	Capt. Wm. C.	Sept. 2nd, 1804	Susanna Perkin Marr
(6)	Sarah M.,	Nov. 25, 1806	_____ King
(7)	Judith W.,	Feb. 25, 1808	_____ Laurance
(8)	Owen H.,	Nov. 19, 1813	Miss Gray
(9)	Louisa W.,	Feb. 15, 1816	_____ Murphy

Name of grand-father James A. Edwards, born Dec. 25, 1801; died about 1875.
Name of grand-mother Susan Ann Goodwin, born Nov. 1, 1803; died about 1867.
They were married January 4, 1825

	Their Children:	Born & Died	To Whom Married
(1)	Amanda C.	(Oct. 16, 1828 (Apl. 23, 1900	Jacob J. Morton 1st Jan. 28, 1846, who died Jan. 15, 1863 Thos. B. Quayle 2nd May 10, 1866, who died Mar. 19, 1876
(2)	Judith M.,	Oct. 18, 1831	Never married.
(3)	Nancy T.,	(Apr. 2, 1834 (Mar. 16, 1901	W. C. Morgan

Their Children:
(Continued)

27

RUTHERFORD COUNTY

(Edwards Family Record p. 2)

Children of Nancy T. Edwards and W. C. Morgan:

    (a)   W. S. Morgan, 8 yrs. Sec'y. State, Tenn., Mar. Fannie Bonner, Fayetteville, Tenn.
    (b)   Blanch, Married G. E. Blake, Nashville, Tenn.
                (Morgan
           Children (Gladys
    (c)   Susan, Mar. W. H. Eaves, Louisville, Ky.
           Children: William & Robert
    (d)   Alex. F., No record
    (e)   Thos. C., No record
    (f)   Arthur L., No record

(4) George W., Edwards   Born & Died   To Whom Married
    Capt. in Civil War   (May 28, 1837   Ann Norvel, Sept. 8, 1858
    Gen. Forest Cav.   (July 17, 1864   (Norvell)

Their Children:

    (a)   Susan, born Oct. 29, 1859 (3 children)
           Mar. Dec. 1878, Jas. E. Horton, Dyersburg, Tenn.
    (b)   Jane, born Aug. 10, 1863 (2 children)
           Mar. Dec. 28, 1887, E. W. Fuller.

                Born   To Whom Married
(5) Jas. K. Polk Edwards   Aug. 4, 1839   Bettie Warren on Dec. 1, 1870
                                           (8 Children)
(6) Arthur Owen   "
    (Capt. of Co. A. 37 Reg.) Oct. 3,1841   Bettie Pryor on Jan. 18, 1915
    Civil War
    Their Children:
        (a)   George, Married Cora Custer
        (b)   Anna, Married Rev. D. M. Stoddard
        (c)   Ed. D. Married Mamie Goetz Hodshire
        (d)   Susie, Mar. Dr. F. E. Walker, Dec. 26, 1900, Lonewolf, Oklahoma.
        (e)   Owen died Nov. 11, 1918.

Date, May 10, 1866.
Name of Father, Thos. B. Quayle, born May 18, 1834- d. Mar. 19, 1876
2nd Mar'ge - Name of Mother, Amanda C. Edwards (Morton) born Oct. 16, 1828,
d. Apr. 23, 1900.
Children of second Marriage ;
                (Born Oct. 13, 1867
        Thos. M., (Died Aug. 18, 1916 Married Maggie May Johnston,
                (Dec. 25, 1903.
                    One son, Thos. Johnston, born Oct. 5, 1904.
        Kathryn,   born Mar. 23, 1870

First Marriage of Amanda C. Edwards was to Jacob J. Morton, Jan. 28, 1846,
who died Jan. 15, 1863.

RUTHERFORD COUNTY

(Edwards Family Record p. 3)

Children of first Marriage:
    Susanna Edwards, b. May 24, 1847, d. July 10, 1864
    Margaret Ann,   b. Sept. 1, 1849, d. Jan. 11, 1854
    Oliver Thomas,   b. Mar. 7, 1853, d. Jan. 18, 1854
    Nancy Elizabeth (Bettie) b. Dec. 22, 1854, d. Aug. 30, 1911
        (See Marriage below)
    William Jacob, b. June 12, 1858, d. Dec. 12, 1918, never married.
    George Arthur, b. Apr. 19, 1861, d. May 1922   "   "

    Nancy Elizabeth Morton was married to Geo. E. Campbell, Oct. 27, 1875 at Tullahoma, Tenn.
        Children of this Marriage - 2
          (1) Alice Elizabeth, b. Oct. 21, 1880,
            Married Oct. 31, 1918 to Rev. J. Hubert Noland.
              Children: Alice Louise, b. Sep. 7, 1919, d. June 4/22
                    James Hubert, b. Oct. 23, 1922.
          (2) H. Curry, born July 19, 1894, Capt. 64th U. S. Infantry, World War.

James A. Edwards, my grandfather
Owen Edwards, my great, grandfather
Arthur Edwards, my great, great grandfather, once lived in Stanton Va. during Rev. War 1786.
John Edwards, my great, great, great grandfather.
Thomas Edwards, my great, great, great, great grandfather 1690.

Owen Edwards and Judith Morton, my great grandparents came to Rutherford County, Tennessee, in 1797.

Norvel (Norvell) ancestors, Welsh descent.
Prince of Wales and his mother a near relative of Elder Adams, and was also closely connected with the Buchanan family, pioneer settlers of the Cumberland region.

Great grandfather, Owen Edwards, one of seven men appointed by the Legislature to select the site for Murfreesboro.

                  Written by Kathryn Quayle,
                  Tullahoma, Tenn. Sept. 1928.

RUTHERFORD COUNTY

ELAM FAMILY RECORD

Taken from an old fragment relating to the
Elam family, owned by Annie E. Campbell,
226 N. Walnut St., Murfreesboro, Tennessee
Copied by Miss Annie E. Campbell, July 5, 1937

1. Edward Elam,   born Jan. 20, 1769
                 died Feb. 15, 1830

2. Jane Elam (Wife of Edward Elam)

                 born July 29, 1772
                 died March 7, 1846

3. Daniel Elam, Born March 21, 1809
                 died December 22, 1829

BIBLE - RECORDS

RUTHERFORD COUNTY

Record from the Fathera Bible.
Owned by Mrs. Emma Reeves, 207 McKnight Drive, Murfreesboro, Tennessee, 1 mile North of Murfreesboro.
Copied by Miss Mabel DuBois, Murfreesboro, Tennessee.
Feb. 8, 1937.

MARRIAGES:
James C. Fathera,
Was married to
Matilda Pace,
September 2nd, 1830.

BIRTHS:
Ebenezer Bester Fathera,
Was borned June 22nd, 1831.

John Randolph Fathera,
Was borned Feb'y 10th, 1833.

Mary Fathera,
Was borned April 5, 1834.

James Willson Fathera,
Was borned May 4th, 1835.

Martha Fathera,
Was borned November 5, 1838.

William Landrom Fathera,
Was borned Novem. 3rd, 1845.

DEATHS:
James Willson Fathera,
Departed this life,
July 8, 1837.

James C. Fathera,
Departed this life,
April 29th, 1858.
Aged 59 yrs. 11 days.

Matilda Fathera,
Departed this Life,
July 19th, 1877.
Age 67 yrs. 10 mo.

E. B. Fathera,
Departed this life,
March 24, 1907.
Age 75 years, 9 mo.

RUTHERFORD COUNTY

FERGUSSON FAMILY RECORD

Family Record of Fergusson Family owned by Miss Nina Fergusson,
Hayesboro Avenue, Nashville, Tenn.
Copied by Miss Annie E. Campbell, August 26, 1938

Duncan Fergusson, of Dalmally, Glen Orchy, Co., Argyll, Scotland,
settled in North Carolina, U.S.A., in 1793. Born 1767; married Isabella McNabb
of Argyll, Scotland, 1793; died 1808.

Adam Fergusson, of North Carolina (son of Duncan Fergusson), born 1796;
married Hester Ann Hazard, daughter of Lot Hazard, of Carthage, Tenn.;
died 1862.
                      of Tenn.
William Wallace Fergusson/son of Adam Fergusson; born 1831;
married Medora Catherine Kerby, daughter of Frank Kerby; died 1922

Their Children

1. Sterling Price Fergusson, Boston, Mass., born Nov. 8, 1868
2. Willard Hampden Fergusson, (West Palm Beach, Fla.,) born 1872.
3. Gen. Frank Kerby Fergusson, (U.S.Army) born 1874; died 1937
4. Ruskin Fergusson, (San Francisco, Calif.), born 1876.
5. Marina Carita Fergusson, Nashville, Tenn; born 1877
6. Nina Minora Fergusson, Nashville, Tenn; born 1881
7. Linton Stephens Fergusson, Hendersonbille, Tenn.; born 1883
8. Charles Marshall Fergusson, (Washington, D. C.); born 1887.

Marriages

Sterling Price Fergusson married Carrie Milton Tucker Sept. 5, 1903
Willard Hampden Fergusson married Betty Temple in 1900
Gen. Frank Kerby Fergusson married Ocie Hardesty Shepherd, 1922
Ruskin Fergusson married Ida Hughes Adams in 1934
Marina Carita Fergusson married A. J. McGaughey in 1902
Linton Stephens Fergusson married Tabitha Dixie Martin in 1916
Charles Marshall Fergusson married Sadie Davis in 1915.

RUTHERFORD COUNTY

GOODWIN, MORTON, QUAYLE FAMILY RECORD

This record is the property of Miss Kathryn Quayle,
209 West Grundy St., Tullahoma, Tenn.
Copied by Mrs. Sadie McLaurine, Sept. 26th, 1938.

A. D. 1633. - From the Pedigree in the Historical Society in the Visitation of London publication.

The first known Henry Goodwin of Buckinghamshire, England, who had one son, Robert Goodwin, who married Jane Dollin, daughter of Anthony Dollin, of Hainault, Flanders.
They had one son, Peter Goodwin, Senr., who married Sarah Hilliard or Highlord, daughter of John Hilliard, of London, Eng.
(Peter Goodwin's Will was dated and was administered by his son James of Virginia).
They had 8 children, as follows:

  1st. Gertrude, married John Piggott, 2nd - Abbott.
  2nd. Suzanna,   "   ___ Stone,
  3rd. Elizabeth, "   John Osborne
  4th. Sarah,   "   Wm. Elwood
  5th. John, died early   No record
  6th. Mathew, died early, No record
  7th. Peter, Jr. "   "   "   "
  8th. James, married   1st Rachel Porter, 2nd - Blanche Porry (?).

(James Goodwin, 8th child settled in Virginia, in 1650, House of Burgeoses in 1658)
James and Rachel Goodwin had 7 children.

  1st. Robert, married Anne ___ York, Co. Va.
  2nd. John,   "   Elizabeth Moore
  3rd. Peter, 3rd "   Rebecca Tiplady
  4th. Mathew, no record.
  5th. Morton, married Barbara ___
  6th. Susanna,   No record
  7th. Elizabeth, married ___ Blinkhorn

Robert & Anne Goodwin had 3 children.

  1st. Martha
  2nd. Robert
  3rd. John, married Mary Elliott, Apr. 22, 1703

John and Mary Goodwin had 2 children.

  1st. George, married 1st, Jane Hazlewood, 2nd, E. Warrick.
  2nd. John, married Jane ___

RUTHERFORD COUNTY

(Goodwin, Morton, Quayle Family Record p. 2)

John & Jane Goodwin had 9 Children,
but it is unnecessary to name all of them
as you are only interested in
George, 7th child, our great grandfather,
in common and your progenitor,
who married 1st, Polly Clark, who was my
great grandmother, and 2nd, Sarah Barrham,
who was your great grandmother.
(Here is where separation begins in the line,
as to our forebears)

George & Polly Goodwin had 9 children:

1st. Nancy Alden, married John Smith in Davidson County.
2nd. John Lamb, married Nancy Greer in Davidson County.
3rd. Sarah Webb, married James Thompson, Davidson Co.
4th. Polly Clark, unmarried, tradition is, killed by Indians.
5th. Tabitha, married Isaac Greer
6th. Levina, " Abner McGaughey, Alabama
7th. Wm. W. Goodwin, married Anne Blackman, Davidson Co.
 (They were my grandparents & lived in Nashville.)
8th. George Goodwin, Jr., married Jane Tindell Buchanan.
9th. Jesse Goodwin, must have died young, no record.

George Goodwin & Sarah Barrham had 2 children, as far as is known:
(Sarah Barrham was the granddaughter of Sir Francis Barrham, of England)
viz:

Sarah Jane, Born Aug. 10, 1807
Susan Ann, Born Nov. 1, 1803.

Sara Jane married Jas. Cloud, on Dec. 20th 1820
(I have no record of this branch beyond the above statement
and have never been able to get any.)

Susan Ann married Jas. A. Edwards on Jan. 4, 1825.

Their Children:

1st. Amanda C.
2nd. Judith M. (no record)
3rd. Nancy T., married Wm. C. Morgan
4th. George W., married Ann Norvell
5th. Jas. K. P., married Betty Warren
6th. Arthur Owen, married Betty Pryer.

My record says:
Amanda married 1st, Jacob Morton, Jan. 28, 1846
 "   "   2nd, Thos. B. Quayle, May 10, 1866.
 "   "   3rd, A. B. Knott

RUTHERFORD COUNTY

(Goodwin, Morton, Quayle Family Record p. 3)

Amanda & Jacob Morton had the following children:

    1st. Susanna E. Morton, Born May 24-47, Died July 10th-64
    2nd. Margaret A. Morton, Born Sept. 1-49, Died Jan. 11-54.
    3rd. Oliver T. Morton,   "   Mch. 7-53, "   Jan. 18-54.
    4th. Nancy E. Morton,   "   Dec. 22-54,
        Married G. E. Campbell
    5th. Wm. Jacob Morton, Born June 12-58, no further record.
    6th. George A. Morton,   "   Apl. 19-61, "   "   "

Amanda & Thomas B. Quayle had the following children:

    7th. Thos. M. Quayle, Born Oct. 13-67,
        Married Maggie Johnson, Dec. 25th 1903,
        She died Oct. 25, 1904, leaving
        one child, Thos. Johnson Quayle,
        Born Oct. 24th, 1904.
    8th. Judith Kathryn Quayle, Born Mr. 23, 1870
        (No further record.)

Wm. C. Morgan & Nancy Edwards, had the following children:

    Alex F. Morgan, no record.
    Thomas C. Morgan, no record.
    Susan Morgan, Married Wm. H. Eaves
      2 children, Wm. & Robert
    Arthur Morgan, no record.
    Wm. S. Morgan, Married Miss Bonner, no further record.
    Blanche Morgan, Married George E. Blake
      1 Son, Wm. M. Blake
      1 Daughter, Gladys Blake

George W. Edwards & Ann Norvell had 2 children -

Susan Ann, 1879,	Jennie, 1864
Married Jas. E. Horton	Married
children	1st. Robt. E. Horton
1. Ann M. Oct. 10 - 80	2nd. E. W. Fuller
2. Blanche M. Aug. 27 - 83	children Horton
3. J. E., Mch. 3 - 99	1. Robrt. E. Mch. 20-83
	2. Georgia Horton
	Sept. 22-84
	3. Elizabeth Horton
	Dec. 88
	4. Elline Fuller,
	Aug. 10, 90
	5. E.W. Fuller, Jr.

RUTHERFORD COUNTY

(Goodwin, Morton, Quayle Family Record p. 4)

(Written to Miss Kathryn Quayle and answered by her)

NOTE: Was Jacob Morton any relation to John W. Morton's father?
Yes, cousin and also cousin to my mother.

           K. Quayle.

Who was Dr. John W. Morton? Dr. Morton married my father's 1st cousin, who was Sara Goodwin. Sarah Goodwin was my grand mother's niece.

           K. Quayle.

The following information was added by Miss Kathryn Quayle of Tullahoma, Tennessee, daughter of Thomas B. Quayle.-

> Thomas B. Quayle was born in Peel, Isle of Man, England, May 18, 1834, also lived in Douglass, Eng.
> Died, Mar. 19, 1876 in Tullahoma, Tenn.
> Married Mrs. Amanda C. Morton, May 10, 1866, Tullahoma, Tenn.
> Came to U. S. 1858, United with the Christian Church 1859, LaPort, Ind.
> Was the first Postmaster at Lavergne, Tenn. & Merchant.
> Elected Magistrate 1875, died before time was out.
> Was a member 9th Indiana Regiment in War Between States, in Commissary Dept. Stationed at Tullahoma during war, and boarded along with other soldiers, with Mrs. Morton.

RUTHERFORD COUNTY

HAYNES BIBLE RECORD

From Family Bible owned by Misses Anna and Sophia McFadden,
226 N. Walnut St., Murfreesboro, Tenn.
This Bible was the property of Mrs. Italla McFadden (Murfreesboro)
who inherited it from her father, Ivy J. C. Haynes of Murfreesboro, Tenn.
Copied by Miss Annie E. Campbell, September 6, 1937.

Marriages

Jeremiah Fletcher was married to
Frances Clay, on the 17th of Feby. 1803.

Ivy J. C. Haynes was married to
Elvira Ann Haynes on the 4th of April, 1839.

I. J. C. Haynes was married to
Julia A. Warren, April 25, 1860

Elvira F. Haynes was married to
J. W. Sage on 25 day of December 1865

M. I. Haynes was married to G. S. McFadden on
5th day of February 1874

Lucy Lorena Haynes was married to
G. C. Batey on 27th day of March, 1876

I. J. C. Haynes was married to
M. J. Suttle Oct. 8, 1878

W. R. Haynes was married to
Sophia Reeves Oct. 16, 1878

Births

Nancy White Fletcher was born on the first of December, 1803
Ivy J. C. Haynes was born on the 19th of June in the year 1816
Elvira Ann Haynes was born on the 26th of May in the year 1820
William Rufus Haynes was born on the 11th of Feb. 1840.
Loretta White Haynes was born on the 3rd November, 1842
Elvira Frances Haynes, on the 22nd July 1845
Mary Itilla Haynes, on the 27th March, 1848
Ann Trabue Haynes, on the 16th July 1851
Lucy Lorena Haynes was born on the 16th of March 1854
Martha Allas Haynes was born on the 11th of July, 1858
Ivy W. Haynes was born May the 12th Anno Domini, 1861
Bill Haynes (col. slave) was born on the 11th of June, 1837

RUTHERFORD COUNTY

(Haynes Bible Record   p. 2)

Deaths

Loretta White, Haynes, departed this life
26th of January 1850

Ann Trabue Haynes, 25th July, 1852

E. A. Haynes, 27th of August in the year 1858.

Martha Alice Haynes departed this life
Jan'y 19, 1873 about 1 oclock noon

I. W. Haynes departed this life May 21st 1861

I. J. C. Haynes departed this life Nov. 30th 1887

Nancy White Fletcher departed this life on the
25th of May in the year 1863.

BIBLE - RECORDS

RUTHERFORD COUNTY

Record from the Henderson Bible.
Present owner: Mrs. W. M. Draper.
Residence: 619 East Lytle St. Murfreesboro, Tenn.
Copied by Miss Annie Campbell, Murfreesboro, Tenn.
January 25, 1937.

Logan Henderson,
Was born April 3, 1785.
Lincolnton, N.C.

Margaret E. Johnston,
Born February 27, 1789.
North Carlina. Married
June 5th, 1807.

THEIR CHILDREN:
Violet Henderson,
Born June 18, 1809.

James F. Henderson,
Born May 4, 1811.

Jane E. Henderson,
Born July 19, 1813.

DEATHS:
Logan Henderson,
Died Tuesday, Dec. 8, 1846.

Margaret Enoch Henderson,
Died August 13, 1863.

Amanda H. Voorhies,
Born Feb. 10, 1817.

James F. Henderson, Married
Amanda H. Voorhies,
Dec. 20, 1832.

THEIR CHILDREN:
Margaret J. Henderson,
Born Dec. 30, 1834.
Died March 14, 1839.

Eugene Henderson,
Born Nov. 8, 1837.

Dewitt Henderson,
Born May 28th, 1840.
Died Aug. 10, 1860.

BIBLE - RECORDS

RUTHERFORD COUNTY

Record from the Hunt Bible.
Present owner: Mrs. Jarman Edwards,(Hallie Hunt.)
Residence: 740 N. Spring St., Murfreesboro, Tenn.
Copied by Miss Annie Campbell, Murfreesboro, Tenn.
January 14, 1937.

Jeremiah Hunt,
Was born in Rutherford
County, Tenn.
November 8, 1803.

Sallie S.(Taylor)Hunt,
Was born October 17, 1811.

Jeremiah Hunt and Sallie
Taylor, were married,
January 13, 1829.

Martha Ann Burgis Hunt,
Was born January 28, 1830.

John P. Hunt,
Was born July 24, 1831.

Nancy G. Hunt,
Was born November 3, 1833.

Mary Susan Hunt,
Was born November 28, 1835.

Eliza F. Hunt,
Was born June 25, 1838.

Sarah Elizabeth Hunt,
Was born September 17, 1840.

Simeon Hunt,
Was born December 4, 1844.

Samuel G. Hunt,
Was born March 11, 1845.

James W. Hunt,
Was born February 15, 1847.

Benjamin M. Hunt,
Was born August 24, 1849.

Thomas J. Hunt,
Was born May 1, 1852.

William J. Hunt,
Was born January 26, 1854.

James W. Hunt and Mattie
C. Stockird, were married,
February 8, 1877.

(Hunt Bible Record p.2.)

Lucy B. and James E. Stockird's Children:

Francis J. Stockird,
Born January 25, 1843.

William F. Stockird,
Born November 19, 1845.

Mary Ann Stockird,
Born June 7, 1847.

Martha C. Stockird,
Born May 1, 1849.

James E. Stockird,
Born June 7, 1851.

Elvira A. Stockird,
Born October 10, 1853.

Nancy F. Stockird,
Born -----, 1855.

Thomas A. Stockird,
Born April 27, 1859.

James E. Stockird,
Was born September 9, 1817.

Lucy B. Stockird,
Was born November 19, 1818,
And were united in marriage,
February 17, 1842.

RUTHERFORD COUNTY

Bible Records

Copied from a Bible owned by Mrs. Anna George Jackson,
Residence Rockvale, Tenn., 1 mile on Versailles Pike
Copied by Annie Campbell Dec. 1, 1934

Francis Jackson I, born in Prince Edward County, Virginia
                                          January 12, 1766
        died at Versailles, Tennessee
                                          February 10, 1845

Married Elizabeth W. Jackson, born in Prince Edward County, Va.,
                                        April 7, 1766
Who died at Versailles, Tennessee,   August 9, 1831

Francis Jackson II, born at Versailles, Tennessee
                                        January 31, 1804
        Died at Versailles, March 1,   1878

Married Elizabeth Hale, who was born July 12, 1809
                            died January 4, 1888

Francis Jackson III, born at Versailles, Tennessee
                                March 28, 1838
              died at Versailles, April 25, 1901

Married (first) Sue A. Covington, who was born March 12, 1841
                                    died May 23,   1877

Married also Rachel Anna George, who was born June 9, 1859
and still survives

RUTHERFORD COUNTY

LOCKE FAMILY RECORD

Owned by Mrs. A. H. McLean, 416 E. Main St., Murfreesboro, Tennessee, whose grandmother was Polly Locke. This family lived at Locke, now known as Carlockville, Tenn.
John Richardson Love, spoken of in this record, was the father of Mrs. McLean.
Copied by Mrs. Sadie McLaurine, December 8th, 1938.

Family Record of Charles & Polly Locke

Elizabeth Locke was born April 2nd, 1791
Susan Locke was born June 29th, 1793
Thomas Batte Locke was born May 25th, 1795
John West Locke was born Dec. 24th, 1796
Judith Mayse Locke was born April 16, 1798
Joseph Locke was born Feb. 16th, 1801
Mary Gilliam Locke was born Apr. 28, 1803
Charles Coppage Locke was born Oct. 16, 1806
Patsey Jones Locke was born Oct. 17, 1808
Gardner Batte Locke was born Aug. 27, 1810
Nancy Berchet Locke was born May 14, 1812

Marriages

Charles Locke & Polly Batt was married July 15th, 1790

The Marriages of their children

Lancaster Glover & Betsy Locke was married Dec. 24, 1807
Clement Cannon & Susan Locke was married Aug. 18, 1810
John West Locke & Eliza Clark was married March 4, 1818
Samuel George Gardner & Mary Gillum Locke was married on Jan. 7th, 1819
Thomas McGowan & Patsy Jones Locke was married Nov. 4, 1824
Joseph Locke & Gilly Moore was married November 24, 1819
Harper H. McGowan & Nancy Berchet Locke was married Nov. 27th, 1828
Gardnier Batte Locke & Mary Jane Prescott was married July 19th, 1836

Deaths of This Family

Thomas Batte Locke died Ap. 1st, 1815
Judith Mayse Locke died Oct. 3rd, 1815
Charles Locke died Nov. 20th, 1849
Polly Locke died Sept. 6th, 1852
Joseph Locke died March 20th, 1854

RUTHERFORD COUNTY

(Locke Family Record p. 2)

Family Record of Samuel G. Gardiner & Mary G. Locke.

Samuel G. Gardiner was born March 4th 1797
Mary G. Locke was born April 28th 1803
Samuel G. Gardiner & Mary G. Locke was married Jan. 7th 1819

Births of their children

Susan E. Gardiner was born Jan 2nd 1820
Caroline Matilda Gardiner was born Dec. 2, 1821.
Edmund Laurence Gardiner was born Feb. 4, 1824
John Fletcher Gardiner was born Sept. 16, 1825
Hibernia Booker Gardiner was born Sept. 24, 1827
Samuel George Gardiner was born May 21st 1830
John Richerson Love was born Nov. 17th 1840
Samuel G. Gardiner died on the 9th of September A.D. 1830

M. E. Daniel & Hibernia B. Gardiner was married
Dec. 24th 1846.

Births of their children

Nancy Josephine Daniel was born 22nd Oct. 1847.
Mary Louise Daniel was born March 30th 1848
Edmund Lawrence Gardiner Daniel was born Jan 6th 1850
Florence Leona Daniel was born Dec. 3rd 1852 &
died June 25, 1854
Duna Josephine & Emma Caroline Daniel twins,
born March 16th, 1850
William Eddins Daniel was born June 22nd 1858.
Hibernia Daniel departed this life on the 8th of
February 1863.

Edmund L. Gardiner & Susan A. Adams was married May 20th
1844.
Samuel Ephraigon Gardiner, their son was born March 9th 1845
Edmund L. Gardiner died Sept. 8th 1845.

April 28th, 1862, the fifty ninth birthday of Mary G. Locke,
hoping in the completion of my labour on this scrap book this day, that
it will be read with interest by my children and
       Grandchildren
and that they may proffit thereby.
          M. G. L.

James Madison Oliphant was born April 20th, 1818
Caroline Matilda Thear Gardiner was born Dec. 2nd 1822

they were married feb. 1st 1838

RUTHERFORD COUNTY

(Locke Family Record p. 3)

Births of their children

Mary Harriet Oliphant was born Oct. 24th 1838
George Presly Oliphant was born July 23rd 1840
Thomas Jefferson Oliphant was born March 22nd 1842
Sarah Ann Oliphant was born Dec. 15th, 1843
Susan Matilda Oliphant was born Febuary 16th, 1846.
Martha Narcissa Cliphant was born August 9th 1848
James Crenshaw Oliphant was born Oct. 13th 1851
Edmund Gardiner Oliphant was born January 8th 1854

Sarah Ann Oliphant, daughter of James and Caroline Oliphant was drowned in a well on May 22nd, 1846,
Aged 2 years and five months.

RUTHERFORD COUNTY

LOWE BIBLE RECORD

W. S. Lowe, born Dec. 20, 1822, Rutherford Co.
       died Feb. 10, 1897   "   "
Martha J. Youree, born Jan. 28, 1826 Rutherford Co.
       died Oct. 12, 1898, Nashville, Tenn.
W. S. Lowe and Martha J. Youree were
       married Oct. 25, 1842

Their Children

	born	married
Jas. G. Lowe	Nov. 9, 1843	Rachel Kelton
Wm. E. Lowe	Dec. 15, 1845	Mollie Prater
Elizabeth D. Lowe	Dec. 12, 1847	Willis Jacobs
Rhoda I. Lowe	July 29, 1850	A. P. Grigg, July 6, 1870
Mary F. Lowe	Feb. 22, 1852	Thos. Kelton
Martha J. Lowe	Jan. 25, 1854	Dr. S. C. Grigg
Hattie T. Lowe	May 2, 1856	Wm. Lowe
Alfred G. Lowe	Feb. 13, 1858	Lester Hollis
Ella M. Lowe	Nov. 6, 1860	Dr. J. D. Hall
Nannie S. Lowe	Aug. 29, 1863	Jimmie Lowe
David C. Lowe	Oct. 1, 1865	Josie Hoover
Joseph A. Lowe	July 1, 1867	Martha Daniel
		Cassie Daniel
		Nannie Benson
Nicholas P. Lowe	Jan. 28, 1871	Semmus Carnahan

Deaths

Jas. G. Lowe	died	March 14,	1923
Wm. E. Lowe	"	Feb.	1890
Elizabeth D. Lowe	"	Oct. 17,	1866
Mary F. Lowe	"	June	1902
Martha J. Lowe	"	Dec. 8,	1912
David C. Lowe	"	Nov. 23,	1937
Joseph A. Lowe	"	Dec.	1929

Father of W. S. Lowe was Wm. Lowe
Mother of W. S. Lowe was Rhoda Plummer
Father of Martha J. Youree was James Youree
Mother of Martha J. Youree was Dolly Hardiman

* * * * * * *

From Bible owned by Mrs. Rhoda Lowe Grigg, 401 N. Spring St., Murfreesboro, Tennessee.
Copied by Miss Annie E. Campbell, February 8, 1937.

RUTHERFORD COUNTY

McADOO BIBLE RECORD

Copied from Bible record owned by Mrs. Hodge McAdoo Smith, 428 East Bell St., Murfreesboro, Tennessee.
Copied by Miss Annie E. Campbell, Feb. 8, 1938.

Births

B. H. McAdoo was borned Decr. 15th 1810
E. T. McAdoo was borned Sept. 2, 1811

Register of the Ages of B. H. & E. T. McAdoo's Children

    Mary E. McAdoo was borned July 10, 1830
    Samuel P. McAdoo was borned Sept. 7th, 1832
    Darthula A. McAdoo, borned Feb. 6th 1835,
    Departed this life August 12th 1857
    Sary F. McAdoo was borned Sept. 16, 1838
    Solon H. McAdoo was borned June 10, 1841
    Lockey C. McAdoo was borned April 26th 1844
    Nancy T. McAdoo was borned Oct. 5th 1845
    Margaret A. McAdoo was Borned 16th August 1848
    Sophia H. McAdoo was borned August 7, 1851
        was borned May 1, 1854
    Eda P. McAdoo was borned Sept. 18th 1858
    died Jan. 21st 1860 age one year 4 months & 3 days
    Eva or Evva D. McAdoo was borned Jan. 7, 1860
    Flora O. McAdoo was borned Dec. 6, 1862
    Robert Hodgie McAdoo was born Oct. 31, 1863
    Virginia H. McAdoo was borned 24 Sept. 1822

B. H. McAdoo was married to Virginia Osborne May 15, 1855.
Virginia H. McAdoo departed this life May 8th 1856

N. E. Anderson was Borned Decr. 8th 1834
B. H. McAdoo & N. E. Anderson were married 25 August 1857

Deaths

E. T. McAdoo departed this life June 25, 1854
Mary E. Sellars died on the 15th September 1855
Samuel P. McAdoo departed this life on the 6th January 1856
Lockey C. McAdoo died Friday morning 6 o'clock on the 22nd Nov. 1844
B. H. McAdoo departed this life March 30th 1863 aged 52 years 3 months and 20 days

RUTHERFORD COUNTY

(McAdoo Bible Record   p. 2)

Slaves of B. H. McAdoo

Births

Manerva was borned May 15, 1820
Liza was borned Dec. 17th 1821
Jas was borned 21 Decr 1823
Porter was borned some time 1825
Harriet was borned June 8th 1823
Isham was borned May 10th 1826
Green was borned July 10th 1828
Jane was borned March 20th 1830
Ephraim was borned August 9th 1833
Joseph was borned Feb. 16th 1836
Henry was borned some time in 1824
Rachel was borned August 14, 1822
Martha was borned August 16th 1838
Mary was borned June 8th 1839
Margaret was borned March 8, 1841
Cambia was borned in the year 1798
Louisa was borned in 1805
Elvira was borned June 26th 1841
Robt. was borned Feb. 10th 1842
Dealia was borned April 30th 1842
Caroline was borned April 1836
Geo Tilor was borned Sept. 18th 1842
Nancy was borned Nov. 28, 1843
Clary was borned May 4th 1844
Albert was borned July 21, 18__
Lucy was borned Feb. 9th, 1845
Lucinda was borned March 10, 1846
Thomas was borned 10 March 1846
Dean was borned August 22, 1846
Vica was borned Sept. 13th 1847
Allen Talor was borned Dec. 1, 1848
Major Nelson was borned August 28, 1849
California was borned July 8th 1853
Sam was borned in 1795
Hebrew was borned in 1792
Pegay was borned in 1784
Edmond was borned in 1826
Noah was borned in Nov. 1842
Hannah was borned some time in the spring of 1804
Matilda F. was borned March 1854, valued at $800.00.

BIBLE - RECORDS

RUTHERFORD COUNTY

Copied from a Record,(Leaf of Elijah McClanahan Bible),
belonging to Mrs.Jarman Edwards,(Hallie Hunt).
Residence: 740 North Spring St.,Murfreesboro, Tennessee.
Copied by Miss Annie Campbell, Murfreesboro, Tennessee.
January 14, 1937.

A List of Elijah McClanahan's Children:

James T. McClanahan,
Was born January 17, 1817.

Sintha H. McClanahan,
Was born May 29, 1819.

Matthew McClanahan,
Was born October 4, 1822.

Robert McClanahan,
Was born March 23, 1825.

Sarah Ann McClanahan,
Was born August 29, 1827.

Cornealy Jane McClanahan,
Was born April 15, 1830.

BIBLE - RECORDS

RUTHERFORD COUNTY

Records from the McClanahan Bible.
Present owner: Mrs. Jarman Edwards,(Hallie Hunt).
Residence: 740 N. Spring St., Murfreesboro, Tenn.
Copied by Miss Annie Campbell, Murfreesboro, Tenn.
January 14, 1937.

Matthew McClanahan, Son of
Samuel McClanahan & Jane Moore,
Was born February 26, 1778. And
Was married to Sarah Bradley,
Daughter of John & Molly Bradley,
On the 21st day of May, 1801.

Mary B. McClanahan, Daughter of
M. McClanahan, and Sarah,
Was born 31st of March, 1802.

Samuel McClanahan,
Was born September 3, 1804.

Jane McClanahan,
Was born September 30, 1807.
(Part of this page torn off.)

Cassandana McClanahan,
Was born December 17, 1815.

James Roulston McClanahan,
Was born April 22, 1818,
At 7 o'clock (P.M.)

Harriett Newell McClanahan,
Was born October 20, 1820.

John Bradley McClanahan,
Was born February 17, 1823.

James R. McClanahan, and
Caroline M. Wallace, Married
February 26, 1840.

Lockey W. McClanahan,
Was born July 12, 1841.

John B. McClanahan, Married
Hannah Kimbro, April 10, ---?

Sarah Matildy McClanahan,
Was born the 16th of May,
1847.

Simeon Taylor and Matilda
McClanahan were married,
September 6, 1833.

Mary B. McClanahan, Was
married to Burwell Ward,
January 24, 1822.

Samuel McClanahan, Was
married to Elizabeth Ward,
----?

Elizabeth McClanahan, Was
married to Robert M. Gibson,
----?

Cassandaney McClanahan, Was
married to Best Ward, ---?

Edwin Amate and Harriett H.
McClanahan, Was married,
June 10, 1841.

Susan Ann Amate,
Was born September 22, 1842.

(McClanahan Bible p.2.)

Simeon Taylor married,
Matilda McClanahan,
Sept. 6, 1833.

Sarah Ann Taylor, first daughter
of Simeon and Matilda,
Was born May 21, 1834.

Matthew M. Taylor,
Was born November 17, 1836.

Mary E.C. Taylor,
Was born December 8, 1841.

David A. Taylor,
Was born August 7, 1844.

Martha B. Taylor,
Was born January 6, 1848.

RUTHERFORD COUNTY

McFADDEN FAMILY RECORD

McFadden Family Record owned by
Misses Anna and Sophia McFadden,
226 N. Walnut St., Murfreesboro, Tennessee
Copied by Miss Annie E. Campbell, August 7, 1837.

Samuel McFadden, son of Guy and Jennie McFadden,
was born July 27th 1794; died April 29, 1848.

Samuel McFadden & Hallie Posey were married
Jan. 18, 1815

Fourteen children were born to them,
9 girls and 5 boys,
names as follows:

    Wm. R.
    James,
    Samuel,
    Henry &
    John;

    Caroline
    Nancy
    Eliza
    Bettie,
    Sarah,
    Susan
    Hallie &
    Lou

Samuel Guy McFadden was born April 4, 1848; died Dec. 8, 1894.

Samuel Guy McFadden and Mary Itilla Haynes were married
Feb. 5, 1874.

RUTHERFORD COUNTY

FAMILY RECORD OF
NICHOLAS MERIWETHER

The Meriwether Family Record is Property of Mrs. B. H. Hyde, Murfreesboro, Tenn. Rt. # 1, 5 miles S. W. from Murfreesboro on Barfield Rd.,(4 miles on Murfreesboro & Eagleville Rd & turn off to left on Barfield Road.

Copied by Miss Annie Campbell, March 23, 1938. Murfreesboro,Tenn.

1st. Nicholas Meriwether, the Welshman, married Elizabeth Wodehouse of Wales.
2nd. Nicholas Meriwether, Kent Co., Va. married Elizabeth Crawford.
3rd. Jane Meriwether, sister of David Meriwether, married Col. Robert Lewis of "Belvoir" Albemarle Co., Va.
4th. Robert Lewis married Frances Lewis
5th. Jane Meriwether Lewis married Swepson Sims, (see Sims Record)

Nicholas Meriwether, known as Nicholas the Welshman, came to America in the early 1600's & settled in Virginia.

William Lewis, son of Col. Robert Lewis and Jane Meriwether Lewis, married Lucy Meriwether and they were parents of Meriwether Lewis.

Col. Robert Lewis, who married Jane Meriwether, was a brother of Col. Fielding Lewis, who married Betty Washington, sister of George Washington.

END

BIBLE - RECORDS

RUTHERFORD COUNTY

Record from the Mitchell Bible.
Present owner: Mr. Tom Brown.
Residence: One mile North-East of Murfreesboro, Tenn., on Halls Hill Pike.
Copied by Miss Mabel DuBois, Murfreesboro, Tennessee.
January 27, 1937.

MARRIAGES:
Effoid D. Booker, and
Eliza L. Corbell,
Was married the
23 Day of Nov. 1843.

Thos. M. Cable &
Mary E. France,
Was married,
16th July 1844.

BIRTHS:
John Preston Hampton Corbell,
Was born March 20th, 1820.

Eliza L. Corbell,
Was born April 15th, 1822.

William Pleasant Henderson Corbell,
Was born Feb. 4th, 1825.

Mark Mitchell, the son of
Joab & Mary Mitchell, his wife,
Was born Jan. the 19th, 1756.

Thomas C. Mitchell,
Was born Nov. 21st, 1794.

Elizabeth Mitchell,
Was born Oct. 18th, 1796.

Louisa Mitchell,
Was born June the 19th, 1798.

Mary Mitchell,
Was born March the 10th, 1801.

Wm. Mitchell,
Was born Oct. the 5th, 1802.

Pleasant H. Mitchell,
Was born March the 3rd, 1804.

Thomas M. Corbell,
Was born the
22nd of April 1820.

Musadora Alice Booker,
Was born March the 28th, 1849.

Thos. I. W. Corbell,
Was born Sept. the 19th, 1809.

Mary Elizabeth Corbell,
Was born the 10th, of Mar. 1871.

Hampton Corbell, Junior,
Was born the 31st of Dec. 1872.

Nancy Jane Corbell,
Was born the 3rd of July, 1874.

Alice L. Corbell,
Was born the 11 of March, 1876.

(Mitchell Bible p.2.)

DEATHS:
William P.H. Corbell,
Departed this life,
Sept. 11th, 1845, at 9 o'clock P.M.

J.P.H. Corbell,
Departed this life,
March 20th, 1848, at 9 o'clock A.M.

Mr. William Corbell,
Departed this life,
July the 10th, 1869, about
3 o'clock A.M. age eighty years.

Mrs. Eliza L. Jones,
Departed this life,
Sept. the 26th, 1873,
About eleven o'clock A.M.

Mrs. Mary E. Corbell,
Departed this life,
the 25th day of November 1881,
Eleven o'clock P.M.

Oston Corbell, Junior,
Died 22 Sec. of August, 1874.

RUTHERFORD COUNTY

MOORE FAMILY RECORD

From the record owned by Mrs. James Herbert Moore,
313 N. Maple St., Murfreesboro, Tennessee
Mrs. Moore's record was a copy from the Bible Record of
Mr. Chas. W. Moore, R.R. #2, Murfreesboro, Tenn. (Franklin Rd.)
Copied by Miss Annie E. Campbell, April 19, 1938.

Ezekiel Moore married Mary King (She first married ____ Bush, had one son, Perseville Bush. Her second husband was Ezekiel Moore. She married the third time ____ Jones; no children of the third marriage.)

Children of Ezekiel Moore & Mary King:

Ezekiel, Hardie Holmes, Thomas, Pheraby Jane, Chas. W., Carroline P., James Henry, Gabriel.

Chas. W. Moore was born Nov. 25, 1820, died Sept. 31, 1887. Lived in Noxubee County, Miss. Moved to Tenn. in 1876. Married Julia Ann King who was born March 28, 1825; died April 15, 1902

Their children

James Ezekiel, born Apr. 8, 1848
    died Apr. 7, 1850
Pattie Jeanette, born July 2, 1850
    died Dec. 29, 1880
Thos. McClure, Born May 9, 1852
    died July 16, 1853
Hardy Henry, Born Jan. 30, 1854
    Died Oct. 16, 1855
Caroline Penelopia, Born Feb. 15, 1856
    Died Jan. 4, 1861
William Chas., Born Nov. 27, 1858
    Died May 13, 1869
Bettie Julia, Born June 11, 1860
    Died June 18, 1912

Chas. William, Born Apr. 3, 1862

Pattie Jeanette Moore married first Thos. W. Ivie, Sept. 3, 1868.
Thos. W. Ivy, Jr. was born Jan. 13, 1870; died May 25, 1900.
Thos. W. Ivy, Sr. died Nov. 14, 1871.

Pattie Jeanette Ivy married (second) J. H. Jamison, Sr., Dec. 22, 1875; had three children: Idalette Pattie, Charles Moore and a child who died unnamed. Pattie J. Ivy died soon after, Dec. 29, 1880.

Bettie Julia Moore married J. H. Jamison, Sr. Dec. 13, 1881.
They had 4 children: James H. Jr., Bettie Julia, a child who died unnamed, & Sarah Dorsey.

RUTHERFORD COUNTY

(Moore Family Record p.2)

Charles William Moore married Mary Sue Beesley Oct. 23, 1889, who was born April 22, 1871.

Their Children:

Chas. Hardie Moore, born Aug. 13, 1890
Married Constance Maxie Sedberry, Dec. 25, 1914.

John Beesley Moore, born May 29, 1892
Married Blanche Virginia Richardson
Dec. 29, 1917. Blanche died Feb. 12, 1928.

Julian Caldwell Moore, born Jan. 3, 1896
Married Eva May Adams, Feb. 15, 1924

William Henry Moore, born Feb. 5, 1898
Married Sarah Elizabeth Bowles, July 23, 1921

Thos. Jefferson Moore, born June 7, 1900
Married Mildred Anna Rose, Sept. 12, 1925

James Herbert Moore, born July 16, 1901
Married Bessie King Wright, May 26, 1925

Mary Elizabeth Moore, born Oct. 25, 1905
Married Herbert Cyril Morris, Feb. 9, 1932

BIBLE - RECORDS

RUTHERFORD COUNTY

Record from the Murfree Family Bible.
Present owner: Miss Fanny N.D. Murfree.
Residence: 225 University St., Murfreesboro, Tennessee.
Copied by Miss Annie Campbell, Murfreesboro, Tennessee.
February 27, 1937.

BIRTHS:
Col. Hardy Murfree,
Was born the 5th of June, 1752.
Died 6th of April, 1809.

William Hardy Murfree,
Was born the 2nd of Oct. 1781,
Hertford Co. N.C., son of
Hardy Murfree and Sally Murfree,
his wife.

Elizabeth Mary Murfree, Daughter of
James Maney and Mary Maney, his wife,
Was born in Hertford Co. N.C., on
the 28th of October, 1787.

William Law Murfree, son of
William H. and Elizabeth M. Murfree,
Was born on the 19th day of July, 1817.
Hertford Co. N.C.

Sally Brichell Murfree, (Daughter of
William H. and Elizabeth M. Murfree)
Was born September, 1821,
Hertford Co. N.C.

Elizabeth Maney Murfree (Daughter of
William H. and Elizabeth M. Murfree)
Was born on the 13th July 1826,
Williamson Co., Tenn.

Fanny Murfree, Daughter of
William L. and F. Priscilla Murfree,
Was born August 2, A.D. 1846.

Mary Noailles Murfree, Daughter of
William L. and F. Priscilla Murfree,
Was born January 24, 1850.

William Law Murfree, Jr.
Son of William L. and
Fanny Priscilla Murfree,
Was born on Tuesday,
March 26th, 1854.

MARRIAGES.
William Hardy Murfree,
and Elizabeth Mary Maney,
Were married in North
Carolina, A.D. 1808.

Married on the 22nd day
of November A.D. 1843,
near Murfreesboro, Tenn.
William Law Murfree, Esq.
to Miss Fanny Priscilla,
daughter of David
Dickinson Esq., and Fanny
Noailles Dickinson.

Married on the 7th day of
December 1881, William
Law Murfree, Jr. to Miss
Louise, daughter of
John Knostman, Esq.

DEATHS:
Elizabeth Mary Murfree,
Consort of William H.
Murfree, departed this
life, on the 13th day of
July A.D. 1826, in the
39th year of her age,
Williamson Co., Tenn.

William H. Murfree,
Departed this life on the
19th day of January A.D.
1827, in the 41st yr. of her
age.

(Murfree Bible p.2.)

William H. Murfree,
Departed this life,
on the 19th day of January, A.D.1827,
In the 41st year of his age.

William Law Murfree,
Departed this life,
August 23, 1892,
At Murfreesboro, Tenn.

William Law Murfree, Jr.
Departed this life,
Jan. 25, 1902,
At Boulder, Colorado.

Fanny Priscilla Dickinson Murfree,
Departed this life,
September 19, 1902,
At Murfreesboro, Tenn.
Aged eighty-six years.

Mary Noalles Murfree, Daughter of
William Law Murfree and Fanny
Priscilla Dickinson Murfree,
Departed this life,
July 31, 1922, Murfreesboro, Tenn.

RUTHERFORD COUNTY

BRICKELL-MURFREE FAMILY RECORD
THE BRICKELLS

This record compiled by (Mrs) Mary Moore Hilliard Hardeman, who died about 1885. The paper from which this copy is made is owned by Miss Fanny N. D. Mufree, 225 University St., Murfreesboro, Tenn.

Copied by Miss Annie Campbell, Murfreesboro, Tenn. April 11, 1938.

Rev. Matthias Brickell of Bertie, N. C, was a clergyman of the Church of England; the first resident preacher west of the Chowan River, He came to North Carolina in 1725, His son Matthias Brickell was a Lt. Colonel in the Revolutionary War.

Lt. Col. Matthias Brickell, my grear-grand father, was born 23rd March 1725, was married to Rachiel Noailles(a French lady) 6th November 1748, died 17th October 1788. His wife Rachaiel Noailles was born the 13th January 1728, died 17th February, 1770. They had 13 children as follows:

1. Marina, born 6th September 1749, died 8th January 1762, 12 years old.
2. Lavinia, born 17th July 1750, died ___1799
3. William, born 30th March 1752, died ___1810
4. Martha, born 25th September 1753, died ___1809
5. Bathsheba, born 28th September 1755, died 7th June 1782
6. Sally, born 26th July 1757, died 19th March 1802, (My grandmother)
7. Matthias, born 23 January 1759, died 3rd June 1797
8. Thomas Noailles, born 11th March 1761, Died ___November 1810
9. John, born 8th September 1762, died ___1798
10. James Noailles, Born 19th January 1765, Died Franklin, Tenn. 25th January 1841
11. Jonathan, born 11th Feburary 1767, Died ____ January 1807
12. Joseph, born 23rd December 1769, Died _____ 1802
13. Ann, born __died ___1770

My great grandfather, Matthias Brickell, married a second time to Mrs. Jones, and they had five children.
1. Benjamin, born 15th December 1773, died ____1812
2. Marina, born 28th May 1780.
3. Rebecca, born 14th June 1780
4. Betsy, born 1st May 1783
5. Nancy, born 17th January 1786

These 18 children of my great-grandparents married as follows:
2nd Lavinia-Married Mr. Dickinson and had three children, Joseph, Matthias, and Rachiel;
Joe married Margaret Gregory and lived in Murfreesboro, N.C.; Rachiel married Dr. Stimpson, was afterwards a widow and engaged to Dr. Kelly when she died and he went deranged. Lavinia Dickinson her mother, married a second time to Dr. Bemburg, My aunt Lavinia Bemburg Burton, was named for her.

3. William Brickell married Nancy Jones who from her termagant disposition obtained the soubriquet, "Blue Hen". They lived at Louisburg, N. Carolina, had no children.

(Brickell-Murfree Family Record)
Page-2

4. Martha and 5th Bathsheba her sister were crossing a bridge in a "gig" when the horse frightened and backed off. Bathsheba was drowned and Martha was saved by the chain of her scissors catching in the bridge. neither of these were married.
6. Sallie, my grandmother, married Col. Hardy Murfree, and had 10 children.
7. Matthias never married, Uncle Matt Murfree named for him.
8. Thomas, married, had five children;
   Rachiel, Betsy, Robert, Thomas, Lavinia. Robert married a Miss Rutland, had no children, lived near Canton, Miss. Thomas was very handsome, very gifted, practiced law in the Courts, with Uncle William H. Murfree who was very fond of him. He lived in Windson, N.C. never married, died in the prime of his life. Lavinia his sister was very pretty and spoiled accordingly. She married Dr. Isaac Jones, and some years after moved from N.C. to Brownsville, Western District of Tennessee, had several children, Eunice her daughter, lives there somewhere.

9. John Brickell, died, never married.
10. James Noailles, Brickell, married Betsy White, of South Carolina (The sister of my friend Col. James J.B. White, of Yazoo City, Miss) late in life, Theymoved to Franklin, Tenn. where he died, aged 76; was buried by the side of my grandfather, Col. Hardy Murfree (his brother-in-law) at the old plantation on west HarpethRiver. He had only two children, William and Henry. William Married Susan Faust of S.C. and had 4 children, James, Daniel, William and Medora. Hanry married Betsy Smith, a daughter of Nicholas P. Smith of Franklin, Tenn. had 4 children, Mary, Lemuella, Agnes, James. They lived in Yazoo City, Miss.
11. Jonathan, married; had nochildren; died in Raleigh, N.C.
12. Joseph died; never married.
13. Ann married Dr. Hill of Franklin County, N.C. had 3 children, Nancy, Lavinia, and Natt; Nancy married Murfree Knight, (a runaway match) was afterwards divorced and married Mark Cook, of Raleigh, N.C. where they lived and died, had no children, Lavinia married Dr. Wheaton. Natt took araenic through mistake and died.

MATTHIAS BRICKELL

(My great-grandfather) married second time to Mrs. Nannie Jones, They had five children;
1st. Benjamin who married Nancy Davis (my father's neice) and they had one child called Benjamin.
2nd. Marina, who married four times; Rollins was her first husband and their daughter Matilda married a Moody and Mrs. Moody's daughter, Lavinia was educated at "Columbia Female Institute" and afterwards Married Mr. Millighan a Baptist preacher, and lived for some years at Jackson, Mississippi.
Aunt Marina Rollins married a second husband named Moore, then a third husband named Saxon, and a fourth named Burns, who was a Baptist preacher and they had a son who was also a Baptist preacher--quite an orator-lived in Memphis, where he preached for some years and died there last winter. I believe there were some Moore and Saxon children but I am not certain.

(Brickell-Murfree Family Record)
Page-3

4. Betsy Brickell--married Mr. Godwin; had three children, a son and two daughters; Their son lived in Mississippi, Ann Married Winston of Alabama and was very rich. Eliza Godwin never married, died a few years ago en route to visit her brother in Miss. He met her in the evening with a carriage at railroad station to take her out across the country to his house next day she spent the night at the Hotel and she was foud dead in her bed next morning from an attach of hemorrhage. She had lived a long time with Mrs. Estelle of Nashville, who adopted her after her mother's death, and when Mrs. Estelle moved to Clinton, Miss. Eliza returned to her childhood home at Huntsville and lived with Mrs. Yeatman, the sister of Mrs. Estelle. She subsequently taught school in Huntsville for a number of years, beloved and respected by all. Her sister and brother are dead also.

5. Nancy Brickell--the greatest beauty beauty that ever lived, married seven times. Her first husband was a Mr. **Lemon**; and Mr. Clark; 3rd Mr. Dickinson, 4th _____ 5th Mr. Drake, a brother of the celebrated Dr. Drake of Cincinnati, Ohio. 6th _____ 7th A **Frenchman**, of Mobile, Alabama, name forgotten. She had a daughter by her fifth marriage (her first child) called "Octavia LaVert". She had a son by the 6th marriage, who when a small boy was in bathing with other boys in Mobile bay; stuck an oyster shell in his foot and died of lockjaw, Aunt Nancy died in Mobile and Dr. Drake went there and carried Octavia, his neice, to Cincinnati where she resided with him and I believe married there.

END OF BRICKELL RECORD

*
3rd Rebecca Brickell6 married Mr. Palmer of Windsor, N.C. Their family numerous, a son called Matt was very talented. He was a class-mate of my husband William Hardeman at Chapel Hill, N.C. and they were very intimate. He died a few years after he left College, never married.

(Brickell Murfree Family Record Page-4)
MURFREE'S

    Hardy Murfree was born in North Carolina, the son of William Murfree and his wife, Mary Moore Murfree, William Murfree was prominent in the patriotic movement of North Carolina, being a delegate from Hertford County to the Provinial Congreee 1775 and 1776, which met at Halifax and Hillsboro He was also a member of the convention which framed the State Constitution of North Carolina.

    Hardy Murfree was an officar in the Continental army throughout the American Revolution. At the age of 23, in 1775, he was Captain; in 1778 he had attained the ranks of Lieutenant Colonel. Detailed accounts of his Military career are given in "The Storming of Stony Point" by Henry Phelps Johnson; Wheeler's Remniscences & Memoirs of North Carolina", and other historical books.

    Hardy Murfree removed from Murfreesboro, N.C. to Williamson Co., Tenn. in 1806, where he died April 6, 1809, age 56 years. He was buried on his plantation 9 miles from Franklin, Tenn. His funeral oration was delivered by Hon. Felix Grundy. Two years after his death, the Tennessee Legislature appointed Commissioners to secure a site and aly off a new town for the capital of Rutherford County, and in an act passed November 19th 1811, directed that "This town shall be forever called and known as Murfreesboro."

    Of the line of Col. Hardy Murfree and Sallie Brickell came the late Mary Noailles Murfree, known as Charles Egbert Craddock, author of stories of the Tenn. Mountains; Southern and historical novels.

    My Great-grandfather, William Murfree married Mary Moore (for whom my mother was named) They had 7 children, three sons and four daughters, Hardy, their first son, was my grandfather, born June 5th, 1752; died April 6th 1809, just before he completed his 57th year.

2nd. William Murfree, never married
3rd. James Murfree, married and left two daughters, Sarah and Mary. Sarah married Henry Sorsbyrg, Mary Married Thomas Finney. My great grandfather's daughters were 1st, Sarah; 2nd Patty; 3rd, Betty; 4th Nancy.

1st. Sarah, married Sam Cryer; had three sons and four daughters.
    The sons were; James, George, and Johnny. The daughters were; Mrs. Parker, Mrs. Pipkin, Mrs. Saurie, Mrs. Barrow. James Was the father of Hardy Cryer of Sumner County, Tenn. (who was my mother's second cousin) John the Brother of James Cryer, married his first cousin Polly Banks, George their brother never married, went blind and lived 25 or 30 years, afterwards.

    Their sister, Mrs. Saurie, has a son living in Nashville; the Rev. William Saurie, a Methodist Preacher, a second cousin of my mother.

2nd. Patty, (my grandfather's sister) married Ben Banks. They had three daughters and three sons. Polly married her first cousin Johnny Cryer, and her sister is Mrs. Boyers of Gallatin, Tenn. Sally theirother sister married Mr. Britt and her daughter is Mrs. Fountain E. Pitts of Nashville, Tenn. Mama's second and my third cousin. Aunt Patty Banks' sons were James, Hardy, and Alexander, who never married.

(BRICKELL-MURFREE FAMILY RECORD Page-5-)
MURFREES

James married Miss Harriett Sketchley, a highly accomplished English lady) and her neice Martha Sletchley married his brother, Hardy Banks. They lived in Murfreesboro, N.C.

3rd Betty, (my grandfather's 3rd sister) married Richard Andrews and had three children, William, Sally and Patty. William was the father of cousin Sally Pugh. Sally married Capt. Dunstan of the Navy and they had a son named William Hardy. Patty and William died of Black tongue in 1812.
4th Nancy (Grandpa's 4th sister) married Jonathan Roberts.
Hardy Murfree, (my grandfather) married Sally Brickell, Thursday 17th February 1780. They had 10 children.

1st. William Hardy, born 2nd October, 1781, died January 1827 in Nashville Tenn. age 45 years; at the house of Mr. John Bell, who married a niece of William Hardy.Murfree, Sally Louise Dickinson.
2nd Fanny Noailles, born 23rd August 1783, died 29th Dec. 1843 (60 Yrs Old)
3&4d. Mary Moore, born 19th March 1786, died Wednesday night 1st March 1848 at the house of her son-in-law, William Hardeman, near Jackson, Mississippi aged 62 years.
4th. Matthias Breckell, Born 26th July 1788, died 15th September 1853, aged 65 years.
5th. Rachiel Dickinson, born 5th October 1790, died 24th August 1794.
6th. Sally Hardy, born 12 February 1793, died 12 August 1857, age 64
7th. Lavinia Benbury, born 3rd April 1795.
8th. A without name born 27 May, 1797, died same day.
9th. A girl without name born 17 June 1798, died 19 June.
10th. Martha Long Ann Croakley, named for two most intimate friends of my grandmother, was born 22nd May 1801, She was 10 months old at her mother's death and was adopted by my mother and father, (Mr. & Mrs. Isaac Hilliard) whom she always called mama and papa. She died at her home in Franklin, Tenn. 19th February 1868, aged 67 years.

The children of my grandparents, Hardy and Sally Murfree, married as follows:
1st. William Hardy Murfree married Elizabeth Maney.
2nd. Fanny N. Murfree married Squire David Dickinson 22nd August 1799, aged 16 years.
3rd. Mary Moore Murfree married Isaac Hilliard, 9th March 1803, aged 17years
4th. Matthias B. Murfree married Mary Roberts May 1816
5th. Sally Hardy Murfree married Dr. James Maney.
6th. Lavinia Benbury Murfree married Col. Frank Burton,
7th. Martha L. A. C. Murfree married Maj. William Maney (the brother of Dr. James Maney and Elizabeth Maney) on the 10th March 1819, 18 years old.
Maj. Maney, born 13 July 1799 was not 20 years old when they were married.

RUTHERFORD COUNTY

MISCELLANEOUS RECORD

Commission of David W. Dickinson as member of House of Representative.

This paper is owned by Miss Fanny N. D. Murfree, 225 University Street, Murfreesboro, Tenn. It was formerly the property of her mother, Mrs. F. Priscilla Dickinson, Murfree, the sister of David W. Dickinson, of Murfrees, Tenn.

Copied by Miss Annie Campbell, Murfreesboro, Tenn. Feb. 9, 1938.

State of Tennessee.
William Carroll, Governor in and over the State.

To all who shall see Those Presents Greetings:
Know ye that whereas, by return made by the proper officers, it has been made known to me, that David W. Dickinson, a citizen of the Eighth Congressional District of this State, hath been duly and Constitutionally electedto Represent the said District, as a member of the House of Representatives, in the Twenty third Congress of the United States.
Now, I, William Carroll, Governor as aforesaid, with all the powers privileges and emoluments incident or pertaining by virtue of the same.

In testimony Whereof, I have hereunto set my hand, and caused the great seal of the State to be affixed at Nashville, this 12th day of August, in the year of our Lord, one thousand eight hundred and thirty three.

    By the Governor,   William Carroll
    Secretary of State,   Sam G. Smith,

END.

RUTHERFORD COUNTY

FAMILY RECORD OF
HARE-DICKINSON
1720

This family record is owned by Miss Fanny N. D. Murfree, 225 University Street, Murfreesboro, Tenn.

Copied by Miss Annie Campbell, Murfreesboro, Tenn. April 11, 1938.

John Hare was born on the 24th Day of March 1720
Priscilla Hare, wife of John Hare, was born the 14th Day of December 1723.
Priscilla Hare, wife of John Hare, departed this life 16th Day of May 1765.
Grace Hare wife of John Hare, Departed this life 30th Day of April 1787.
The ages of John Hare and his wife Priscilla and their children.
Mary Hare was born September the 6th 1742
Luke Hare was born June 20th 1745
Sarah Hare, was born in Dec. the 14th 1748
Elizabeth Hare, was born in October the 24th Day 1750
John Lawrence Hare, was born in March the 18th Day 1754
Moses Hare, was born in August the 28th 1757
Benjamin Hare, was born in October the 3rd 1760
Penelope Hare was born in February the 11th Day 1764

The above list of the names and ages of the children of John Hare and his wife Priscilla Hare was copied from an old blank book.
The births of three other children are noted, probably by the second wife, Grace Hare (the date of whose death is given above) as these dates are subsequent to the death of the first wife, Priscilla Hare, May 16, 1765.

These entries are as follows:
September 5th 1766, Lucresy Hare, was born
Jesse Hare was boen 14th Day of May 1769
on another page in this entry
Bryan Hare was born the 17th Day of December 1783.
In the same book occurs these entries:
David Dickinson, son of David Dickinson was born the 11th Day of October 1774.
David William Dickinson son of David Dickinson was born 10th day of June at 8o'clock in the morning Friday 1808.
The items below are copied from old memorandum found among Dickinson papers.
David Dickinson son of John Dickinson and Rebeckah, his wife was born June 2nd 17-7, (third figure of date is obliterated by book worm hole, but it may be presumed to be "3" making the date 1737, and his age at his marriage in 1764 twenty-seven.

(Family Record of Hare-Dickinson)

Sarah Hare, daughter of John Hare and Priscilla, his wife, was born December the 14th 1748

David Dickinson and Sarah Hare was marry Sept. 25th day 1764
Priscilla Dickinson, daughter of David Dickinson and Sarah his wife, was born December 17, 1765
Mary and Sarah Dickinson daughters of David Dickinson and Sarah his wife was both born January 22nd Day 1770.
David Dickinson son of David Dickinson and Sarah his wife was born November 13th day 1774.
Luke Dickinson son of David Dickinson and Sarah his wife, was born December 10th Day 1776.
Sarah Dickinson, departed this Life February 27th 1778.
David Dickinson Departed this Life the 25th of November 1783.

This is the last entry on the old memorandum.

David Dickinson son of David Dickinson and Sarah his wife, was born November 13th 1774
Fanny Noailles Murfree daughter of Hardy Murfree and Sally Brickell, Murfree, his wife, was born August 23, 1783.
Hardy Dickinson son of David Dickinson and Fanny his wife was born in 1800, died in infancy.
Sarah Louisa Dickinson, daughter of David Dickinson and Fanny his wife was born in 1802 and died in 1832, married John Bell.
David William Dickinson son of David Dickinson and Fanny his wife, was born June 10, 1808, died 1845, married first Miss Eliza J. Gtantland, (who died in 1838) and second Miss Sallie Brickell Murfree, daughter of William Hardy Murfree.
Lavinia Dickinson daughter of David Dickinson and Fanny his wife, was born next, died about thirteen or fourteen years of age.
Benjamin Dickinson son of David Dickinson and Fanny his wife, was born about 1814, died about 1824.
Fanny Priscilla Dickinson and Fanny his wife was born Sept. 24, 1816, died 1902, Sept. 19th, married Nov. 22, 1843, William Law Murfree.
William Dickinson Dickinson, son of David Dickinson and his wife, Fanny born, ___ died about four years of age.
Martha Elizabeth Dickinson daughter of David Dickinson and Fanny his wife, was born June 10th 1823, andJames Dickinson son of David Dickinson and Fanny his wife, died in infancy.

Their last child was a daughter dying in infancy.

END

RUTHERFORD COUNTY

FAMILY RECORD OF MANEY-BAKER

This record is owned by Miss Fanny N. D. Murfree, 225 University Street, Murfreesboro, Tennessee.

Copied by Mrs. Sadie McLaurine, Murfreesboro, Tennessee, April 11, 1938.

The Maneys were Franch Hugenots who fled from France to England at the Massacre of St. Bartholmeis day. The first James Maney mentioned in the record, came to America and is supposed to have settled on Long Island going from there to Virginia and then to North Carolina, ascended the Chowan River and established a settlement in Hertford County, the place taking its name from him and called "Maneys Neck" It is said that the beauty of the yellow jessamine then in full bloom caused him to settle in that place. He married in North Carolina.
James Maney the first, married Susanna Ballard, left one son, James.

James Maney the second, married Elizabeth Baker. Had four children James, Henry, Susan, and Priscilla. Henry died, young, killed by lightning, Susan married Gen. Thomas Wynns, no children, Priscilla married Mr. Burgess, no children.
James Maney the third married Mary Roberts, six children, James, Elizabeth, Meredith, Thomas, Mary, Henry and William.

James Maney,(4th) married Sallie Murfree, eight children, James, Fannie, William, and John died young, Thomas married Fannie Bell, daughter of Hon. John Bell. David Married Mary, daughter of Hon. John Bell, Louis married Adeline Daughter of Gov. Cannon, Mary married Hon. Edward Keeble.

Elizabeth Meredith Maney, married William H. Murfree. Three children William H. Who married Priscilla Dickinson, Sallie who married David Dickonson, Bettie who married Henry Frazier.

Henry Maney married Mary Brown, four children, Priscilla married John Bright, Virginia married Mr. Dunehoo, Henry married Miss Erskine Bettie married Mr. ErskineSamuel.

William Maney, married Martha Murfree, twelve children, William, Bettie who married Maj. Bowman, Martha ann who married Dewitt Clinton Douglass, Susan who married Charles Boddie, Fannie Dickinson who married John Bell Jr. Margaret who married Drs Parkson, Eliza who married Gen. Cook, Hardy, David Thomas and Sallie./ Lawrence who married Miss Abston/

The home of the second James Maney was burned during the Revolution by a party of Brittish and Torics. Hechimself made a narrow escape. Is said to have been possessed of a large estate.

(Family Record of Maney-Baker Page-2)

Mary Roberts wife of the third James Maney, was a daughter of the first marriage of her mother who for her second husband married Mr. Meredith In this way the name of Meredith comes into the family. He was a highly cultivated gentleman, she was a lade of grand and stately manner. She lived to a ripe old age.

Traditions and recollections of the Baker family, as given by Dr. Simmons Baker, when seventy-two years old, Born Feb. 15th 1775.

Four brothers said to be from Sussex England, Two settled in northen part of United States, the other two in Virginia on James River.
An old seal brought by one of these has on it a coat of arms, a castle, and three keys, surmounted by three white roses as a crest. In 1793, Sir George Baker, physcician to George the the Third, had the same arms, hit the crest, an arm extending from the top of the castle with a stone clenched in the hand.

Tradition in family os that they are descended from Admirial Blake, Maney descendants of the family named Blake.
Little is known of the immediate descendants of these emigrants from England The last of the name and family on James River was Laurence Baker. He died about 1807, leaving no issue at his death he gave to the father of Dr. Simmons Baker, a mourning ring with name of Elizabeth Baker, who died in 1764, in the inside. Not knownwho this Elizabeth Baker was.

Another branch of the family settled at South Quay in the Black water.

Henry Baker married Angelica Bray, a lady said to be of great beauty. There is a tradition that she could claim descent from the Royal house of England. From her son, The Maneys branch of the family are descended.

Henry Baker, son of the first marriage, married Caty Booth, of Isle of Wright, Va., Had four sons, Lawrence, Henry, William, and Bray, and threedaughters, one of whom Elizabeth married the second James Maney, and after his death, married a Mr. Figures.

The will of the older Henry Baker, is said to be still oreserved. Bears date of Jan. 9th 1737-He died 1739.

The above is taken from a record in my fathers writing, dated March 1866, In oneor two places I have written a little that has been gathered from other sources.

Rebecca Kimberly

END

RUTHERFORD COUNTY

NEWSOM BIBLE RECORD

From Newsom Family Bible Record Property of Roy S. Newsom, 449 Bell St., Murfreesboro, Tenn. Formerly the property of Roy's great grandfather, Balaam Newsom, handed down to his son, J. K. Newsom. At the death of J. K. Newsom, 1937, this Bible came into possession of Roy S. Newsom.
Copied by Miss Annie E. Campbell, March 3, 1938.

Marriages

Balaam Newsom and Ann E. McRae
was married Dec. 23, 1847

A. G. Newsom and Alice E. Hill
was married Oct. 18, 1871

James K. Newsom and Mary Christopher
was married Jan. 12, 1881

James K. Newsom and Amma Jones
was married Sept. 9, 1885

W. S. Newsom and Susie Layne
was married Feb. 1, 1906

W. S. Newsom & M. Annie Burk
was married Oct. 15, 1919

Births

Balaam Newsom was born February the 8th 1824
(Rutherford Co.)

Ann E. Newsom was born April the 1st 1829

(Children of Balaam & Ann E. Newsom)

Albert G. Newsom was born Nov. 8th 1848
Wm. S. Newsom was born Feb 2nd 1855
James K. Newsom was born Oct. the 28th 1857

(Wife of Albert G. Newsom)
Alice E. Newsom was born Nov. 17, 1853

RUTHERFORD COUNTY

(Newsom Bible Record   p. 2)

Births (Continued)

Children of Albert G. & Alice E. Newsom

    Thomas B. Newsom was born Feb. 7th 1873
    Laura A. Newsom was borned Aug. 21st, 1874
    Tillie McGuire Newsom was borned March 24th 1876
    Balaam R. Newsom was borned Aug. 10th 1877.
    Samuel G. Newsom was borned June 22nd, 1882
    Francis P. Newsom was born Jan. 13, 1885
    Maud Louise Newsom was born Dec. 2, 1891
    Willie Newsom was borned Dec. 30th 1881 (Child of
    James K. Newsom & Mary C. Newsom)
    Eliza P. Newsom was born Sept. 9, 1888 (Child of
    J. K. & Amma Jones Newsom)
    Susie Layne was borned Jan. 10, 1860

Deaths

Wm. McRae died Sept. the 20th   1855
Francis H. McRae died March 4th   1883
Tillie M. Newsom died May 12th   1881
Willie Newsom died Jan. 8th 1882
Mollie Newsom the wife of J. K. Newsom died Jan. 28, 1882
Nancy Newsom died April 11th 1856
Thomas B. Newsom died May 10th   1936
Balaam Newsom died July 10, 1901
Ann E. Newsom died Jan. 27, 1906
Albert G. Newsom died April 28, 1912
Susie Newsom died February 22nd 1915
W. S. Newsom died Feb. 19, 1929
J. K. Newsom died Oct. 14, 1937

RUTHERFORD COUNTY

NUGENT BIBLE RECORD

From the Nugent Family Bible, owned by Mrs. Walter K. Wood (Louise Nugent), 308 E. Lytle Street, Murfreesboro, Tennessee.
Copied by Mrs. Sadie McLaurine, March 17th, 1938.

Marriages

D. D. Nugent and Louise A. were married October 22nd, 1843.
D. D. Nugent, Jr. and Lizzie Jones were married Dec. 23rd, 1874.
J. S. Nugent and Euphemia Clark were married Nov. 3rd 1875.
Louisa Ann Nugent was married to Walter K. Wood, Aug. 23rd, 1903.
Orville Nugent was married to Kate Billings, Jan. 6, 1903.

Births

D. D. Nugent was born June 12th 1821.
Louisa Ann Nugent was born Oct. 8, 1821.
Mary E. Nugent was born Nov. 6th 1825
Americus T. Nugent was born Feb. 6, 1829
John H. Nugent was born Dec. 25th, 1834
James S. Nugent was born June 23rd, 1851
D. D. Nugent Jr. was born March 24th, 1854
Henry C. Nugent was born March 17th 1856
Lizzie Jones was born Sept. 15th, 1854
Euphemia Clark was born Nov. 29th, 1851.
Charles R. Nugent was born December 17th, 1875
Nina Nugent was born Dec. 29th 1878
David Ralston Nugent was born June 10th 1886.
Orville C. Nugent was born Aug. 18th 1876
Louise Anna Nugent was born February 17th, 1883
Margaret May Nugent was born Oct. 19th, 1888.
Marguerite Nugent Wood was born June 12th, 1904.
Wandena Nugent Wood was born March 26th, 1906.
Orville Clark Nugent, Jr. was born Oct. 2, 1904
James Billings Nugent was born July 11th, 1900

Deaths

William H. Nugent departed this life Aug. 13th, 1851
Henry C. Nugent departed this life December 9th, 1856
David D. Nugent Sr. died March 2nd, 1899
Louisa A. Nugent, died Nov. 4, 1907.
Maggie (Marguerite) Nugent died March 29th, 1903
Daniel McAllister, Sr. died Aug. 1851
Mrs. Elizabeth McAllister died Feb. 20th, 1873.
Clara L. McAllister died July 15th 1888.
Jas. S. Nugent, died March 18th, 1937.

RUTHERFORD COUNTY

(Nugent Bible Record p.2)

NOTE: This record was given by Mrs. Walter K. Wood of Murfreesboro, whose Mother was Euphemia Clark.

"Grandma Margaret Clark's Mother was Phemia Moore and she married James Johnson. Carroll Clark Sr's Mother was Margaret Durham and married Isiah Clark.

Carroll Clark had four brothers and two sisters.
The boys' names were: James, William, Absolum, and Gilliam.
The girls were Elizabeth, Sarah, Elvira and Theresa.

Margaret Clark had one sister and three brothers.
The sister Elizabeth who married a Scott, & the brothers were Bert, William & Thomas.

David Dickson Nugent's mother was Margaret Clark, who was born in Raleigh, N. C. She was related on her father's side to Andrew Johnson.

Euphemia Clark, daughter of Margaret Clark, married Jas. S. Nugent, Nov. 3rd, 1875."

RUTHERFORD COUNTY

(NUGENT Record p. 3)

"The Romance of your name."

This is an ancient French name and can be traced to Normandy, long before William the Conqueror invaded England. The Nugent family is a branch of the great house of Belesme, being descended from Wulke de Belesme, Lord of Nogent le Rotrou, who accompanied the Conqueror & fought in the battle of Hastings.

The root word from which the name derived is "gent" signifying pleasantness of place or person. The old words, no, one, non & none were applied to a low meadow or land frequently unundated.

In the course of time No-gent became the name of a number of towns ideally situated on the banks of a river such as Nogent-sur-Seine, and Nogent-sur-Marne-- Gilbert de Nugent, consuis of the Lord of Nogent le Rotrou, founded the name & family in Ireland in the time of Henry de Lacy's expedition into that country. They settled in West Meath and for many generations. Many American Nugents are descendants of that branch of the family that went to Canada from Ireland.

Daniel Clive Nugent, a representative of this branch, came to the United States from Canada during the latter part of the eighteenth century, and became a prosperous merchant.

RUTHERFORD COUNTY

PATTERSON BIBLE RECORD

Family Bible Record of A. J. Patterson Bible owned by Mrs. Lee McClaren, 403 N. Academy St., Murfreesboro, Tenn., formerly owned by A. J. Patterson, Murfreesboro, Tenn.

Births

A. J. Patterson was born (Rutherford Co.) October 18th A.D. 1842
Olivia J. Patterson was born March 4th A.D. 1856
Finis E. Patterson, Son of A. J. & Olivia J. Patterson was born Nov. 3rd A.D. 1876
James B. Patterson son of A. J. & Olivia J. Patterson was born April 18, A.D. 1878
Martha P. Patterson Daughter of A. J. & O. J. Patterson was born Sept. 17th A.D. 1879
Annie Patterson Daughter of A. J. & O. J. Patterson was born June 26, A.D. 1881
Frank R. Patterson son of A. J. & O. J. Patterson was born April 7th A.D. 1883
Infant Daughter of A. J. & O. J. Patterson, born August 14, A.D. 1885
Bessie Olivia Patterson daughter of A. J. & O. J. Patterson was born Oct. 2nd A.D. 1886
William O. Patterson son of A. J. & O. J. Patterson was born June 18th A.D. 1888
Nannie R. Patterson was born Jan. 31, 1892

Deaths

Annie Patterson Daughter of A. J. & O. J. Patterson departed this life April 26th A.D. 1887 Age 5 years 10 months
Infant Daughter Died August 17th A.D. 1885 Age 3 days
Martha Polemia Patterson daughter of A. J. & O. J. Patterson departed this life May 16, 1915
James Bates Patterson son of A. J. & O. J. Patterson departed this life July 24, 1916
Wm. Osborne Patterson son of A. J. & O. J. Patterson departed this life December 12, 1921 (World War Veteran) Murfreesboro, Tenn.
Samuel A. Patterson son of A. J. & O. J. Patterson departed this life March 8, 1924, Murfreesboro, Tenn. (World War Veteran)
A. J. Patterson departed this life February 9, 1928 Age 85 years 4 months
Olivia Jane Patterson departed this life Jan. 31, 1931 age 74 yrs 10 months
Bessie Olivia Patterson Henson died Jan. 13, 1932 at San Angelo, Texas.

Marriages

A. J. Patterson was united in marriage to Miss Olivia J. Rankin Nov. 22, 1875
F. E. Patterson was united in marriage to Miss Eva Cawthon Dec. 26, AD 1900
James B. Patterson was united in marriage to Miss Lorena Litton, July 9, 1906

RUTHERFORD COUNTY

(Patterson Bible Record p. 2)

Marriages (Continued)

Frank R. Patterson was united in marriage to Miss Bertha McCrane
Dec. 25, 1907
Bessie Olivia Patterson was united in marriage to Samuel A. Henson
Dec. 22, 1914
Samuel A. Patterson was united in marriage to Miss Lillie Mae Beasley
April 25, 1919
Nannie R. Patterson was united in marriage to Jas. Lee McClaran
July 6, 1922

* * * * * * *

Above copied by Miss Annie E. Campbell, Feb. 9, 1938.

RUTHERFORD COUNTY

REEVES - SHAW FAMILY RECORD

This record is the property of Mrs. W. R. Haynes, 528 East College Street, Murfreesboro, Tennessee.
Copied by Miss Annie E. Campbell, May 13, 1938.

REEVES FAMILY RECORD

Moses Guinn Reeves was born in Orange County, N. C. Jan. 5, 1800
                died Apr. 22, 1861
Catherine Shields Reeves was born in Philadelphia, Pa., March 20, 1804
                died Dec. 2, 1894

Their Children

    Daniel L. Reeves was born December 14, 1828
    Levi W. Reeves was born Dec. 9, 1830
    Daniel Leinau Reeves was married to Miss Mary Butler Shaw
    of Bedford County, Tenn., July 26, 1853, by Rev. G. T. Henderson.
    Daniel Leinau Reeves was married to Mary Lewis Garner,
    Oct. 12, 1858.
    Capt. C. W. Bell was married to Catherine Reeves Nov. 26, 1896
    William Rufus Haynes was married to Miss Sophia Reeves Oct. 13, 1878
    Charles Reeves was born June 29, 1854
    Mary Sophia Reeves was born March 6, 1856
    Levi W. Reeves was born July 18, 1857
    Lewis G. Reeves was born August 1, 1859
    Catherine Reeves was born Dec. 3, 1860
    Lewis Green Reeves was born Dec. 3, 1862
    Addie Reeves, born March 6, 1864

NOTE: Information below given by Mrs. W. R. Haynes.

    Moses Guinn Reeves removed with his father to Rutherford County in 1806, became a citizen of Murfreesboro in 1817.
    In 1823 he was elected to the office of Register of Rutherford County, which office he held for many years. He was married to Miss Catherine Shields in 1828, at Murfreesboro, Tenn. Moses G. Reeves died in Atlanta, Ga., enroute home from a visit to relatives, is buried at the old City Cemetery on Vine St. in Murfreesboro, Tenn.

SHAW FAMILY RECORD

Christopher Columbus Shaw, a Revolutionary soldier, was born in Greene County, S. C., Oct. 25, 1765. Removed to Bedford County, Tenn. 1808. Died Feb. 23, 1832.

RUTHERFORD COUNTY

(Reeves - Shaw Family Record p. 2)

Mary Butler, wife of Christopher Columbus Shaw, was born in 1779
died in 1861, aged 82.

Mary Butler Shaw, granddaughter of C. C. and Mary Butler Shaw, was born
Aug. 25, 1836
died Nov. 12, 1857
She was married July 26, 1853 to Daniel Lineau Reeves of Murfreesboro, Tenn.

RUTHERFORD COUNTY

BIBLE RECORDS

Bible record copied from Family Bible of Mrs. John M. Pickard, Sr., (formerly Rossie Rucker), of Lascassas Tennessee.
Copied by Sadie McLaurine Dec 1 1936

    Samuel Reed Rucker,   Born Jan. 27, 1794
                                              Died Dec. 3, 1862

    Mattie Bedford Martin,   Born Dec. 2, 1808
                                              Died Mar. 4, 1896

    Robert M. Rucker,   Born Dec. 3, 1830
                                              Died Sept. 22, 1908

MARRIAGES

    Samuel R. Rucker was united in holy bonds of wedlock on the 11th day of February 1828, with Mattie Bedford Martin.

    Robert. M. Rucker was united in holy bonds of wedlock on 24th July, A.D. 1867 with Mrs. A. L. Cowen.

RUTHERFORD COUNTY

Bible Records

Copied from a Bible owned by Mrs. Sarah Searcy Tompkins
Residence 313 North Maple Street, Murfreesboro, Tenn.
Copied by Annie Campbell Dec. 1936

MARRIAGES

William W. Searcy, and Elizabeth Harris of Warren County, N. C.
    January 22, 1797

William W. Searcy, and Sarah Morton of Rutherford County, Tenn.
    September 18, 1806

William W. Searcy and Sarah Campbell   May 6, 1838

BIRTHS

William W. Searcy,	January 1, 1769
Sarah Morton, his wife,	March 30, 1783
Isham G. Searcy	October 20, 1797
William W. Searcy,	July 4, 1800
Lucy W. Searcy	August 4, 1802
James Morton Searcy	March 15, 1808
Catherine Morton Searcy	October 26, 1809
Anderson Searcy	September 12, 1811
John Searcy	February 21, 1814
Sarah M. Searcy	May 23, 1816
Robert W. Searcy	April 6, 1818
Tabitha Searcy	July 10, 1820
Judy Searcy	February 19, 1824
Lafayette Searcy	April 8, 1827
William W. Searcy, son of John W. and Ann Searcy,	October 25, 1840
A. B. Fisher	December 20, 1820

Searcy Bible Record (Continued)
P. 2.

DEATHS

Elizabeth Searcy, wife of William W. Searcy, September 22, 1804, aged 25 yrs.

James Morton Searcy   August, 1809

Sarah M. Searcy, wife of William W. Searcy,   April 29, 1832

Sarah M. Battle   October 3, 1835

Isham G. Searcy   July 24, 1841

John W. Searcy   September 18, 1843, aged 29

Ann Searcy, wife of John W.,   September 15, 1843

Catherine M. Yandell, wife of Dr. Wm. M. Yandell, September 12, 1843

James T. Richardson   September 3, 1846

William W. Searcy   January 8, 1846, aged 27

Anderson Searcy, son of Wm. W. & Sarah,   April 3, 1847

Tabitha Batey, wife of Benjamin Batey &
       daughter of Wm. W. and Sarah Searcy, May 31, 1849

Robert M. Searcy, son of Wm. W. & Sarah,   January 24, 1851

Lafayette Searcy, son of Wm. W. & Sarah,   March 15, 1852

Lucy W. Searcy, wife of Beverly Randolph,   December 30, 1891

W. W. Searcy, son of W. W. Searcy &
                  Elizabeth Searcy,   September, 1880, aged 80 years

RUTHERFORD COUNTY

SHORT BIBLE RECORD

Short Family Record from a Bible owned by Mrs. Fanny Short Wrather, Route 3, Murfreesboro, Tenn., located on Lebanon & Murfreesboro Pike, 7 miles from Murfreesboro, 2 miles from Walter Hill.
Copied by Miss Annie E. Campbell, from notes of Miss Mary Short, Murfreesboro, Tennessee, Aug. 10, 1937.

Births

Anderson Short was born Oct. 15, 1793
Winefred White was born Mar. 18, 1797
James I. Leach was born July 19, 1817, son of Thomas and Winefred Leach.

Children of Anderson and Elizabeth Short:

Jas. H. Short was born Oct. 6, 1819
Samuel W. Short was born Dec. 24, 1820
Martha Short was born Sept. 22, 1822

Children of Anderson and Winefred Short:

John Short was born Oct. 22, 1825
William Short was born Dec. 31, 1827
Patrick Short was born July 17, 1830
Ann Roberty Short was born Jan. 15, 1838

Peter White was born Mar. 31, 1809
Thomas Leach was born Sep. 21, 1793
Wm. Leach was born June 2, 1795
John Leach was born May 18, 1798

Deaths

Elizabeth Short died Mar. 12, 1823
Winefred Short died Jan. 1, 1839
Anderson Short died Oct. 12, 1876
Peter White died Mar. 9, 1828
Thomas Leach died July 5, 1822

Marriages

Anderson Short and Elizabeth Warren were married in the year 1819
Thomas Leach and Winefred White were married Sep. 27, 1813
Anderson Short and Winefred Leach were married Dec. 23, 1824

BIBLE - RECORDS

RUTHERFORD COUNTY

Record from the Short Family Bible.
Present owner: Mrs. S.D. Short, Walter Hill, Tennessee, on the
Walter Hill and Jefferson Pikes, North-West of Murfreesboro.
Copied by Miss Annie Campbell, Murfreesboro, Tennessee.
March 3, 1937.

BIRTHS:
William Short,
Was born Dec. 31, 1827.

Mahala Elizabeth Williams,
(His wife) was born,
June 17, 1843.

Susan Roberty Short,
Was born Aug. 22, 1861.

Willie Elizabeth Short,
Was born Nov. 14, 1862.

Robert Lee Short,
Was born Jan. 22, 1865.

Franklin Cheatum Short,
Was born Apr. 22, 1866.

Virginia Parthena Short,
Was born Dec. 1, 1867.

Frances Short,
Was born Aug. 23, 1869.

Juliet Short,
Was born Apr. 7, 1871.

Presley Alexander Short,
Was born Aug. 6, 1872.

Ashkenas Short,
Was born Jan. 12, 1874.

Sarah Lizette Short,
Was born Feb. 23, 1876.

Spencer Dillon Short
Was born July 3, 1877.

John Houston Short,
Was born Dec. 22, 1879.

Mattie Lee Short,
Was born Jan. 28, 1888.

MARRIAGES:
William Short and
Mahala Elizabeth Williams,
Were married Nov. 21, 1860.

John Houston Phillips, and
Susan Roberty Short,
Were married Sep. 18, 1879.

DEATHS:
Spencer Dillon Short,
Died Sept. 19, 1931.

RUTHERFORD COUNTY

FAMILY RECORD OF LEONARD SIMS

INDEX

A

B
Bass, Arthur, 2
Bass, Eliza, (Lida) Howse, 2
Bass, Hartwell Jordon, 2
Bass, Hartwell P. 2
Bass, Mary Yeargan, 2
Bates (or Batey) Christopher, 3
Batey, Louisa, 1
Batey, Luisa, 1
Battle, Adelaide, 2
Battle, Allen, 2
Battle, Elizabeth, 2
Battle, Jennie, 2
Battle, L.H. 3
Battle, Lucian, 2
Battle, Robert, 2

C
Caney, Springs, 2
Cooper, Sarah, 2
Crockett, Granville, 1

D
Davidson, B.H. (Dr) 1 - 3

F
Fletcher, Jim, 1

G
Gentry, Camilla, 2

H
Hall, (Mr) 1
Huff, Gertrude, 2

J

K
King, H.A.J. 3

L
Lanier, Sarah, 2
Lawrence, Mary A. 2
Lewis, Jane Meriwether, 1
Lawrence, Edmund, 2

M
Mansfield, Alexander, 3

Marshall Co, 2
Minor, Mary, 2

P
Patterson, Alex, 2
Patterson, Annie, 2
Patterson, Nancy, 2
Patterson, Sam, 2
Patterson, Tom, 2

R
Reid, Benjamin, 2
Reid, Mary, 2
Rutherford Co. 1

S
Sims, Alexander Mansfield, 2
Sims, Artilla Jane, 1
Sims, Bessie, 2
Sims, Camilla, 2
Sims, Charles Yancy, 1
Sims, Charlotte, 1
Sims, Charlotte Amelia, 2
Sims, Clinton, 3
Sims, Dewitt, 2
Sims, Edmund, Bartlett, 2
Sims, Elizabeth Jamison, 1
Sims, Elizabeth Kennon, 1
Sims, Fruzelle, 3
Sims, James Ganaway, 1
Sims, Jane, 1
Sims, Jane M. 1
Sims, Jane Meriwether Lewis, 2
Sims, Jeffie, 2
Sims, John, 1
Sims, John Lewis, 1
Sims, Joseph, 1
Sims, Leonard, 1-2
Sims, Leonard H. 1
Sims, Leonard H (Jr) 1
Sims, Leonard Mansfield, 2
Sims, Lewis S. 2
Sims, Lewis Swepson, 2
Sims, Maggie Bart, 2
Sims, Mai, 3
Sims, Martha Frances, 1
Sims, Mary Ann Elizabeth, 2
Sims, Mary Yeargan, 2
Sims, Mary S. Yeargan, 2

Sims, Nicholas Howell, 2
Sims, Rebecca Frusanna, 2
Sims, Robert Y. 1
Sims, Roxanna J. 1
Sims, Sarah, 1
Sims, Sarah Jane, 2
Sims, Sarah Jane Meriwether, 2
Sims, Sarah Louise, 1
Sims, Sumner, 2
Sims, Susan Barnes, 1
Sims, Susan Francis, 2
Sims, Susie, 2
Sims, Swepson, (Dr) 1-2
Sims, Thomas, 1, 2
Sims, Thomas C. 1
Sims, Thomas Hilary, 2,3
Sims, William Batey, 1
Sims, William S. 1
Snell, Lucy, 3
Snell Sarah Jane, 2
Swepson, Sarah, 1

T
Texas, 1

Y
Yeargan, Mary S. 1

RUTHERFORD COUNTY

FAMILY RECORD OF
LEONARD SIMS

Sims Family Record is property of Mrs. H. B. Hyde, Murfreesboro, Tenn. Rt. #1, about 5 miles S. W. from Murfreesboro, on Barfield road, (4 miles on Murfreesboro & Eagleville Road, turn to left on Barfield Rd)
The Sims family was English.
This family record copied by Miss Annie Campbell, March 22, 1938.

Leonard Sims, Born July 2, 1738, died 1804, (married Sarah Swepson) who was born Oct. 27, 1752, died June 14, 1811.
Their Issue:
Elizabeth Jamison, died Feb. 3, 1835
William Batey Sims, born May 1, 1760. died Jan. 11, 1855, age 95.
Dr. Swepson Sims, (of Rutherford Co) Born May 16, 1775, died Sept. 22, 1850
Dr. Swepson Sims married Jane Meriwether Lewis, born July 31, 1776, died July 22, 1843,
THEIR ISSUE:
Sarah, who married 1st Granville Crockett, 2nd Mr. Hall,
Elizabeth Kennon Sims, who married John Smith
Leonard H (Sims) who married Luisa Batey, (Leonard H Sims was Senator and Congressman) record on pg. 3,
Jane Sims married Jim Fletcher
Susan Barnes, born Jan. 3, 1801, died May 10, 1851
Thomas Sims, married Mary S. Yeargan, (names of their 13, children elsewhere
John Sims (brother to Dr. Swepson perhaps) born 1773, died 1841
Charlotte Sims (his wife) born July 29, 1774, died Oct. 7, 1837
Joseph Sims, born ___died Dec. 1850, (in Texas) (perhaps brother of Dr. Swepson.

Leonard H. Sims (son of Dr. Swepson Sims and Jane M. Sims) born Feb. 27, 1807, (Senator & Congressman) died Feb. 28, 1886, married Louisa Batey Dec. 8, 1824, Louisa Batey was born Jan. 19, 1808, died Feb. 17, 1887

Their 12 children:
William S. Sims, born March 17, 1826, died October 11, 1847
Roxana J. Sims, born April 26, 1828, __d__
Robert Y Sims, born March 2, 1830, __D__
Thomas C. Sims, born Jan. 26, 1832, __d__
Artilla Jane Sims, (wife of Dr. B. H. Davidson) born July 18, 1834, died April 14, 1871
Leonard H. Sims Jr., born Sept. 22, 1836, died July 9, 1854
John Lewis Sims, born Feb. 21, 1839, __died__
James Ganaway Sims, born Feb. 2, 1841, ___d__
Sarah Louisa Sims, born July 2, 1843, died Feb. 22, 1848
Martha Frances Sims, born May 19, 1845, died Jan. 25, 1848
Charles Yancy Sims, born May 10, 1847, died March 9, 1886 (or 1856)
Elizabeth Kennon Sims, born Nov. 3, 1850, d____

(Family Record of Leonard Sims Page-2)

Thomas Sims (son of Dr. Swepson Sims and Jane Meriwether Lewis Sims) was born May 22, 1813, died Jan. 3, 1864.

Mary S. Yeargan Sims, was born May 22, 1813, died Jan. 3, 1864

Thomas Sims was married to Mary S. Yeargan, April 26, 1832.

THEIR CHILDREN
1. Sarah Jane Sims, born April 3, 1833, Died June 22, 1850
2. Lewis Swepson Sims, Boen Dec. 8, 1835, died ___
3. Leonard Mansfield Sims, born Jan. 15, 1838, died Oct. 20, 1856
4. Edmund Bartlett Sims, born Jan. 9, 1840
5. Nicholas Howell Sims, born April 4, 1842, died Jan. 3, 1908,
6. Mary Ann Elizabeth Sims, born April 29, 1844, died June 25, 1886
7. Susan Francis Sims, Born Aug. 29, 1846, died June 9 or 10, 1875,
8. Charlotte Amelia Sims, born March 22, 1849, died Oct. 10, 1868
9. Sarah Jane Meriwether Sims, born March 25, 1851, died April 28, 1914
10. Rebecca Frusanna Sims, born Oct. 2, 1853, died Jan. 4, 1908
11. Thomas Hilary Sims, born Jan. 8, 1856
12. Infant born and died March 4, 1858
13. Alexander Mansfield Sims, born July 29, 1861, died a small child.

Mary A Lawrence was the only daughter of Edmund Lawrence and Sarah Lanier, an English family.
Lanier

Marriages of the children of Thomas Sims & Mary Yeargan Sims.
1. Sarah Jane Sims, never married, died at 17 years of age.
2. Lewis S. Sims, married 3 times.
   1st Sarah Jane Snell, Dec. 13, 1865, (she died Jan. 1, 1867)
   2nd Sarah Cooper, by whom he had a daughter, Bessie, who married Arthur Bass.
   3rd Miss Camilla Gentry, (spinster) who survived him several years, returning to Caney Spring, Tenn. (Marshall Co) to keep house for her two aged brothers.
3. Leonard Mansfield Sims, never married
4. Edmund Bartlett Sims, married , 1. Nancy Patterson, Mch. 7, 1867 they had two children, Sumner and Camilla.
   2. (wife) Gertrude Huff, their issued, Jeffie, Susie, Dewitt, & Leonard, Maggie Bart died young.
5. Nicholas Howard Sims, married Mary Minor (no children)
6. Mary Ann Elizabeth Married Benjamin Reid, Dec. 20, 1876, (1 girl Mary)
7. Charlotte Amelia Sims, married. Hartwell P. Bass, Nov. 21, 1867 (wife and baby died first year.)
8. Susan Francis Sims, married Alex Patterson, (their children, Tom, Sam and annie.
9. Sarah J. M. Sims, married Hartwell P. Bass, (they had 5 children, 1st and last died infants)
   Mary Yeargan Bass,
   Eliza (Lida) Howse Bass, and Hartwell Jordan Bass, were reared to be grown & married.
10. Rebecca Frusanna Sims, married Lucian Battle. Their children, Allen, Jennie, Elizabeth, Adelaide, and Robert, all married.

(Family Record of Leonard Sims Page-3)

11. Thomas Hilary Sims, married Lucy Snell,(4 children) baby died, Clinton, Mai and Fruzelle, all married but, fruzella and baby died.
12. Infant born and died same day
13. Alexander Mansfield died when a child
    Dr. B. H. Davidson died Oct. 9, 1875
    Christopher Bates or Batey, died 1849
    H. A. J. King was born Nov. 1, 1822, died Aug. 2, 1839
    L. H. Battle, died June 20, 1925.

END

BIBLE - RECORDS

RUTHERFORD COUNTY

Record from the Spain Family Bible.
Present owner: Mrs. S.D. Short, Walter Hill, Tennessee, North-
West of Murfreesboro, on the Walter Hill & Jefferson Pikes.
Copied by Miss Annie Campbell, Murfreesboro, Tennessee.
March 3, 1937.

Gideon Wiseman Thomas,
Was born Mar. 12, 1821.
His wife, Nancy Eleanor
McEwen, was born July 16, 1821.

Mary Ann Thomas,
Was born Sep. 27, 1854.

Sarah Eleanor Spain,
Was born June 21, 1880.

Mary Alice Spain,
Was born June 9, 1882.

Martha B. Sims,
Was born May 1, 1831.

James Alexander McEwen,
Was born May 8, 1818.

John Peterson Spain,
Was born May 19, 1811.

Sara (Bond) Spain, Wife of
John P. Spain,
Was born May 19, 1815.

Eliza Green Spain, Daughter,
Was born Oct. 10, 1832.

John W. Spain, Son,
Was born May 22, 1834.

Matilda C. Spain,
Was born Dec. 19, 1835.

Mary Ann Spain,
Was born Oct. 4, 1837.

George L. Spain,
Was born Sep. 30, 1839.

Sion W. Spain,
Was born Nov. 22, 1841.

Delvina Jane Spain,
Was born Nov. 8, 1843.

David Sneed Spain,
Was born Aug. 16, 1847.

Nancy Edney Spain,
Was born Sep. 10, 1845.

Stephen Samuel Spain,
Was born Feb. 25, 1850.

Elizabeth Geneva Spain,
Was born March 20, 1851.

Malissa P. Spain,
Was born May 12, 1854.

Thomas Spain,
Was born Sep. 23, 1857.

MARRIAGES.
Jas. A. McEwen, and
Martha B. Sims, were married,
Mar. 24, 1850.

(Spain Bible p. 2.)

John Peterson Spain, and
Sara Bond, were married,
Dec. 14, 1831.

James F. Jordan and
Eliza Green Spain, were married,
Jan. 10, 1855.

David Sneed Spain and
Mary Ann Thomas, were married,
Nov. 20, 1877.

Samuel Stephen Spain, and
Mrs. Mary McClaren Comer,
Were married May 29, 1904.

Sarah Eleanor Spain, and
Spencer Dillon Short,
Were married Jan. 22, 1899/

Samuel Leland Pettus, and
Mary Alice Spain, were married,
June 10, 1903.

DEATHS:
Nancy Eleanor Thomas,
Died May 8, 1898.

Gideon Wiseman Thomas,
Died Jan. 1, 1908.

Sara Spain, Wife of
John P. Spain,
Died June 5, 1876.

Malissa P. Dosier,
Died April 23, 1900.

Matilda C. Spain, daughter
of John P. & Sara Spain,
Died Sep. 1, 1862.

Elizabeth Geneva Spain,
Died June 15, 1875.

Nancy Edney Spain,
Died July 26, 1895.

Mary A. Spain Taylor,
Died June 9, 1907.

John Peterson Spain,
Died Jan. 1, 1901.

Stephen S. Spain,
Died Nov. 27, 1914.

Milly Spain, Wife of
John Spain,
Died Nov. 22, 1857.

John W. (Jack) Spain,
Died Dec. 8, 1901.

Mary Alice Spain Pettus,
Died Feb. 26, 1905.

David Sneed Spain,
Died June 25, 1915.

Mary Ann Spain, (His wife)
Died July 22, 1924.

RUTHERFORD COUNTY

Bible Records

Copied from a Bible owned by Mrs. Emma Tatum Hayes,
Residence 210 South Spring Street, Murfreesboro, Tenn.
Copied by Annie Campbell Dec. 1, 1936

William Travers	was born	November 15, 1770
John A. Travers	was born	July 15, 1803
Jane C. Travers	was born	November 10, 1805
Samuel Travers	was born	December 10, 1810
William Travers, Junior	" born	September 11, 1813
Benjamin Travers	was born	October 3, 1816

RUTHERFORD COUNTY

Bible Records

Copied from a Bible owned by Mrs. Bettie Shepherd, Residence 410 North Maple Street, Murfreesboro, Tenn. Copied by Annie Campbell Dec 1, 1936

MARRIAGES

Wm. C. Trousdale and Martha J. McDonald,   February 6, 1851.

J. K. Trousdale and Cynthia Tittle,   November 24, 1881

Brice Trousdale and Lona Herod,   November 28, 1879

Bettie Trousdale and John Shepherd,   November 15, 1876

Mary Jane Trousdale and Lee Thompson,   December 1886

BIRTHS

Sarah H. Trousdale,   November 11, 1851

John K. Trousdale,   June 19, 1853

Brison Trousdale,   February 22, 1855

Elisabeth M. Trousdale,   May 30, 1858

Mary Jane Trousdale,   September 25, 1861

DEATHS

Sarah H. Trousdale,   April 15, 1862

Fannie Trousdale,   September 11, 1900

Martha J. Trousdale,   April 12, 1906

William C. Trousdale,   September 15, 1906

RUTHERFORD COUNTY

Bible Records

Copied from a Bible owned by Mrs. Emma Tatum Hayes,
Residence 210 South Spring Street, Murfreesboro, Tenn.
Copied by Annie Campbell Dec. 1, 1936

Marriages

Rev. Alfred C. Tatum and Ann Eliza N. McAdow,	December 31, 1850
Edward T. Hays and Mary M. Tatum,	December 10, 1873
Charles B. New and Martha C. Tatum,	November 1, 1876

Births

Alfred C. Tatum was born	November 22, 1824
Ann Eliza N. Tatum was born	October 8, 1835
Jane Franklin Tatum was born	November 9, 1851
Mary Mason Tatum was born	December 24, 1852
George Donnell Tatum " born	January 6, 1855
Martha Caledonia Tatum born	March 4, 1857
Eliza Hatton Tatum was born	August 21, 1859
Emma Charlotte Tatum " born	January 12, 1862
Julia Milton Tatum was born	April 29, 1864
William Ivy Tatum was born	June 13, 1866
Willis Hickerson Tatum born	September 7, 1868
Edwin Alfred Tatum was born	December 5, 1870
Rev. Nuborn McAdow Tatum was born	March 27, 1876

Tatum Bible Record (Continued)
P. 2.

DEATHS

Jane Franklin Tatum	Died	January 17, 1852
Wilis Hickerson Tatum	died	March 12, 1889
Mary M. Hayes	died	December 30, 1889
William Ivy Tatum	died	June 22, 1890
Edwin Alfred Tatum	died	July 6, 1892
I. D. Tatum	died	May 19, 1908
Ann Eliza N. Tatum	died	July 31, 1903
Julia Milton Kirby	died	March 16, 1908
Rev. Alfred Carroll Tatum died		February 17, 1909

RUTHERFORD COUNTY

TAYLOR - WAIR BIBLE RECORD

Taylor-Wm. King Wair Family Record from the Bible of Mrs. Maria Frances Wair Gaines by her son, Hon. John Wesley Gaines. This copy is owned by Annie E. Campbell, 226 N. Walnut St., Murfreesboro, Tennessee
Copied by Miss Annie E. Campbell, July 7, 1937.

Marriages

November the 6, 1828, Wm. K. Wair was married to Miss Permelia Taylor, all of Davidson County

Wm. K. Wair was married to Miss Eliza Hamlet November 25, 1869

Births

Permelia Taylor   Born   January 21 - 1813
Fanny Taylor   Aprile   5 - 1814
Benjamin Taylor   Sept.   7 - 1815

Martha Ann Wair   February the 29, 1832
Maria Frances Wair daughter of William K. Wair and Permelia his wife was born August 11th at 8 o'clock in the morning in the year of our Lord 1834.
Georgia Ann Wair   B   September 26, 1836
Thos. H. Wair   Sept   7   1838
Lenora Louisa Wair was born November the eighteenth 1840

Births

(Children of Thomas Taylor I and his wife Martha _____ Taylor of Davidson County, Tenn.)

James Taylor, B. July 11th   1771
Susana Taylor, B. Jany. 2nd   1773
John Taylor, B. January 2nd   1775
Mary Taylor, B. March 4th   1777
Robert Taylor, B. April 28   1779
Fanny Taylor, B. April 22   1784
Sarah Taylor, B. March 2,   1786
Thos. Taylor, B. January 27,   1790
Margaret Taylor, B. July 7,   1792
Martha Taylor, B. Oct. 22,   1794

Lenora Lou was born the 18 of November 1840
Wm. Thomas Wair was born Aug. 12th, 1870

RUTHERFORD COUNTY

(Taylor - Wair Bible Record p. 2)

Deaths

Thos. Taylor (I) died August the 9 1815
Martha Taylor wife of Thos. Taylor died August 17 18(26)?
   aged 76 years old

        Sarah Taylor decd June the 10   1805
        Susan Woods   April 5   1811
        Fanny Taylor decd August 5   1814
        Timothy Tracy   1810
        Martha Taylor Feb 10   1816
        Benjamin Taylor Janu 1816
        Thos. Taylor   March 26, 1824
        Susanna Shaw   Sept. 10 1822
        Jonathan Clay   May   19 1825

Thomas Henry Wair departed this life on the twenty-first
day of November aged three years two months and fourteen
days

Thomas Taylor (II) departed this life on the 27 of December 1852

W. K. Wair departed this life on the 5th day of February,   1887

RUTHERFORD COUNTY

TAYLOR FAMILY RECORD

From record of the Taylor family owned by Annie E. Campbell,
226 N. Walnut St., Murfreesboro, Tennessee
Copied by Miss Annie E. Campbell, July 5, 1937.

Children of Robert Taylor and Eliza Branch Taylor, who were
married April 4, 1806 in Davidson County, Tenn.

```
Sally S. Taylor   born Jan.  5, 1807 in Davidson Co. Tenn.
Benjamin B. Taylor born Dec. 4, 1808   "      "        "
Martha Ann Taylor   "    Sept. 13, 1810 "      "        "
Thomas Taylor       "    Sept.  6, 1812 "      "        "
Grizzy Taylor       "    June   6, 1814 "      "        "
Robert Taylor       "    March 24, 1816 "      "        "
Eliza Taylor        "    Nov.  25, 1817 "      "        "
July Wilmoth Taylor "    Feb.  16, 1820 "      "        "
James Morrow Taylor "    Jan.   3, 1822 "      "        "
Frances Taylor      "    Nov.  15, 1823 "      "        "
John Joseph Taylor  "    Aug.  21, 1826 in Rutherford Co. Tenn.
Maria Amandy Taylor "    Feby.  5, 1828 "      "        "      "
William Carol Taylor"    Nov.   6, 1830 "      "        "      "
```

TENNESSEE

RUTHERFORD COUNTY

FAMILY RECORD
A HISTORY OF THE WALTON FAMILY

HISTORICAL RECORDS PROJECT
OFFICIAL PROJECT NO. 465-44-3-115

COPIED UNDER WORK'S PROGRESS ADMINISTRATION

MRS. JOHN TROTWOOD MOORE
STATE LIBRABRIAN & ARCHIVIST, SPONSOR

MRS. ELIZABETH D. COPPEDGE
DIRECTOR OF WOMEN'S & PROFESSIONAL PROJECTS

MRS. PENELOPE JOHNSON ALLEN
STATE SUPERVISOR

MISS MATILDA A. PORTER
SUPERVISOR

COPIED BY
MISS MABEL B. DUBOIS

TYPED BY
MRS. MERVILLE M. COWAN
MISS MABEL B. DUBOIS

JUNE 29, 1938

RUTHERFORD COUNTY

FAMILY RECORD
A History of the Walton Family

The owner of the Walton Family Record is;
Mrs. Josephine Weakley, 203 2nd Ave, No.
Murfreesboro, Tenn.

RUTHERFORD COUNTY

FAMILY RECORD
A HISTORY OF THE WALTON FAMILY

NEW INDEX

A

Ala, 4
Alexandria (Va) 2
Amelia County, 2
America, 2, 4
Augusta, 3
Augusta Chapter D.A.R. 3
Augusta (Ga) 4

B

Betts, Sally, 1
Boonesborough, (Ky) 2
Boyd's Creek, 1
Beautiful Land, 4
Bedford County (Va) 1,2
Bible, 2
Booth, Edwin, 4
Bush River, 1

C

Callaway, 2,3
Callaway, Frances Walton, 1,2
Callaway, George, 1
Callaway, Richard, 2
Camber, Dorothy, 3
Cherokee, 1
Curuch of England, 2
Clay, Henry, 4
Cumberland County (Va) 2, 3
Cumberland Parish, 1

D

Delaware, 2

E

Elizabeth City (Va) 2
England, 2,3

English Bible, 2
Episcopal Church, 2
Europe, 4

F

Florida, 3,4
Franklin State of, 1

G

George, 1, 2
Georgia, 2,3,4

H

Halifax County (Va) 1
Hanover County (Va) 1,2
Hughes, Isaac, 1,3
Hughes, Martha, 1
Hughes, Sally, 1,3

I

Irving, Washington, 4

J

Jefferson, Thomas, 1
John B, 1
Jones, Willis, 1
Jonesbourgh, 1
Judith, 2

K

Kentucky, 2
Knight, 1,2
Knight, Lucian Lamar, 4
Knight, Woodson, 1
Knight & Yarbrough, 1

L

LaFayette, 4
Levert, Henry (Dr) 4
Levert, Madame, 4
Longfellow, Henry W. 4
Louisa County, 2
Lunenburg County (Va) 1

M

Mackain, James, 2
Martha, 1, 2
Meadow Garden, 3
Meherrin Station, 1
Mobile, Ala, 4
Moore, (Mrs) 1
Moore, Fanny, 1
Morton, 1
Morton, Hugh, 1
Mosby, Edward, 2

N

Nancy, 1
New Kent County, 1, 2
New Orleans, 4
North Carolina, 1, 2

O

Old Dominion, 2

P

Patty, 1, 2
Penn, William, 2
Peter's Parish, 2
Philadelphia, 2, 3
Prime Edward County (Va) 3

R

Reab, George Walton, 4
Rebecca, 2
Richmond County, 3
Robert, 1, 2
Robert, Jr. 2
Rochambeau, 4
Rosney, 3
Russell's Creek, 1

S

St. Paul Parrish, 3
St. Peter's Parrish, 2
Sand Hills, 3
Savannah, 3
Scott, Elizabeth, 1
Sherwood, Joseph Frances, 2
Sims, Mary, 2
Susannah, 1

T

Tallahassee, 4
Temperance, 1
Tennessee Eastern, 1
The Draper MSS, 2
Thomas, 1, 2

V

Virginia, 2, 3
Virginia County, 1
Virginia Land Grants, 1

W

Wales, 2
Wall Town, 2
Walton, 2
Walton, (Bishop) 2
Walton, (Gov) 4
Walton, Edward, 2
Walton, Elizabeth, 2
Walton, Frances. 2
Walton, George, 1, 3
Walton, George (Gov) 3
Walton, George, (Jr) 3
Walton, Izaak, 2
Walton, Jesse, 1, 2
Walton, John, 2, 3
Walton, Joseph, 2
Walton, Mary, 2
Walton, Mizapena, 2
Walton, Newell, 2
Walton, Octavia, 4
Walton, Polly, 2
Walton, Polly, 2
Walton, Rebecca, 2
Walton, Robert, 2, 3
Walton, Robert, (Jr) 3

Walton, Robert,(Sr) 1,2
Walton, Sherwood, 2,3
Walton, Simeon, 2
Walton, Tillman(Capt) 2
Walton, William, 2
Washington County, 1,2
Watkins, Robert,(Col) 3
Watkins, Sally (Mrs) 3
Welsh,(town) 2

Y

Yarbrough, 1
Yarbrough, Joseph, 1

RUTHERFORD COUNTY

FAMILY RECORD
A History of the Walton Family

Governor George Walton of Georgia and his cousin, George Callaway of Bedford county, Va., were both named in honor of their wealthy uncle, George Walton, son of Robert Walton, Sr., and brother of Frances Walton Callaway. He was born Feb. 6, 1724-5 in St. Peter's Parish, New Kent county, and died in Lunenburg county Va. 1780. Married in Cumberland county, Va., May 22, 1749, Martha Hughes, daughter of Isaac Hughes and sister of Sally Hughes. From 1753 to 1756 he was a vestryman of Cumberland Parish, Lunenburg county, Va. In 1762 he conveyed 262 acres in Bedford county, Va. The same year he bought 400 acres in Bedford county, Va., where from year to year his grants increased rapidly, the selection of much of the land being made by his brother, Sherwood, the surveyor. (See Virginia County Records, Vol 6, page 276) Virginia Land Grants, Volume C, pg 197, show that Feb. 1, 1781, Thomas Jefferson conveyed to George Walton 1850 acres in Halifax county, Va., on the branches of Russell's creek.

Knight's Reminiscences state that George Walton had a plantation of 2700 acres on Bush river and lived about four miles north of Meherrin Station (now on the Southern R.R.). Knight relates the family tradition that, when Tarleton's cavalry reached what is now Meherrin, George Walton heard of the approach of the raiders. He was then 56 years of age, but somewhat of an invalid and unequal to heavy exertion. But he hastened to bury an earthen jar of gold coins. The exertion was too much for him. He died the next morning. For more than fifty years afterward efforts were made to discover the whereabouts of the jar of gold, but it was never found.

The Virginia Court of Appeals shows the case of Knight & Yarbrough in the year 1820. This states that the will of George Walton was recorded July, 1798 (a long time after his death!) and the will of his wife, Martha, was recorded in October, 1814. This document proves untrue a statement I have sometimes run across, that Martha died in middle age and he then married her sister, Nancy. The Court of Appeals records the following children of George and Martha, as being alive in 1820:
 (1) "Thomas, who has issue."
 (2) John B.
 (3) "Robert has issue, Robert and Thomas"
 (4) " Mrs. Moore has issue, including Fanny Moore."
 (5) "Temperance, wife of Joseph Yarbrough, who has issue"
 (6) "Susannah, wife of ____ Morton, who has issue, among others Hugh Morton"
 (7) Mrs. Sally Betts
 (8) Martha (Patty) wife of Woodson Knight. This couple were married in Prince Edward Co., Va., June 18, 1781.
Besides the above there was at least one other child, viz.:
George, who moved to Georgia, but returned to Virginia, where he died about 1806; he had married Elizabeth Scott; among his descendants was a grandson, William Scott Walton. In some lists Jesse Walton, well known in early history of Eastern Tennessee, is given as a son of George and Martha. Jesse Walton in 1780 commanded a division at the battle of Boyd's Creek in the Cherokee expedition; he represented Washington county (now Tenn) in the general assembly of North Carolina and introduced a bill for the establishment of Jonesborough, named in honor of Willie Jones, a leading politician. Jonesborough was the first capital of the state of Franklin and is still

the seat of justice of Washington county, Tenn. The Draper MSS mentions Jesse Walton as a "near relative" of Sherwood Walton and his sister, Frances Walton Callaway, but does not indicate the exact relationship. If he was a son of George and Martha, he had died before the Court of Appeals in 1820 listed the children then surviving.

Knight believes that these brothers and sisters, Robert, Jr., Rebecca, George, Joseph Frances and Sherwood, were the sons of the immigrant, and that this immigrant probably accompanied William Penn on the ship "Welcome" that anchored in the waters of the Delaware Oct. 3, 1682. But we find the father of this family, Robert Walton, Sr., an Episcopalian, living in New Kent (now Hanover) county, Va., in 1717, when his eldest child was born. It is somewhat difficult to believe that a member of the Church of England would have a colony of Friends to America. There was a John Walton in Elizabeth City, Va., in 1621, and other Waltons lived in the Old Dominion in the 17th century. Indeed the name was far from uncommon in Cumberland county, or elsewhere. In the 18 the century the records show numerous Waltons. There was a Thomas Walton, who March 27, 1750, signed a deed in Cumberland county, and later documents show that he had a son, Robert, also a daughter, Patty (deceased in 1794) wife of Edward Mosby (who died intestate in 1769). This Thomas might have been a nephew of Robert Walton, Sr. There was an Edward Walton in Cumberland county, father of two daughters, Martha and Judith. Judith, born 1770, married 1787 her first cousin, Capt. Tillman Walton, a Revolutionary soldier who died in North Carolina. In Hanover county lived John and Mary (Sims) Walton, parents of Edward (born 1743), George (of Amelia county) John (of Louisa county) and Simeon Walton, whose daughter, Polly Walton, married James Mackain 1793, and they were at Boonesborough, Ky. in 1795. Other children of John and Mary were Mary, Jesse, Elizabeth, Robert, Frances, William, Mizapena and Newell (born 1763).

It is said the name Walton was derived from the Welsh town where the family lived. A high wall built around the town caused outsiders to call it Wall-Town, which name soon came to be attached to the people living within the walls. Records show that the Waltons moved from Wales to England, but just when this line of the family settled in the new world is not positively known. Nor do we know if they were related to Izaak Walton, beloved fisherman; or to Bishop Walton, a compiler of the polyglot edition of the English Bible.

THE WALTON FAMILY OF VIRGINIA

The Walton family of Virginia became allied with the Callaway family through the marriage, in 1745 in Bedford county, Va., of Richard Callaway and Frances Walton, daughter of Robert and Frances Walton. The records of St. Peter's Parish, New Kent county (now Hanover county) Va., (which are now in the semnary at Alexandria, Va.,) show the Walton family to have been identified with the Episcopal Church and preserve the birth dates of the following children of Robert and Frances:

(1) Robert Walton, Jr., born Jan. 7, 1717-18, in St. Peter's Parish.
(2) Rebecca, born April 20, 1720, in the same parish. No. record.
(3) Joseph Walton, born Feb. 10, 1721-2. One of his sons, William Walton, of Georgia, was a member of the Revolutionary Congress at Philadelphia in 1781.
(4) George Walton, born Feb. 6, 1724-5, also in St. Peter's Parish,
(5) Frances Walton, born Jan. 14 1726-7, in St. Peter's Parish; married 1745 Richard Callaway; died 1766.

(6) Sherwood Walton, born July 1, 1728 a distinguished citizen of
Virginia; well-known as surveyor and land owner; a friend
of the Callaway family.

Robert Walton, Jr., the eldest of this family, married Sally Hughes, daughter of Isaac Hughes, of Cumberland county, Va., (will proved in 1758). He died while still in life's prime. In his family there were four children, namely:
(1) Mrs. Sally Watkins
(2) Robert, who died in Charlotte county, Va.
(3) George Walton, signer of the Declaration of Independence 1776; governor of Georgia 1779-80 and 1789-90.
(4) John Walton, a pioneer of Georgia, who represented the parish of St. Paul in the Provincial Congress July 4, 1775; a member of the Council of Safety; a member of the Continental Congress in 1778; and a signer of the Articles of Confederation. He died in 1783 while acting as surveyor of Richmond county, and while living near Augusta, Ga. His brother, George, was one of his executors. The other brother, Robert, was at the time serving as an officer of the colonial army in Virginia.

GOV. GEORGE WALTON, SIGNER

GOVERNOR GEORGE WALTON of Georgia, son of Robert Walton, Jr., and nephew of Frances Walton Callaway (wife of Richard Callaway). was born in Prince Edward county, Va., 1749; was named for a wealthy uncle. George Walton, of whom more hereafter. Was apprenticed to a carpenter. Went to Georgia at the age of 20; studied law at Savannah; was admitted to the bar; in 1777 married Dorothy Camber, said to have been the daughter of an English nobleman. He was present at the meeting, July 27, 1774, to protest against the tyrany of England; was a member of the Council of Safety; was secretary of the Sons of Liberty July 4, 1775, and had the honor of formulating the document that set forth the reasons for dissolving relations with England. He was at Philadelphia July 4, 1776, to sign the Declaration of Independence and represented Georgia in Continental Congress until the close of the war, excepting only the term of his service as governor. He was commanding colonel of the First Georgia battalion and narrowly escaped death when the British captured Savannah in 1778. But he as seriously wounded and held as a prisoner of war until finally exchanged for a naval captain. He was repeatedly returned to the Continental Congress and in 1789 was again elected governor. He represented Georgia in the United States senate, served as judge of the superior court for 15 years, and also as chief justice of the supreme court of Georgia. No man in the entire history of Georgia was ever more signally honored by the state than Governor George Walton. He owned a summer home on the Sand Hills and a winter home at Meadow Garden near Augusta; the latter is now the property of Augusta Chapter, D.A.R. It was in this home that his death occurred Feb.2, 1801, said to have been hastened by the death of his eldest son, Thomas Camber Walton. Interment was in the family burial ground of his sister's son, Col. Robert Watkins, at Rosney, but fifty years afterward the body was exhumed and placed under the monument at Augusta, erected to the Georgia signers.

Governor George Walton was survived by his widow and a son, George Walton, Jr. The latter served as secretary of the territory of east Florida;

one of the counties of Florida was named for him. The state capital was named Tallahassee (or Beautiful Land) by his daughter, Octavia Walton (afterward Madame LeVert). She was born near Augusta, Ga., in 1810, and married Dr. Henry LeVert of Mobile, Ala., whose father came to America as fleet surgeon under Rochambeau. Madame Levert was not only beautiful, but cultured as well. She spoke most of the tongues of Europe fluently. She won the friendship of Lafayette, Washington Irving, Henry W. Longfellow, Edwin Booth, Henry Clay and many other illustrious men. When the monument to Clay was unveiled at New Orleans, she delivered the address of the occasion. and it attracted wide attention for depth of thought and clarity of diction. When she died, it is said that her only living descendant was a grandson, George Walton Reab, of Augusta, Ga. For detailed information regarding the Governor Walton family read that interesting book, Reminiscences of Famous Georgians, by Lucian Lamar Knight.

--- End ---

BIBLE - RECORDS

RUTHERFORD COUNTY

Record from a Bible owned by Mrs. N. Y. Wilburn.
Residence 9 miles on the Bradyville Pike, South-East of
Murfreesboro, Tennessee.
Copied by Miss Mabel DuBois, Murfreesboro, Tenn.
February 17, 1937.

MARRIAGES:
Benjamin B. Patillo, To
Nancy E. Ward,
Sept. 19, 1838.

BIRTHS:
Burrell Ward,
Was born June 21, 1794.

Mary B. McClanahan,
Was born Mar. 31, 1802.

Tennessee Texana Ward,
Was born June 10, 1846.

DEATHS:
Burrell B. Ward,
Died June 14, 1856.

Benjamin A. Ward,
April 29, 1864.

Tennessee Texana Ward,
Died Feb. 7, 1848.

Mary B. Ward,
Died April 23, 1873.

Raiford Ward,
Died Dec. 10, 1934.

Mary C. Ward,
Died ---, 27, 1910.

Robert M. Ward,
Died April 17, 1920.

BIBLE - RECORDS

RUTHERFORD COUNTY

Record from the Bible of Burwell Ward.
Present owner: Mrs. Jarman Edwards, (Hallie Hunt)
Residence: 740 N. Spring St., Murfreesboro, Tenn.
Copied by Miss Annie E. Campbell, Murfreesboro, Tenn.
January 15, 1937.

Children of Burwell Ward, &
Mary B. Ward, his wife.

Nancy L. Ward,
Was born October 17, 1822.

William D. Ward,
Was born April 16, 1824.

Sarah Ann Ward,
Was born December 12, 1825.

Matilda Jane Ward,
Was born October 15, 1827.

James Ward,
Was born April 23, 1830.

Raiford C. Ward,
Was born February 27, 1832.

Robert McGulkin Ward,
Was born August 13, 1834.

Benjamin A. Ward,
Was born October 10, 1836.

Mary C. Ward,
Was born January 31, 1844.

RUTHERFORD COUNTY

Bible Records

Copied from a Bible owned by Miss M.B. McDonald.
Residence Smyrna, Tenn.
Copied by Mabel B. DuBois Dec. 1, 1936

Marriages

James J. Ward and Mary J. Leath, June 18, 1850

George W. McDonald Sr. and Isabella Ward, Feb. 6, 1866

Births and Deaths

James J. Ward	Born August 23, 1817 Died Feb. 1, 1886
Louisa Ward	Born Sept. 25, 1819 Died March 29, 1849
Mary J. Leath Ward	Born Dec. 20, 1824 Died Nov. 21, 1912
Mary E. Ward	Born Nov. 18, 1838
Martha Ward	Born Sept. 5, 1840
Josephine Ward	Born Oct. 18, 1846
Andrew J. Ward	Born March 21, 1849 Died June 12, 1892
William E. Ward	Born April 17, 1851 Died Aug. 15, 1909
Charles A. Ward	Born June 15, 1852 Died Aug. 3, 1902
Frances C. Ward	Born Sept. 29, 1855
Fanny Ward Sherrell	Born Sept. 5, 1853 Died April 23, 1916
Isabella Ward McDonald	Born Jan. 5, 1843 Died Feb. 18, 1917
Jennie McDonald	Born Aug. 15, 1804
George W. McDonald Sr.	Born Jan. 12, 1834 Died May 13, 1904

BIBLE - RECORDS

RUTHERFORD COUNTY

Record from the Williamson Family Bible.
Present owner: Mr. W. T. Snell.
Residence: 4 miles North-East of Murfreesboro, Tenn., on the Lascassas Pike.
Copied by Miss Mabel Baird DuBois, Murfreesboro, Tenn.
January 8, 1937.

Richard W. Williamson &
Charlotte Dixon,
Was married May 17, 1838.

Richard W. Williamson &
Sarah Glenn,
Was married August 29th, 1841.

Richard W. Williamson &
Mary Ann House,
Was married December 25th, 1849.

BIRTHS:
Richard W. Williamson,
Was born the 9th, Oct. 1814.

Charlotte, the Wife of
Richard W. Williamson,
Was born November 18th, 1812.

Mary A., Wife of
Richard W. Williamson,
Was born November 2, 1825.

Thos. Daniel, Son of
R.W. & C. Williamson,
Was born Aug. 20th, 1840.

John H., Son of
R.W. & S. Williamson,
Was born November the 22nd, 1844.

Martha Jane, Daughter of
R.W. & S. Williamson,
Was born August 12th, 1847.

Richard Thomas, Son of
R.W. & M.A. Williamson,
Was born October 21st, 1850.

Catharine Raney, Daughter of
R.W. & M.W. Williamson,
Was born January 17, 1853.

Louisa Jane, Daughter of
G. A. & M.A. House,
Was born January 23rd, 1843.

William George, Son of
G.A. & M.A. House,
Was born September 6th, 1844.

Mary A.L. Snell, Daughter of
James H. & L.J. Snell,
Was born July 22nd, 1861.

DEATHS:
Charlotte, Wife of
R. W. Williamson,
Died March 19th, 1841.

Thos. Daniel, Son of
R. W. & C. Williamson,
Died June 19th, 1841.

Sarah, wife of R.W. Williamson,
Died the 6th of August, 1849.

Richard T. Williamson, Son of
R.W. Williamson, Died May 6, 1856.

Richard W. Williamson,
Departed this life, April 13, 1886

TOMBSTONE - INSCRIPTIONS

BEESLEY CEMETERY
RUTHERFORD COUNTY

Located Six Miles West of Murfreesboro, Tenn., between the Manson and Franklin Pikes.
Copied by Miss Mábel DuBois, Murfreesboro, Tennessee.
February 8, 1937.

Lillian Orlean Beesley,
Born Jan. 8, 1888.
Died ---, 13, 1888.

John Beesley,
Born Sept. 3, 1840.
Died July 3, 1891.

Daughter of
Christppher & Bettie Beesley,
Born July 18, 1886.
Died Feb. 28, 1888.

Christopher Beesley,
Born July 19, 1804.
Died Mar. 10, 1879.

Cascendre Beesley,
Born May 28, 1782.
Died Sept. 27, 1873.

In Memory of, S. Beesley,
Born June 15, 1779.
Died Feb. 27, 1862.

Rachel Beesley,
Born April 6, 1800.
Died July 12, 1887.

In Memory of
N. W. Beesley,
Born June 16, 1838.
Died Oct. 16, 1867.

Benjamin I. Haynes,
Born Jan. 1, 1855.
Died April 17, 1872.
Age 17 y. 3m. 17 d.

Wat J. Hollowell,
May 6, 1849.
June 5, 1872.

Mollie L. Hall, Wife of
Charles A. Beesley,
May 2, 1876.
Feb. 19, 1906.

RUTHERFORD COUNTY

BLACK – COLEMAN GRAVEYARD

Located 5 miles North of Murfreesboro & Lebanon Highway. Graveyard to left of & adjoining Highway, on farm settled by Samuel P. Black, Sr., now owned by Sam Black Wade, Murfreesboro, Tenn. R.R. #2.
Copied by Miss Annie E. Campbell, Murfreesboro, Tenn., June 18, 1938.

Sacred to the memory of
John R. Wilson, M.D.
Born April 4th 1799
Died Aug. 8th 1854

To our Mother, Eliza P.,
wife of John R. Wilson, M.D.,
daughter of Samuel P. &
Fanny Black
Born Oct. 1, 1806
Died Jan. 17, 1864

Two old fashioned box tombs with inscriptions too worn to read. One of these marks the grave of Samuel P. Black, Sr., who settled this place.

Nannie L., wife of William A. Wilkinson, daughter of Thos. G. & Catharine Black
Born Nov. 19, 1839
Died Nov. 5, 1866

Samuel P. Black
Born April 10, 1837
Died March 24, 1898
  "Into thy hands I commend my spirit."

Catharine W., wife of Thomas C. Black, M.D.
Born Jan. 11, 1817
Died Jan. 15, 1891
  "Even so Father; for so it seems good
   in thy sight."

Thomas C. Black, M. D.
Born Mar. 18, 1809
Died May 29, 1873
  "Mark the perfect man and behold the
   upright, For the end of that man is
   peace."

Mary Eliza Coleman
Born 1857
Died 1873
(Inscription unreadable)

Fanny J. Coleman
wife of Walter P. Coleman, M.D.
daughter of Samuel P. &
Fanny Black
Born Aug. 4, 1821,
Died May 11, 1862

Sacred to the Memory of
Mrs. Fanny Black
Consort of the late
Samuel P. Black
Born 1779
Died Oct. _____ 1854.
(Part of inscription on the
above old fashioned box tomb
is unreadable.)

Walter Preston Coleman, M.D.
Born Feb. 7, 1823
Died June 10, 1870
  "As we believe that Jesus
   died and rose again even so
   them also which sleep in
   Jesus will God bring with
   him."

Ellen Douglas
daughter of W. P. & Sally N.
Coleman
Born Mar. 7, 1889
Died Nov. 19, 1889

Nannie Black
wife of Hinton J. Baker
Nov. 30, 1879
Dec. 18, 1914

Mattie V. Chadwick
Died Jan. 17, 1921
Aged 85 yrs.

TOMBSTONE - INSCRIPTIONS

OLD BRADLEY GRAVEYARD
RUTHERFORD COUNTY

Located 2 miles North-East of Murfreesboro, Tennessee, on Halls Hill Pike, on farm owned by Mrs. John Lillard.
Information given by Mrs. Jarman Edwards.
Residence: 740 N. Spring St., Murfreesboro, Tenn.
Copied by Miss Annie Campbell, Murfreesboro, Tenn.
January 15, 1937.

There is no trace of this old grave-yard left, the tombstones have moved away. This is the burial place of John Bradley, a Revolutionary Soldier, noted as a Race-Track man, and a Trainer of Horses. Bradley's Race Track was noted in this section of Tennessee.
    Bradley's Academy was given by John Bradley. For many years this school was attended by the young men of this town, and the youth of other towns came to Murfreesboro to study.
  James K. Polk came here prior to his entering University of North Carolina. "Major" Jack Bradley was a well known figure of this section for many years.

TOMBSTONE - INSCRIPTIONS

OLD BUTLER GRAVEYARD
RUTHERFORD COUNTY

Located 4 miles South of Murfreesboro, Tennessee, on the
Murfreesboro and Shelbyville Highway, on farm owned by
W. T. Todd; property for many years of Mr. and Mrs. James
M. Knight & settled by Wm. S. Butler. This is the burial
place of two Confederate Soldiers.
Copied from notes of Mrs. W. T. Todd, by Miss Annie Campbell,
Murfreesboro, Tennessee.
June 16, 1937.

Wm. S. Butler,
Mar. 26, 1798.
Jan. 30, 1873.

I. W. Butler,
1841 - 1863.
Soldier-1861-1865-C.S.A.

Nancy E. Campbell, Wife of
Wm. S. Butler,
Feb. 15, 1812.
Oct. 22, 1888.

Henry W. Butler,
1850 - 1876.
Brave-Generous-True.

Our Babies:
Dennis S., Warner,
Lewis, James K.P.

Little Children of
Dr. R.J.& Laura B. Turner,
Joe, Annie Laurie.
"Jesus took them up in his
arms and blessed them."

Joe E. Butler,
1839 - 1868.
Soldier-1861-1865-C.S.A.

TOMBSTONE - INSCRIPTIONS

OLD CAMPBELL GRAVEYARD
RUTHERFORD COUNTY

Located 3½ miles South-West of Murfreesboro, Tennessee, on Midland Road, (off Murfreesboro and Eagleville Pikes) now owned by J.J. Harlan. This place is known as the "Campbell Spring" Place, having been settled in 1803 by Samuel Campbell, and owned by his son and grandson until 1895; since when there have been several changes of ownership. The present house was built in 1858 or 1859.
Copied by Mrs. Sadie McLaurine and Miss Annie Campbell.
May 25, 1937.

CAMPBELL:
Wm. E. Campbell,
1845-1924.
His wife,
Eleanor Taylor,
1845-1930.
Foot-Stones Marked:
W.E.C.-E.T.C.

S.Side-
Rev. Wm. Eagleton, Pastor of
Presbyterian Church,
Murfreesboro, Tenn. 36 yrs,
Born in Blount Co. E. Tenn.
Mar. 25, 1796.
Died Mar. 28, 1866.
North-Side-
Margaret Ewing, consort of
Rev. Wm. Eagleton,
Born in Blount Co. E. Tenn.
Aug. 4, 1795.
Died July 7, 1864.
East-Side-
In Memory of,
Father and Mother.

David S. Campbell,
Born Mar. 26, 1847.
Died Feb. 7, 1879.

James W. Lowe,
Born March 2nd, 1837.
Died July 29th, 1897.
"Asleep in Jesus."

(5 Graves marked with limestone markers, no inscriptions. Information as to dates, etc., supplied by Annie E. Campbell, Murfreesboro, Tennessee.)

Samuel Campbell, Sr.,
Born in Campbell County, Va.
Jan. 15, 1769.
Died Sept. 7, 1846.

Nancy Mann Campbell, Wife of
Samuel Campbell, Sr.
Born in Georgia in 1778.
Died Aug. 28, 1841.

Samuel Campbell, Jr.,
Born Jan. 9, 1816, in
Rutherford Co. Tenn.
Died Apr. 28, 1875.

(Campbell Graveyard p.2.)

Elvira Eagleton Campbell,
Wife of Samuel Campbell,Jr.
and daughter of Rev. Wm.
Eagleton &Margaret Ewing Eagleton.
Born in Blount County,Tenn.
Born July 27, 1821.
Died Jan. 6, 1878.

Margaret Angeline Eagleton,
Daughter of Rev.Wm.Eagleton,
& Margaret Ewing Eagleton,
Born Jan. 27, 1817,in
Blount County, Tenn.
Died Aug. 18, 1895.

(8 Unmarked Graves)
Josiah Campbell,
Born Dec. 25, 1809.
Died ---,---, 188-?

Arabella Smith Sumpter,
Born in Giles County,Tenn.
Widow of Dr.Volney Sumpter.

Vira Belle Campbell,Infant
daughter of John A.Campbell,
and Nettie Sumpter Campbell.
Born Oct. 15, 1878.
Died Nov. 28, 1878.

Children of Wm.E Campbell,&
Eleanora Taylor Campbell;
Infant son,Samuel Campbell,III,
Born October 24, 1872.
Died Feb. 17, 1902.

Harry Elam Campbell,
Born May 13, 1877.
Died March 28, 1928.

David Campbell,
Born March 9, 1879.
Died July --, 1881.

Mahala Floyd,(col.)
Faithful servant for many years,
Died in 1894.

TOMBSTONE - INSCRIPTIONS

CARLTON GRAVEYARD
RUTHERFORD COUNTY

Located 1 mile North of Rockvale, Tenn., on Snail Shell Cave Road, on C. E. Yeargan farm,(West of Murfreesboro,& Eagleville Pikes.)
Copied by Miss Annie Campbell, Murfreesboro, Tenn.
December 26, 1936.

Willis Jackson,
Born September 24,1810.
Died August 1, 1869.

Martha Ann Carlton,Daughter of
Benagea & Mary Carlton,
Born September 8, 1823.
Died April 16, 1874.

Mary, Wife of Benagea Carlton,
Born 1780.
Died December 25,1847.

Benagea Carlton,
Born October 17, 1782.
Died October 1850

Hannah, Wife of
Kinion Carlton,
Born September 3,1820.
Died October 11, 1859.

Henry Frazier Carlton,Son of
Kinion & Margaret Carlton,
Born November 9, 1871.
Died June 23, 1872.

Mary J.,Daughter of
Kinion Carlton,
Born September 18,1839.
Died October 6, 1840.

Margaret L.,Daughter of
Kinion Carlton,
Born February 22, 1832.
Died August 2, 1837.

Christopher G.,Son of
Kinion Carlton,
Born December 20, 1841.
Died October 22, 1844.

Horace L. Holder,
Born April 8, 1901.
Died April 30, 1931.
James B., Son of
P.B. Smotherman,
Born Nov. 11, 1869.
Died August 10, 1890.

-Kirby G., Son of
M. B. & Tabitha Carlton,
------------------?

William. Son of
Benagea & Mary Carlton,
Born September 30,1812.
Died May ----, 1847.

Wm. Blake Carlton,
Born January 11, 1814.
Died August 17, 1856.
"Our Mother",Mary Carlton,
Born March 17, 1818.
Died May 27, 1898.

Kinion Carlton,
Born -----1815.
Died November 5, 1880.
(Monument adorned with
Masonic Emblems.)

(Carlton Graveyard, p.2.)

Alice, Daughter of
Kinion & Margaret Carlton,
Born September 1, 1875.
Died in Infancy.

Charles B., Son of
Kinion Carlton,
Born August 28, 1866.
Died March 15, 1867.

Lucinda Elizabeth(Carlton),
Wife of Marion Jackson,
Born August 4, 1846.
Died April 5, 1872.

Willis M., Son of
Kinion Carlton,
Born December 20, 1858.
Died February --, 1859.

Tennessee, Daughter of
Kinion Carlton,
Born June 30, 1855.
Died January 30, 1859.

Robert M. Smotherman,
Born January 26, 1846.
Died December 9, 1875.
(Monument adorned with
Masonic Emblems.)

Leila E., Daughter of
M.B. & Tabitha Carlton,
Born May 18, 1884.
Died December 4, 1909.

Martha M. Carlton, Loftin,
Born October 16, 1850.
Died July 5, 1894.

John A. Loftin,
Born September 7, 1846.
Died November 25, 1905.

David Walker Carlton,
Born September 13, 1878.
Died August 15, 1879.

Herbert Carlton,
Born February 29, 1888.
Died September 15, 1889.

Robert Carlton,
Born February 9, 1890.
Died June 24, 1890.

F. Elam Carlton,
Born March 24, 1881.
Died July 4, 1903.

F. M. Carlton,
Born June 14, 1851.
Died September 20, 1906.

Mrs. F. M. Carlton,
Born August 3, 1853.
Died February 5, 1927.

RUTHERFORD COUNTY

OLD CITY CEMETERY

MURFREESBORO

The Old City Cemetery is located in Murfreesboro, between Vine and State Streets, 4 blocks from the public square.
Many of the monuments and markers are broken and defaced, some of the stones are face down on the ground and the inscriptions are fast becoming unreadable.
Copied by Mrs. Sadie McLaurine, Miss Annie Campbell and Miss Mabel DuBois, Jan. 13, 1938.

Pvt. William Burnett
    Jeffries Co. Va. Troops
    Rev. War
        1845

John Bradley
    Virginia
    Major
    Rev. War
        1833

Samuel McClanahan
    Virginia
    Major
    Rev. War
        1850

William Smith
    Sgt. 7, Va. Regt.
    Rev. War
        1830

(Maj. John Bradley was buried at his family burial ground a mile from Murfreesboro on Halls Hill Pike Northeast of Murfreesboro, long since this graveyard has disappeared.)

(The burial places of William Burnett, Samuel McClanahan & William Smith are not known.)

    Richard Keele
    Pvt. Sevier's N. C. Regt.
        Rev. War
            1849

Sacred to the Memory of
    Samuel Wilson
died the 11th Sept. 1830
Aged 72 years.
  "Here lies the brave
    the virtuous
    the independent and
    honest man the lover
    of liberty and truth in
    (defaced) which
    was respected by all
    who knew him in life and
    lamented in death."

(Samuel Wilson was buried about 3 miles from Murfreesboro near National Cemetery on Nashville & Murfreesboro highway. The original stones were removed to the old City Cemetery in Murfreesboro by the Capt. Wm. Lytle Chapter D.A.R., 1937.)

    Robert Smith
Capt. Va. Continental Troops
    Rev. War
    Sept. 30, 1822

(Note: The above stone was placed 1937 by the Capt. Wm. Lytle Chapter D.A.R. Capt. Smith is said to be buried at the old Washington graveyard on Manson Pike.)

Note: Government Markers were placed by Capt. Wm. Lytle Chapter, D.A.R. to the above Revolutionary Soldiers of Rutherford County.

RUTHERFORD COUNTY   (Old City Cemetery p. 2)

Greenville T. Henderson
    Born
  Sept. 28, 1803
    Died
  March 1, 1888
"A Preacher of the Gospel for 66 years,
  Honored in life,
  Remembered in Death!"

    Matilda
Daughter of Chas. & Catherine Keyser,
    Wife of
Rev. G. T. Henderson,
  was born in Philadelphia, Pa.
  Oct. 21, 1803
After serving God and her generation,
  A teacher of school Half a century,
  She died Jan. 11, 1874
"Trusting in Christ,
The Resurrection and the Life."

    Eliza Wingo
   Consort of
  Thos. R. Wingo
 Born Dec. 6th 1832
 Died Aug. 6th 1858
Aged 25 yrs. 8 mo. 10 da.
"She was lovely & amiable in life
& died in the full triumph of a Christian
faith."

   Jno. Wm. Wingo
    Born
  Feby. 17th, 1855
  Died March 6th ___
  Aged 18 days.

    Sacred
    To the
   Memory of
Melville C. Henderson
Born May 12, 1835
Died Oct. 25, 1889

    MOTHER
 Emily C. McFarlin
    Born
  March 6th, 1832
  Died March 29, 1878
  Aged   46 years

   One Stone
The Mother & Daughter
  In Memory of
  Mrs. Martha
  Consort of
 Dr. James Brook.
daughter of the late
Thomas & Sophia
   Jordan
Born Feb. 12, 1826
Died Nov. 21, 1858
    Also
    Lula
Infant daughter of
James & Martha
   Brook
Born Aug. 25, 1856
Died July 7, 1858

   Sacred
To the Memory of
  Mary I. Ray
  Daughter of
John C. & A. T. Ray
Born May 29, 1850
Died Sept. 29, 1851
Aged 1 year & 4 months

  In Memory of
William C. Ray
Son of Jno. C. & A. T. Ray
  Born Sept. 10, 1852
  Died Aug. 6, 1853
Aged 10 mos. 27 days

  In Memory of
Martha C. Fletcher
  Daughter of
Granderson & Ann Fletcher
  Born Nov. 5, 1852
  Died Sept. 18, 1853

Sacred to the Memory of
Benjamin Smith
  Died Feb. 26, 1882
  Aged 77 years
"He lived a consistent
Christian throughout life."

Sacred to the Memory of
Judyann Smith
  Born July 10, 1837
  Died Sept. 21, 1846

RUTHERFORD COUNTY   (Old City Cemetery p. 3)

Sacred to the Memory of
James S. Smith
Born Aug. 10, 1834
Died Nov. 2, 1853
Aged 19 yrs. 2 mo. and 22 days

Sacred to the Memory of
Artemesia M.
Daughter of Jas. M. & Mary A.
Weatherly
Consort of Shirwood W. Smith
Died Aug. 4, 1860
Aged 18 years & 25 days
"Weep not my _____
Dry up your tears
For I must ly here
Till Christ appears."

In Memory of
Mrs. Rosia A. B. Smith
Consort of H. P. Smith
born in Granville County, N. C.
Oct. the 27th 1827, died June 24th, 1851

Sacred to the Memory of
Stacy Taylor
who died 5th Dec. 1825 in the
19th year of his age

(top of stone broken off)
of Edward Infant son of Frances &
W. A. O'Callathan, born May 14, 1853
died Jan. 12, 1854, aged 7 months
& 29 days.
"Thus youth in its loveliest bloom
must waste & wither in the tomb."

Sallie wife of A. M. Cawthon
Born Jan. 9, 1867
Died Dec. 22, 1890

Rhoda V. Wife of A. M. Cawthon
Born Oct. 6, 1844
died July 15, 1887

James Cawthon
Born Oct. 6, 1807
Died April 17, 1882
"A devoted Father."

Richard C. Cawthon
Born Apr. 25, 1867
Died Sept. 1, 1917

(Masonic Emblem & Open Book)
Ard P. Davis was born
February the 16th 1822
and died February 5, 1846

In Memory of
Mary W. R. Ganaway,
consort of
John Ganaway
Born April 20th 1795
Died March 19, 1855

In Memory of
John Ganaway
Born March 23d 1788
Died July 12th 1851
"Son of Temperance."

In Memory of
Matthias Lepard
Born May 2, 1821
Died Dec. 20, 1858

(On One Stone)
South side
In Memory of Bennett Smith
died in his 85th year
North side
In Memory of Isabella Smith
Died in her 84 year.

Sacred to the Memory of
Rev. James Porter Rankin
Born May 10th, 1805
Died Sept. 11th, 1831
Aged 26 years 1 mo. & 1 day

Sacred to the Memory of
Maj. Samuel H. Hodge
Born 1st. Jan. 1800
Died 29th March 1846
"In the midst of his years
& usefulness
He fell Lamented by his
family by the Presbyterian
Church & by the Community."

RUTHERFORD COUNTY   (Old City Cemetery p. 4)

R. M. Searcy
Lieut. 34th Ala. Rgt.
Born at Tuscaloosa, Ala.
   Mar. 20, 1844
Died at Murfreesboro, Tenn.
   Jan. 7, 1863

Our loved and honored
   Father
Dr. James Maney
Born in Hertford Co. N. C.
   Feb. 9, 1790
Died at Murfreesboro, Tenn.
   Nov. 12, 1872
Aged 82 yrs. 9 mo. 4 d.

Sacred to the
Memory of
Doctr. Wm. L. Thompson
Who died Nov. 10, 1833
Aged 28 years

To the Memory of
The Lamented
Dr. John M. King
Who departed this life
Nov. 23d. 1824
In the 30th year of his life.

RUTHERFORD COUNTY

Tombstone Inscriptions

Old City Cemetery, located 4 blocks from public square,
Between Vine and State Streets, Murfreesboro, Tenn.
Copied by Sadie McLaurine and Annie Campbell
September 14, 1936

Sacred to the Memory of William D. Baird
    Who was born in N. C. in 1780
        died April 17 1843, Aged 63 years
He was diligent in business, Fervent in Spirit,
Serving the Lord. He was prudent in conduct, Steadfast
in principle, persevering in Exertion; withal a devoted
Friend of the Presbyterian church, in which he was a
Ruling Elder for 30 years.

In Memory of Abigail Baird Consort of Wm. D. Baird
        died April 12, 1855
        aged 71 years

    Adam Baird dec'd March 24th 1825
    in the 38th year of his age

        Shemuel M. Golightly
    departed this life July 1, 1851
    In the 18th year of his age

The tombstone of Jonathan Currin bears only his name. The
stone is close to the path on the left, facing south. He
was one of the early merchants of Murfreesboro.

(Many of the records in the Old City Cemetery were copied
and printed in "Tombstone Inscriptions and Historical
Manuscripts", by Mrs. J. H. Acklen.

TOMBSTONE - INSCRIPTIONS

OLD CITY CEMETERY
RUTHERFORD COUNTY

Located in Murfreesboro, Tennessee, 4 blocks East of the
Public Square, East Vine Street.
Copied by Miss Annie Campbell, Murfreesboro, Tennessee.
May 20, 1937.

(On South Side of Monument)
Sacred to the Memory of
Lavinia H. Hilliard, Wife of
Isaac Hilliard, and only child
of Daniel and Eliza Leinau.
   (East Side)
Born in the City of
Philadelphia, State of
Pennsylvania, on the
9th day of October, In the
year of our Lord, 1817.
   (North Side)
Departed this life at
Beersheba Springs, State
of Tennessee, on the
11th day of August 1837.
With a glorious hope of
Eternal Life.
   (West Side)
Reader, whomsoever thou art,
or wherever thou art from,
Envy me not the small space
of Earth that covers my
clay cold ashes.

In Memory of
Susan R. McKinley,
Born June 4, 1826.
Died August 5, 1855.

In Memory of
John McKinley,
Born May 7, 1797.
Died March 15, 1842.

In Memory of
Rebecca McKinley, Consort of
John McKinley,
Born Decr. 15, 1799.
Died August 12, 1810.

In Memory of
Henry W. Todd,
Born April 25, 1854.
Died July 25, 1855.

In Memory of
Mrs. Margaret F. Todd,
Born Sept. 2nd, 1818.
Died Dec. 18th, 1851.

In Memory of
J. Wendell Todd,
Born Oct. 10th, 1850.
Died Sept. 21, 1851.

The Leiper Vault, bearing
only the Inscription,
"John Leiper"-Vault-
It is situated midway of
the East side of the
Cemetery. The original
covering of the underground
Vault has been replaced
with concrete. The stone
bearing the above inscription
seems to be original, and is
placed in the center of the
concrete work.

RUTHERFORD COUNTY

Tombstone Inscriptions—

Dickinson Cemetery, at old Grantland Estate, now owned by City of Murfreesboro, about one mile on the Nashville Highway-
Copied by Annie Campbell
October 13, 1936

    David Dickinson,   Died July 20th, 1848
                                    in the 75th year of his age.

        "Honest, just, kind and true."

In memory of Fanny N. Dickinson, wife of David Dickinson, Born Aug. 22, 1782
                                                                      Died Dec. 28, 1843

Martha, wife of L. G. Gallaway,   Born June 10, 1823
                                                                     Died Feb. 27, 1850
    This monument is erected by her bereaved husband to
    commemorate her love, truth and devotion.

David W. Dickinson, born June 10, 1808, Franklin, Tenn.
                          died April 27, 1845, near Murfreesboro
Member of Congress from 1833-1835, and 1843-1845

Eliza J. Grantland, wife of David W. Dickinson

Sallie Brickell Murfree, second wife of David W. Dickinson

 (The tombs of David W. Dickinson and his two wives, Eliza J. Grantland of Georgia and Sallie Brickell Murfree of Franklin, Tenn., were broken by a tree falling across them. The box tombs were repaired, but the inscriptions were not restored. The information above was obtained from Miss Fanny Noailles Dickinson Murfree, 225 University Street, Murfreesboro, Tenn.)

RUTHERFORD COUNTY

Tombstone Inscriptions

Evergreen Cemetery, located ½ mile from public square
of Murfreesboro, Tenn., between Highland street and Greenland
Drive
Copied by Sadie McLaurine and Annie Campbell
      Date, September 18, 1936

Capt. Ed Arnold, Husband of Harriet Arnold
      Born in Mecklenburg Co. Va. Apr. 13, 1818
      died in M'boro, Tenn.   Nov. 11, 1884

  Harriett N. Arnold, Born Oct. 20, 1820
      Died Oct. 7, 1895

      EATON
  March 2, 1813   April 22, 1886
  Esther M. wife of Joseph H. Eaton

Joseph H. Eaton, L.L.D., born Sept. 10, 1812
      died Jan. 12, 1859
He was the son of Joseph Eaton
Who was the son of David Eaton
Who was the son of John Eaton
Who was the son of Joseph Eaton
Who was the son of John Eaton
Who emigrated from Wales A. D. 1686

      Wm. Baird
    died July 8, 1914

  Bennettie Patillo, wife of W. D. Baird
    born July 19, 1845
    died Sept. 8, 1908

  Jas. Pinkney Baird, born Aug. 9, 1808
      died Feb. 17, 1900

  Sara A. Baird, Consort of J. P. Baird
  and Mother of Mary T. and J. R. Baird
    born Dec. 12, 1825
    died March 3, 1898

  Leland Jordan, born Dec. 2, 1846
      died Feb. 24, 1935

  Letitia Perkins Jordan, born Apr. 30, 1858
      died Nov. 4, 1910

    Isaac M. Hicks, born Nov. 22, 1818
      died Apr. 16, 1865

Evergreen Cemetery (Continued)
P. 2.

In Memory of M. B. Murfree
born July 26, 1788, Hertford Co. N. Carolina
died Sept. 15, 1858, Murfreesboro, Tenn.

In Memory of Mrs. Mary Ann Murfree
Born Aug. 12, 1797, in Murfreesboro, Hertford Co., North Carolina
Died July 15, 1857, at Murfreesboro, Tenn.

In Memoriam, Annie M. Murfree
born Dec. 2, 1840
died Nov. 17, 1888

In Memory of William H. Murfree
born September 13, 1828
died March 14, 1861

In Memory of Hardy Murfree
born October 23, 1827
died November 11, 1880

Rev. Eugene A. Taylor, D. D.
born Oct. 16, 1853
died Nov. 9, 1898

Dr. Samuel H. Freas
born January 8, 1843
died May 29, 1877

Mary F., wife of Dr. Samuel H. Freas,
born May 19, 1849
died July 3, 1890

Harris B. Northcut, born May 27, 1855
died May 1, 1890

William B. Byrn, Born February 27, 1811
Died August 4, 1883

Sarah C., wife of William B. Byrn
Born December 20, 1824
Died June 25, 1886

Sarah P. Hicks,
Born Petersburg, Va., Mar. 17, 1817
Died Sept. 19, 1897

Evergreen Cemetery (Continued)
P. 3.

J. Addison Smith, D.D.
Born Lockhart, Texas, July 22nd 1851
Died Murfreesboro, Tenn. April 21, 1920
Beloved Pastor of First Presbyterian Church, Murfreesboro, Tenn.
October 1909- to April 1920.

Will Allen Dromgoole
daughter of John Easter and Rebecca Mildred Blanch Dromgoole
of Murfreesboro,
Author, Poet, Song Writer
30 years Literary Editor, Nashville Banner
Died September 1, 1934

"To love and serve,
this only is a great life."

RUTHERFORD COUNTY

TOMBSTONE - INSCRIPTIONS

Evergreen Cemetery, located ½ mile from public square, Murfreesboro, Tennessee, between Highland Avenue and Greenland Drive.
Copied by Miss Annie Campbell.
Date: November 14, 1936.

Bromfield Ridley - Born in Granville County, North Carolina,
August 1, 1804.
Died August 11, 1869.
At Murfreesboro, Tenn. Aged 65 years.
"An up-right Judge, A Devoted Patriot,
An Exemplary Christian, An Indulgent Father."

Rebecca T. Ridley -Born 1810, Married in 1829-Died July 1870-Aged 60 years. "A Woman of Christian Graces".

Virginia Rebecca Ridley, Daughter of Bromfield and Rebecca T. Ridley, Died at LaGrange Ga., July 2, 1859. Aged 17 years.

A. G. Cosby -   Born Jan. 20, 1809.
                                     Died March 19, 1863.

Sarah McKinley, wife of A.G. Cosby - 1821-1909.

C. B. Cosby -   Born May 19, 1851.
                                     Died Feb. 4, 1863.

Captain William Ledbetter -   Born --- --, 1831.
                                     Died Apr. 6, 1906.

Dr. Robert Searcy Wendel -   July 14, 1821.
                                     June 24, 1892.

Emma Claiborne James, Wife of Dr. Robert Searcy Wendel -
                                     March 14, 1833.
                                     July 27, 1886.

David Wendel - Born January 14, 1785, at Winchester, Va.
       Died October 8, 1840, at Murfreesboro, Tenn.

Sarah Hale Neilson, wife of David Wendel-Born May 22, 1788.
                                     Died August 17, 1838.

Sally Hudson Neilson, daughter of D.D.& S.J. Wendel,
       Died Feb. 21, 1875. Aged 26 years.

David D. Wendel -   Born February 4, 1811.
                                     Died April 20, 1873.

Evergreen Cemetery (continued Page 2)

Sarah Jane Wendel -   Born November 7, 1814.
                                            Died March 16, 1873.

Martha Collier -   Born January 10, 1801.
                                            Died December 12, 1863.
                                            Age 62 years, 8 mos.

Edmond G. Cock -   Born October 11, 1810.
                                            Died December 16, 1857.

Emily H. Cock -   Born March 10, 1820.
                                            Died August 15, 1849.

James M. son of E.G.&Emily H.Cock- Born November 3, 1848.
                                              Died August 4, 1852.

Thomas M. Hill -   Born October 3, 1825,
                                            Died May 5, 1869.

Wm. Henry Hill -   Born March 24, 1858.
                                            Died August 6, 1880.

Adam Bock -   Born in Germany, 1853.
                                            Died in Murfreesboro, 1916.

Virginia C. Jordan, wife of Adam Bock   Born   1848.
                                              Died   1918.

Amon Boring -   Born   1791.
                                            Died   1839.

Nancy Boring -   Born   1795.
                                            Died   1839.

In Memory of Sallie B. Henry, wife of William Elliott -
                                              Born October 23, 1802.
                                              Died April 29, 1860.

Nannie G. Henry, wife of J.H.Elliott- Born in Culpepper, Va. Dec. 1832.
                                              Died Feb. 2, 1899.

J. H. Elliott -   Born February 11, 1834.
                                            Died December 27, 1902.

Dr. James Wendel -   Born November 29, 1812.
                                              Died December 21, 1898.

Jane Caroline, wife of Dr. James E. Wendel, daughter of
Hon. Edwin Ewing - Died February 14, 1871. Aged 34 years, 1 month,
                                              15 days.

TOMBSTONE - INSCRIPTIONS

EVERGREEN CEMETERY
RUTHERFORD COUNTY

Located ½ mile North-East of Public Square, Murfreesboro,
Tennessee, between Highland Avenue and Greenland Drive.
Copied by Miss Annie Campbell, Murfreesboro, Tenn.
December 20, 1936.

Walter K., Son of
D.D. & S.J. Wendel, Lieut.
Co. A., 2nd Regt. Tenn. Vols C.S.A.
Fell in the Battle of Richmond, Ky.
August 30, 1863. Aged 23 years.

In Memory of Wm. F. Arnold,
Born January 26, 1845,
Killed at Atlanta Ga., July 13, 1864.

In Memory of John F. Arnold,
Killed in Battle at Atlanta, Ga.,
July 19, 1864.

TOMBSTONE - INSCRIPTIONS

EVERGREEN CEMETERY
RUTHERFORD COUNTY

Located ½ mile North-East of Public Square, Murfreesboro,
Tennessee, between Highland Avenue and Greenland Drive.
Copied by Mabel B. DuBois, Murfreesboro, Tenn.
January 2, 1937.

Victoria, Wife of
Hugh P. Baird,
Born January 4, 1845.
Died July 16, 1884.

Giles Scales Harding, Jr.
Born 1854.
Died 1922.

Dr. Medicus Ransom,
Born Sept. 11, 1827.
Died Dec. 31, 1891.

Lorena Peck Ransom Harding,
Born 1862.
Died 1932.

Temperance Amanda Peck,
Born in Weakley Co., Tenn.
December 17, 1836.
Died 1875.

RUTHERFORD COUNTY (Evergreen Cemetery p. 9)

In Memory of
William F. Arnold
Born Jan. 26, 1845
Volunteered in the Confed.
Army, in the 2nd Tenn. Reg.
8th May 1861 & was killed
13th July 1864

In Memory of
John F. Arnold,
Who enlisted in the
2nd Tenn. Reg. & was a
faithful & gallant soldier-
fought in about 15 hard
fought battles & was killed
fighting the enemy at
Atlanta, Ga. on the
19th July 1864

"Here lies two gallant heroes who fought and fell for right.
Long may they dwell in glory with angels pure & bright."
"Sleep on my dearest boys. We have laid you side by side."

Capt. James Clayton
1833 - 1913

T. U. Parrott
Co. A. 2nd Ky. Reg.
Died Dec. 18th, 1862
From a wound received at Hartsville, Tenn.
Dec. 7, 1862
Age 24 years & 4 mo.

Carter B. Harrison, United States Marshal
Brother of President Benjamin Harrison.
(Buried in Evergreen Cemetery in box tomb
without inscription. This information
was given by the caretaker.)

Capt. Wm. Ledbetter
Born 1831
Died April 4, 1907

Benj. McCulloch Hord
Born Mar. 20, 1842
Died June 14, 1922
Capt. in Walker's Brigade

Blufford B. Swain
Co. E
45 Tenn. Inf.
C.S.A.
Aug. 22, 1889
Mar. 10, 1926

Granville Ewing Smith
Tennessee
Pvt. 60 Pioneer Inf.
February 13, 1929.

Private Porter E. Compton
Dec. 31, 1891
Feby. 14, 1919
Co. A. 16th Inft. 31st. Div.

Gen'l Joseph B. Palmer
Nov. 1, 1825
Nov. 4, 1890

Walter K. Wendel,
Lieut. Co. A. 2nd Reg.
Tenn. Vols. C.S.A.
Aug. 1863, Aged 23 years.

Mordicae Lillard
Born May 20, 1834
Died Mar. 17, 1899

Henry Frazier Bell
Tennessee
Engineman 1 cl.
U. S. Navy
March 11, 1928

Dr. H. H. Clayton
Born Dec. 27, 1826
Aug. 11, 1888

RUTHERFORD COUNTY (Evergreen Cemetery p. 10)

J. Addison Smith   D.D.
  Born Lockhart, Texas
  July 29, 1854
  Died Murfreesboro, Tenn.
  Apr. 21, 1920
Ordained to the Ministry
St. Louis Mo. Apr. 1880
Beloved Pastor of first
Presbyterian Church
Murfreesboro, Tennessee,
Oct. 1909 to Apr, 1920
  "For me to live is Christ
  and to die is Gain."

  Dr. Medicus Ransom
    Born Sept. 11, 1827
    Died Dec. 31, 1891

  Maj. John Woods
    Born Sept. 11, 1807
    Died May 23, 1896
"His words were kindness
His deeds were love
His spirit humble, he
  rests above."

  Charles Ready
    Born Dec. 22, 1802
    Died June 4, 1873

  James McCullough
    Born Feb. 14, 1807
    Died July 20, 1892
"In life beloved
In death lamented."

  Capt. Richard Beard,
    C.S.A.
  1842   -   1931
"One of Lee's men of
gentle birth and of a
goodly presence - a man
noble and true"-

  Orville Ewing, slain in the
Battle of Murfreesboro, 31st Dec. 1862,
  Aged 22 years.

  Rev. C. D. Dillon (Bapt.)
    May 13, 1861
    Apr. 13, 1935

  In Memory of
Dr. James Brickle Murfree
  Son of
Matthias B. and Mary Roberts Murfree
  Born Sept. 16, 1835
  Died Apr. 24, 1912
"Precious in the sight of the
Lord, is the death of his Saints."

"A kind and loving husband,
devoted father, true friend.
Brave soldier, respected and
beloved citizen.
"His children rise up and
call him blessed."
"He like the great physician,
went about doing good."-
"Blessed are the pure in heart
for they shall see God."

(NOTE: He is the father of
our present Dr. Matt Murfree)

  Mary Noailles Murfree
  (Chas. Egbert Craddock)
  Daughter of
  William Law Murfree
    and
  Priscilla Murfree
Jan. 24, 1850 - July 31, 1922
"Know that my redeemer liveth."

  Rev. Eugene A. Taylor, D.D.
  Oct. 16, 1853 - Nov. 9, 1898
"He trusteth in the Lord."

  Judge John Whitsitt Childress
    Apr. 20, 1845
    Mar. 29, 1908

  Dr. Earnest M. Holmes, M.D.
May 14, 1877   - Jan. 19, 1918

  Rev. John W. Jamison
    Aug. 24, 1868
    July 22, 1926

  Claud Compton
  Tennessee Prvt.
  Coast Artillery Corps
    Feb. 10, 1937

RUTHERFORD COUNTY (Evergreen Cemetery p. 11)

Elvie McFadden
1878 - 1926
"She being dead, yet sleepeth."
(NOTE: It is for her that the
McFadden school here is named.)

Dr. Wm. H. Lytle
Sept. 30, 1827
July 12, 1915
"My trust is in God."

Gen. Henry H. Norman
July 4, 1839 - Sept. 8, 1906

Major Ferdinand Molloy,
Comm. of Subsistence C.S.A.

Lieut. Robert S. Brown
Killed in action on
Oct. 4, 1918 - Defending
Apermonte, Argonne Forest, France.
Aged 21 years.

Col. Richard H. Keeble
Killed in the battle
at Petersburgh, Va.
June 30, 1864
Aged 33 years
"I will say of the Lord,
He is my refuge and
my fortress."

Dr. Samuel H. Freas
Born Jan. 8, 1843
Died May 29, 1877

"Come ye blessed."
Dr. Joe M. MClain
Oct. 25, 1830
Nov. 12, 1906

"Sacred to the Memory of DAVID WENDEL whose purity
of life and stern regard for truth whose candour
and firmness whose zeal in promoting morality and
whose conscientiousness in the discharge of every
duty rendered him an ornament to society and a
blessing to his family the faculties of whose
cultivated mind were never idle and always employed
upon objects worthy of a man and a christian.

Born at Winchester, Va.
Jan. 11th, 1785
Died at Murfreesboro, Tenn. Oct. 8, 1810."

"David Deaderick Wendel
Born February 4, 1811
Died April 29, 1873

As a ruling elder in the Presbyterian Church
Magnified his office and walked blameless.
As a Mason, a citizen and friend, he was
without reproach.
As a husband he was tender, affectionate
And as a father he was kind and gentle
As a Christian his walk and conversation were
such as becoming the Gospel of Christ."

RUTHERFORD COUNTY

FARRIS GRAVEYARD

Located 12 Miles S. W. from Murfreesboro on Murfreesboro and Eagleville highway, on farm owned by W. R. Frazier, Rockvale, Tenn. Formerly property of Rev. C. B. Farris who settled the place and lived there until his death in 1887.

John F. Holden
Born 7-11-1854
Died 1 - 1883

Rev. Charles Blackman Farris
member Tennessee Conference
Born June 4, 1813
Died Aug. 4, 1887

Anna F. Dicus
Died Oct. 29, 1932

Nancy Williamson
Born about 1804
Died   1861

Margaret T. Farris
Daughter of C. B. & Mary J. Farris
Born Jan. 15, 1851
Died Sept. 5, 1864

T. S. Smotherman
Born April 2, 1869
Died May 29, 1908

Little Tommie L. Smotherman
Born Aug. 19, 1906
Died Aug. 18, 1907

Infant son of A. L. & T. H. Howard,
Born and died March 26, 1918.

Charlie Rough Farris
Born July 5, 1873
Died Aug. 24, 1890
   "The Lord giveth and the Lord
   taketh away, Blessed be the
   name of the Lord."

In Memory of
John Wesley Farris
Born Sept. 30th 1840
Died March 17th 1931

10 Graves marked with inscriptions.
10 Graves with markers without inscriptions.
No unmarked Graves noted.

Copied by Miss Annie Campbell, June 18, 1938.

TOMBSTONE - INSCRIPTIONS

OLD GANNAWAY GRAVEYARD
RUTHERFORD COUNTY

Located 4 miles South-West of Murfreesboro, Tenn., on Midland Road, off Murfreesboro & Eagleville Pikes, on farm owned by Mrs. John A. Jordan, formerly owned by M. C. Jordan, who bought it from the estate of Burrell Gannaway.
Copied by Mrs. Sadie McLaurine and Miss Annie Campbell.
May 25, 1937.

Sarah E.W. Mitchell, consort of
G. C. Mitchell,
Born Oct. 19, 1820.
Died July 22, 1854.

Burrell Gannaway,
Born Dec. 19th, 1785.
Died May 26th, 1853.

(1 stone lying on ground,
Inscription on bottom side,
Could not be moved, probably
Wife of Burrell Gannaway.)

Fanny, M.L.E. Gannaway,
Born June 28, 1812.
Died Oct. 24th, 1847.

TOMBSTONE - INSCRIPTIONS

HAYNES CEMETERY
RUTHERFORD COUNTY

Located 9 miles West of Murfreesboro, Tenn., on Franklin Pike.
Copied by Miss Mabel DuBois, Murfreesboro, Tennessee.
February 8, 1937.

In Memory of
Julia Ann Haynes, Wife of
W. A. Haynes, & daughter of
John & Jane D. Covington,
Born Apl. 18, 1820.
Died July 16, 1859.

In Memory of
C. C. Haynes, Son of
W.A. & J.A. Haynes,
Born Feb. 11, 1862,
At Jordan Spring, near
Winchester, Va. Member
Co. I, 1st Tenn. Confederate Vol.

In Memory of
Hyram H. Haynes, son of
W.A. & Julia Ann Haynes,
Born May 25, 1839.
Died April 5, 1860.

William Airchaball Haynes,
Born Aug. 15, 1810.
Died Oct. 5, 1887.

Marquis Lafayett Covington,
Who was born, Aug. 26, 1815, &
Died Sept. 10, 1846.

Jessee Covington,
Was born Dec. 20, 1793, and
Departed this Lifth,
Mar. 28, 1834.

In Memory of
Jane D. Covington,
Born Sept. 13, 1776.
Died May 14, 1853.
Age 76 years, 8 months, 1 day.

John Covington,
Was born Feb. the 15, 1772.
And departed this life,
Jan. the 24th, 1847.

W.J. Maxwell,
Born April 25, 1811, &
Died June 22, 1841.

C. C. Wray,
Born Oct. 4, 1835.
Died Sept. 2, 1889.

RUTHERFORD COUNTY

FRANCIS JACKSON GRAVEYARD

Located on farm now owned by W. H. Williams, address: Rockvale, Tenn. Formerly and for many years the property of Francis Jackson, Senr., & his son Francis Jackson. This place is 3 miles from Rockvale, 13 miles S. W. of Murfreesboro, 2 miles on Versailles pike, & turn to left on road called Versailles & Shelbyville Pike.

Sacred to the Memory of
Francis Jackson, Senr.
born in Prince Edward County Va.,
on the 12th of January 1766 &
departed this life Feb. 10, 1845.

Sacred to the Memory of
Elizabeth W. Jackson
Consort of Francis Jackson Senr.
born in Prince Edward County
Virginia on the 7th day of April 1766
departed this life August 9th 1831

    Oddfellows Emblem
    Francis Jackson
Born Jan. 31, 1804, Died March 1, 1878
(last line of inscription unreadable
on account of broken stone)

Elizabeth Hale, wife of
Francis Jackson
Born July 12, 1809,
Died Jan. 4, 1888
  "Asleep in Jesus, oh! how sweet
  From which none ever wakes to weep."

Sacred to the Memory of
Emlyann V. Jackson
daughter of Francis Jackson Jr.
& Elizabeth Jackson
born Dec. 20, 1833 departed this life
Jan. 16, 1844

Mary L. E. Jackson
Born Jan. 6, 1836
died Feb. 21, 1853
Aged 17 yrs. 1 mo. & 15 days

Mary A., wife of T. N. Jackson
Died Feb. 21, 1888, Aged 56 years
  "Our Mother at rest."
On reverse of Mary A., wife of T.N.J. Marker
T. N. Jackson Husband of Mary A. and
Loyola S. (Lovejoy) Jackson
Born April 18, 1832
Died June 2, 1896
  "Our Father at rest."

Judith Jackson,
wife of Jasper Jackson
born Feb. 21, 1823;
died Jan. 17, 1882

Oceana B.,
Daughter of W. J. & J. A.
Jackson, born May 27, 1859;
Died Jan. 17, 1882

Mary B., Daughter of John G. &
Mary J. Jackson,
born Jan. 7, 1881;
died Aug. 18, 1881.

Sacred to the memory of
Anna Johnson, wife of
W. T. Johnson, who was born
March 28, 1838 and
departed this life
Sept. the 4, 1863
Aged 25 years five months and
six days

One marble marker for baby's
grave on which inscription is
invisible.
One field stone marker without
inscription, probably grave of
a slave, according to
Miss Carmine Jackson, Rockvale,
Tenn.
14 Graves with markers.
No unmarked graves discovered.
4 stones on ground, but
inscriptions read.

Copied by Miss Annie Campbell,
May 15, 1938.

RUTHERFORD COUNTY

JACKSON (CAPT. F. M.) GRAVEYARD

Located on farm of Mrs. Annie George Jackson, address: Rockvale, Tenn., one mile from Rockvale on Versailles Pike; 11 miles Southwest from Murfreesboro. At Rockvale, on Murfreesboro & Eagleville highway, turn to left as the Pike forks.
5 Graves, 2 readable markers with inscriptions, 1 grave with wooden marker, and 2 Graves with field stones without inscriptions.
Copied by Miss Annie Campbell, May 15, 1938.

"Lead Kindly Light."
Mrs. Jane George
Born Dec. 6, 1821
Died Apr. 16, 1904
   "Asleep in Jesus."

Capt. F. M. Jackson
Confederate soldier
Born Mar. 28, 1838
Died Apr. 25, 1901
   "Gone but not forgotten."
(On reverse side of stone)
Susan A. wife of F. M. Jackson
Born March 12, 1841
Died May 23, 1877.
The above inscription is in memory of Mrs. Susan A. (Covington) Jackson, who is buried a mile away in the Ransom graveyard.

Grave of infant child of
Grover and Valera Jackson
with wooden head and foot marker
is beside the grave of
Capt. F. M. Jackson.

The above 3 Graves are enclosed in an iron fence.

Outside iron fence:

Grave with head & foot markers of field stone, no inscription.
Grave with head & foot marjers of field stone, no inscription.
(Information below given by Mrs. Annie Jackson)
The above two graves are of Confederate Soldiers, names forgotten, who died at the Jackson home during the War Between the States. A beautiful wild grape vine forms a canopy for these two graves.

TOMBSTONE - INSCRIPTIONS

OLD JORDAN GRAVEYARD
RUTHERFORD COUNTY

Located 4 miles South-West of Murfreesboro, Tenn., on the Midland Road, off the Murfreesboro and Eagleville Pikes, on farm owned by Mrs. John A. Jordan, formerly owned by M.C. Jordan, who bought it from the estate of Burwell Gannaway. Copied by Mrs. Sadie McLaurine and Miss Annie Campbell. May 25, 1937.

Henry C. Johnson,
June 14, 1853.
July 12, 1906.

Robt. L. Jordan, Son of
M.C. & E.W. Jordan,
Born Aug. 8, 1864.
Died Jan. 18, 1884.

E. W. Jordan,
Born Mar. 12, 1827.
Died July 12, 1892.
M. C. Jordan,
Born Sept. 28, 1820.
Died Feb. 14, 1879.

E. Addie Beasley,
Born Aug. 1, 1858.
Died June 28, 1883.

Starnes Jordan, (Unmarked grave)
Born July 4, 1862.
Died Oct. 18,---?
(Information supplied)

Martha J. Jordan, Wife of
D. S. McCollough,
Born Sept. 22, 1843.
Died Sept. 4, 1891.

Joshua M. Johnson, Son of
Minerva Jordan Johnson Dodson,
Head & Foot stone marked,
J.M.J.

Jordan (Johnson)
Mrs. Minerva Dodson,
Marked with stone bearing
no Inscription.

(6 stones with Inscriptions.
1 stone without Inscription.
1 unmarked grave.)

TOMBSTONE - INSCRIPTIONS

OLD LILLARD GRAVEYARD
RUTHERFORD COUNTY

Located 6 miles South-West of Murfreesboro, Tennessee, on the Murfreesboro & Eagleville Pikes, Highway No. 51, on farm owned by Dr. S. B. Smith, Overall (Salem) Tennessee, formerly owned by Mordecai Lillard. The Lillard family have removed remains of their people to another Cemetery.
Copied by Mrs. Sadie McLaurine and Miss Annie Campbell.
June 16, 1937.

To the Memory of
Obadiah Smith, who
Died 4th Aug. 1815.
Aged 1 year, 4 months, &
21 days.
To the Memory of
Samuel H. Smith,
Who died 12th Jan. 1823.
Aged 1 year & 10 months.

(Note: Both of the following inscriptions are on separate stones of different size and shape, not even near each other, except in same graveyard; Both plain to read.)

In Memory of
Lucy A. McGowan,
Born Oct. 30, 1840.
Died Oct. 13th, 1854.

In Memory of
Lucy H. McGowan,
Born Oct. 30th, 1840.
Died Oct. 13th, 1854.

(One Marker contains the following lettering; no names nor dates.)

O.M.S. & S.H.S.

Susan G. Brady,
Born March 8, 1843.
Died June 8, 1859.
Wife of W.T. Brady.

In Memory of
Thos. H. McGowan,
Born June 1, 1838.
Died July 29, 1859.

RUTHERFORD COUNTY

Tombstone Inscriptions

Miles Graveyard, located on Chloe Bond's farm, 7 miles from Murfreesboro half mile to the left off Nashville Highway
Copied by Mabel Dubois
October 13, 1936

Thomas Miles Sr., Lieut. Foley's Company North Carolina Troops
Revolutionary War
Died April 15th, 1838

Elizabeth V. Moore, wife of F. W. Miles, Born Jan. 10, 1840
                                          Died Dec. 13, 1890

B. M. Miles, Son of F. W. & E. V. Miles, Born Dec. 2, 1868
                                          Died Nov. 12, 1890

Sallie Russworm, wife of C. M. Miles,   Born Feb. 17, 1828
                                          Died Nov. 21, 1884

Mary Ida Miles   Born Mar. 17, 1862
                                          Died Oct. 7, 1873

Nancy W. Miles, consort of C. M. Miles   Born June 27, 1825
                                          Died April 8, 1851

TOMBSTONE - INSCRIPTIONS

MOLLOY CEMETERY
RUTHERFORD COUNTY

Located 3 miles South-West of Murfreesboro, Tenn., off Salem
& Eagleville pikes, on Midland Road; on the farm owned by
Mr. Dorsey Cantrell.
Copied from notes of Mrs. Eleanor M. Gillespie.
Residence: 305½ 28th Avenue North, Nashville, Tennessee.
Copied by Miss Annie Campbell, Murfreesboro, Tenn.
December 17, 1936.

In Memory of
Fannie M. Molloy,
Born April 16, 1775.
Died September 2, 1855.

In Memory of
John Molloy,
Born Buckingham Co. Va.
January 17, 1802.
Died October 29, 1857.
(Married Nancy Elam.)

In Memory of
Judith L. (Molloy) Young,
Consort of Hiram Young,
Died 19th of June, 1839.
Aged 31 years-(Born 1808)

In Memory of
Dan. E. Molloy,
Born September 14, 1845,
Died of a wound at the
Battle of Murfreesboro,
January 1, 1863.

Sacred to the Memory of
Fanny M.G. Barlow, consort
of Benj.D. Barlow,
Died on Thursday,
May 9, 1833, In the 18th
year of her age.

In Memory of
Nancy Molloy,
Born June 20, 1810.
Died July 28, 1854.

In Memory of

In Memory of
William Molloy,
Born May 28, 1799.
Died July 17, 1852.

Sacred to the Memory
of John L. Molloy,
Born April 11, 1834.
Died October 25, 1853.

Lucius N.B. Molloy,
Born August 14, 1831.
Died November 17, 1852.

Dr. G.D. Molloy,
Born August 23,----?
Died September 23, 1853.

Elizabeth Molloy,
Born October 30, 1797.
Married John Jones,
October 16, 1821.
Died January 3, 1863.

Martha Woodson Molloy,
Born 1806-Married William
Gilliam, May 8, 1823, Died
near Trenton, Tenn., during
War between the States, and
is buried there.

RUTHERFORD COUNTY

RANSOM GRAVEYARD (Also Called Mt. Rose)

Located on farm of J. T. Adcock, address: Rockvale, Tenn., formerly owned by Joseph Ransom, on Versailles Pike, 12 miles Southwest from Murfreesboro. At Rockvale, 10 miles on Murfreesboro & Eagleville highway, turn to left as the Pike forks.

This graveyard is owned by Messrs. Willis & Ellis Ransom, Murfreesboro, Tenn., who keep it in beautiful order.

11 Graves with markers and inscriptions and 1 Grave with field stone marker without inscription. No stones on which inscriptions were unreadable.

Elizabeth Covington
Born Jan. 26, 1810
Died July 16, 1905

Col. C. D. Venable
5th Tenn. Regt.
Confederate Soldier from
Henry County Tenn. who
died Christmas 1862 at
home of Elizabeth Covington
during War between the States.
Information given by
Mrs. Annie Jackson.

Lutie A., daughter of
W. S. & E. R. Ransom
Born Oct. 31, 1860
Died Jan. 1, 1861

Willis Snell Ransom   Masonic Emblem
Born Aug. 23, 1832
Died Dec. 17, 1889

Ellen R. Ransom
Born Sept. 4, 1841
Died June 22, 1893

Alfred Ransom
Born Oct. 13, 1867
Died July 20, 1894

                    Masonic Emblem
Captain John Childress Jackson
Born Feb. 6, 1822
Died Apr. 10, 1898

Sue Adalade
Wife of F. M. Jackson
daughter of M. L. & E. Covington
Born March 12, 1841 Died May 23, 1877
  "Living she was true to me
   Dying she trusted in God."
            F.M.J.

Mrs. Mary Jane,
Wife of John C. Jackson and
daughter of M. L. &
E. Covington
Born June 6, 1839
departed this life
Dec. 28, 1884
  "She is not dead but sleeping."

Williams Lafayette
son of John C. & Mary Jane Jackson
born Feb. 11, 1858
died July 17, 1879
Aged 21 yrs. 5 months & 6 days

RUTHERFORD COUNTY

Tombstone Inscriptions

Old Ready Burial Ground, Readyville, Tenn., 12 miles from Murfreesboro on Woodbury Pike
Copied By Sadie McLaurine
Date October 13, 1936

    In Memory of Lucinda Ready, daughter of C. H. Ready
                            Born December 29, 1810
                            Died March   12, 1830
                  Aged 19 years and two months

ALSO:

Colonel Charles Ready SR. Esquire
b. 1 APR. 1770 SALISBURY, WICOMICO, MARYLAND
d. 9 SEP 1859 READYVILLE, RUTHERFORD, TENNESSEE
                                    89 YRS. 4 MO. 3 DA.

MARY READY, HIS WIFE
b. 1 SEP 1773   NORTH CAROLINA
d. 3 SEP 1848   READYVILLE, RUTHERFORD, TENNESSEE
                                75 YRS. OLD

RUTHERFORD COUNTY

OLD BILLY "BOOTS" COLEMAN CEMETERY
ROOKER FAMILY GRAVEYARD

Located on farm owned by young Billy "Boots" Coleman, on old Jefferson road. Turn to left 7 miles from Murfreesboro on Murfreesboro & Lebanon road, 2 miles from pike, 9 miles Northwest from Murfreesboro.

There are 22 graves in this cemetery; 16 Graves marked with limestone markers without inscriptions; 1 Grave marked with limestone marker without inscription, with little wooden grave-house in dilapidated condition, over it. 5 Graves have markers and inscriptions.
Copied by Miss Annie Campbell, Sept. 30, 1937.

Jennings Rooker
Born 1796
Died May 30, 1869
Aged 73 years

William M. Rooker
Born March 16, 1849
Died July 21, 1866

Nannie D. Rooker
Born Aug. 29, 1836
Died July 20, 1863

Mary A. Spain
Sept. 27, 1854
July 22, 1924
  "At Rest."

D. S. Spain
Aug. 16, 1842
June 25, 1915
  "Here is one is sleeping
  in faith and love,
  with hope that is treasured
  in heaven above."

RUTHERFORD COUNTY

SEARCY GRAVEYARD

Old Searcy Graveyard is located 12 miles northwest from Murfreesboro on "Old Jefferson" road. (Turn to left 7 miles from Murfreesboro on Murfreesboro & Lebanon road.)
This was the place settled by Col. Sm. W. Searcy in 1804.
Owned at present by Miss Mackie Malone, 1427 E. Main St., Murfreesboro, Tenn.

The Searcy family graves are enclosed by a rock fence, now in bad condition, the graves of Letitia Dance and O. H. P. Abbott being located outside this fence.

The Searcy Graveyard is very old and the family long ago left the community. The graveyard is in a very dilapidated condition. Col. Wm. W. Searcy was buried in a vault underground, walled up with brick and native limestone. Over this was the box tomb and a wooden grave-house was placed over the tomb. The vault is open and the tomb in pieces (not broken pieces but apart.)
The slab on which the inscription is engraved is in excellent condition, having been protected by the house.
The Graves of the three wives were marked by box tombs, these are all apart on the ground and the inscriptions are all but defaced by exposure to weather. There are 8 Graves with stones and inscriptions; 1 Grave with stone, without inscription; 3 unmarked Graves.
Copied by Miss Annie Campbell, September 30, 1937.

COL. WILLIAM W. SEARCY

"Col. William W. Searcy, who was born in Granville County, North Carolina, on the 1st day of January, 1769, and died on the 8th day of January 1846, in his 77th year. He removed from the state of his nativity to Kentucky with his widowed mother, in 1785, where he resided until 1804, when he removed to Rutherford County, Tennessee, where he ended his earthly career. He enjoyed in a high degree, the confidence of the community in which he resided, at different periods, having filled various offices civil and miletary, and amongst othes, the office of Senator in the Legislature of Tennessee. He was for the last ten years of his life, an acceptable member of the Baptist Church. He was an affectionate Husband, Kind Father, and lived and died with the deserved repetation of an honest man."

"Elizabeth T. Searcy, Consort of Col. William W. Searcy, was born 1781, and departed this life The 22nd of Sep. 1804."

"Sarah M. Searcy, Consort of Col. William W. Searcy, who was born the 30th of M(arch 1783) She departed this life April 29, 18(32)" (These dates supplied from Bible record).

"Sacred to the memory Sarah Searcy, Consort of Col. Wm. W. Searcy, who was born Aug. 8, 1776 and departed this life April 27, 1845. She was a prominent member of the Primitive Baptist Church."

"Sacred to the memory of John W. Searcy, Son of Sarah M. & William W. Searcy Who was born on 2nd February 1814 and departed this life on the 10 September 1843 in the 29th year of his life."

RUTHERFORD COUNTY

SEARCY GRAVEYARD   p. 2

"Sarah M. Battle, Consort of Gen. A. Battle and daughter of Col. W. W. Searcy was born the 23 of Apr. 1816 - Departed this life 3rd Oct. 1835."

"In memory of Letitia Dance, Born March 23, 1824   Died Sept. 17, 1850."

"In memory of O. H. P. Abbott, Born May 23rd, 1818 Died Jun2 8th, 1850."

There are also in this enclosure the unmarked Graves of:

        Anderson Searcy
        Fayette Searcy
        Robert Searcy

And One Grave marked with limestone marker without inscription.

TOMBSTONE - INSCRIPTIONS

OLD SIMS GRAVEYARD
RUTHERFORD COUNTY

Located 5 miles from Murfreesboro, Tennessee, off the Murfreesboro & Eagleville Pikes, Highway No. 51, on Barfield Road 1 mile. This graveyard joins the farm of Felix Snell, but not identified with Snell place. Was originally part of Sims estate, settled by Dr. Swepson Sims, later owned by Thomas Sims & his wife, Mary S. Sims, & is still used by Sims descendants.
Copied by Miss Annie Campbell, Murfreesboro, Tennessee.
June 16, 1937.

Howard Smith,
Sept. 8, 1881.
Oct. 9, 1881.

Alma Smith,
Sept. 8, 1881.
Oct. 14, 1881.

Katie K. Smith,
Oct. 1, 1870.
Nov. 23, 1873.

In Memory of
Sarah Louisa Sims,
Born July 2d, 1843.
Died Feb. 22d, 1848.

In Memory of
Martha Frances Sims,
Born May 19, 1845.
Died Jan'y 25th, 1848.

In Memory of
Sarah Jane Sims, daughter of
Thomas & Mary S. Sims,
Born April 3, 1835.
Died June 22d, 1850.
"I'll Rest, I'll Rest."

Leonard M. Sims, Son of
Thos & Mary Sims,
Born Jan'y 15th, 1838.
Died Oct. 20, 1856.

In Memory of
An Infant son of
Thos. & Mary Sims,
Born & Died March 4, 1858.

Our Mother:
Mary S., Wife of
Thomas Sims,
Born Nov. 13, 1817.
Died Nov. 28, 1887.
"-- now can no longer stay,
To cheer us with thy love;
We hope to meet with thee
again, In a brighter world
above."

In Memory of
Robert L. Sims,
Born Aug. 26, 1810.
Died Nov. 23, 1856.
"Do not misunderstand me;
All is Right. Dedicated
by his wife & son, whose
irreparable loss will be
ever Felt."

(Old Sims Graveyard p. 2.)

Sacred to the Memory of
Leonard Jo. C. Sims,
Born Feb. 25, 1843.
Died Sept. 10, 1845.

In Memory of
Edward H. Sims,
Born Feb. 7th, 1832.
Died Jan'y 10, 1836.

In Memory of
Thomas Sims, Son of
Swepson & Jane M. Sims,
Born May 22, 1813.
Died Jan. 3, 1864.
" Blessed are they that
Die in the Lord."

1 stone,
Inscription not legible.

6 unmarked graves.

Clifford G. Smith,
1872 - 1931.

Robert A. Smith,
Feb. 16, 1846.
Sept. 16, 1916.
His Wife,
Florence McLean,
Feb. 3, 1846.
Jan. 21, 1901.

Lewis Sims, Son of
H. P. & Jennie S. Bass,
Sept. 21, 1882.
July 7, 1883.

Hartwell P. Bass,
Jan. 12, 1844.
Feb. 23, 1897.
Jennie S. Bass,
Mar. 25, 1851.
Apr. 28, 1914.
BASS.

Benjamin Franklin Reid,
Born June 3, 1848.
Died Apr. 14, 1914.
Mollie Sims Reid,
Born Apr. 29, 1844.
Died June 25, 1886.

Mary E. Wife of
B. F. Reid,& daughter of
T. & M. S. Sims,
Born April 29, 1844.
Died June 25, 1886.
"Gone to rest."

M. J.,Wife of
G. A. Crockett,
Feb. 20, 1849.
Sept. 26, 1885.
"At Rest"

In Memory of
Irene Frances Owen,
Consort of
Chas. L. Owen,
Born Mar. 25, 1856.
Died Oct. 5, 1887.
"A Treasure on Earth,
An Angel in Heaven."

J. Dink Lawrence,
Born May 16, 1844.
Died May 6, 1914.
"Gone, but not forgotten."

Emma B. Smith,
Aug. 31, 1855.
Feb. 6, 1932.

Lucian Smith,
Dec. 29, 1854,
Mar. 6, 1932.

Eugene M. Smith,
Feb. 18, 1850.
Feb. 12, 1917.

Sacred to the Memory of
Dr. Swepson Sims,
Born May 16th, 1775.
Died Sept. 22d, 1850.

Sacred to the Memory of
Mrs. Jane M. Sims,
Born July 31st, 1776.
Died July 22d, 1843.
FAREWELL:
Elizabeth Smith,
Died Oct. 8, 1885.
Age 73 yrs.5 mos.18 days.

RUTHERFORD COUNTY

Tombstone Inscriptions

Taylor Graveyard, located 5 miles from Eagleville off Murfreesboro
and Eagleville Highway on "Ditch Road, 1 mile from highway
Copied by Annie Campbell
Date, November 18, 1936

The oldest graves in this cemetery are the unmarked graves of
Robert Taylor and his wife, Eliza Branch Taylor, who were pioneers of this
community, coming here from Davidson County in 1825. Eliza Branch Taylor
died about 1840, Robert Taylor died about 1850.

> Sacred to the Memory of R. H. Taylor, son of B. B. and
> M. A. Taylor, who was born November 7, 1840, and departed
> this life December 1, 1864, aged 24 years
> and 24 days. (Member of 20th Tennessee Regiment, killed
> at Franklin)

> Minerva A. Taylor, Born August 13, 1813
> Died February 16, 1895

> In Memory of B. B. Taylor, Born in Davidson County
> December 4, 1808
> Died July 11, 1889
> Aged 80 years, 7 months, 7 days

> J. T. Taylor, Born April 1, 1850
> Died February 14, 1909

RUTHERFORD COUNTY

Tombstone Inscriptions

Warren Burial ground, located on N. F. Molloy's farm, one mile from Murfreesboro, on the Salem Pike-
Copied by Sadie McLaurine
Date, October 13, 1936

In Memory of William Warren, Born April 19, 1785
                                      Died January 18, 1852

In Memory of Catherine Warren, consort of William Warren-
                    Born March 2nd, 1796
                    Died August 6th, 1832-

RUTHERFORD COUNTY

WOODFIN CEMETERY

Located on farm owned by Horace Watkins, formerly the _____ Woodfin place, three quarters of a mile from Fosterville, Tenn., off Murfreesboro-Shelbyville Highway one quarter mile, 16 miles from Murfreesboro. This is known as the Woodfin Cemetery, but is used as a public burial place. 38 inscriptions copied, 1 stone in Woodfin Lot on ground, 1 ledger stone near Woodfin Lot with inscription illegible. 1 box tomb overgrown with vines. 1 grave house with no marker. About 12 markers not copied. 3 Graves unmarked.
Copied by Miss Annie Campbell and Mrs. Sadie McLaurine, Sept. 12, 1938.

In memory of Mrs. Hahhah Woodfin
wife of _____ Woodfin
who departed this life
Aug. 8th 1815.
In the 80th year of her age.

In memory of Nicholas Woodfin
Born Aug. 2, 1759
Died Dec. 21, 1832

In memory of Miss Jane Woodfin
Born 22 April 1803
Died 31 March 1826

James Woodfin
Born Sept. 19, 1819
Died Aug. 21, 1876
  "Meet me in heaven."

Thomas M., son of
J. H. & E. W. Woodfin
Born Nov. 12, 1865
Died Mar. 29, 1882
  "Our Darling."

_____ Woodfin
Born
Died Nov. 26, 1889

Farewell, Mother
   Mariah
wife of Samuel Woodfin
Born Dec. 9th, 1796
Died Mar. 8, 1863
Aged 66 yrs. 2 mos. 29 days.

Farewell, Father
   Samuel Woodfin
Born 1791   Died Apr. 29, 1863
   Aged 72 years

Nannie
Dau. of
E. H. & M. E. Hale
Born July 30, 1856
Died July 26, 1890

Miss S. J. Hale
June 4, 1844
Aug. 3, 1890

Mal
Wife of John W. Hale,
Born Dec. 4, 1828
Died June 22, 1901

Sacred to the memory of
   Bettie Hale
Born March 1, 1861
Died May 18, 1880

Sacred to the memory of
   E. H. J. Hale
Born Feb. 5, 1856
Died Jan. 12, 1882

J. Harley Hale
1883 - 1900

One Stone
Father
Andrew H. Edwards
1852 - 1896
Mother
Nannie J. Edwards
1852 - 1900

Blanche A., Daughter
   of
A. H. & N. J. Edwards
Born Nov. 28, 1885
Died Oct. 12, 1886

Edwards
Raleigh Overton
1903 - 1934

W. M. Williams
July 24 - 1856
May 23 - 1931
"Gone but not forgotten."

Mary Lee
Daughter of W. M. & Stacy
   Williams
Mar. 14, 1882 - July 23, 1921

David S. Williams
Aug. 9, 1837   Mar. 25, 1916

Lucy Williams
Nov, 12, 1912   Jan. 10, 1913
"Budded on Earth
In Bloom in Heaven."

Wavie G.
Infant daughter
of
W. D. & Leatha Williams
Oct. 3, 1918   Oct. 19, 1918

William D. Williams
Feb. 7, 1885   Oct. 24, 1918

N. P. Agee,
May 29, 1837   Oct. 3, 1911
"No pains, no griefs, no anxious fear
Can reach our loved one sleeping
   here."

Elder H. F. Agee
Sept. 10, 1840   Nov. 18, 1907
"Earth has no sorrow,
That Heaven cannot heal."

Tennie Agee
Born July 4, 1865
Died Nov. 27, 1909
"Sheltered and safe from sorrow."

Ruth Agee
wife of L. D. Agee
Born Sept. 16, 1874
Died June 3, 1905

One Stone
John D. Gilmore
April 6, 1841   April 24, 1914
   His Wife
Mary Luvenia
Jan. 6, 1844   Nov. 19, 1923

Mary Elizabeth
   wife of
L. D. Roulstone
Born 1884   Died Aug. 1, 1904

Chas. Bingham
June 9, 1858
September 24, 1911
53 years 3 months

Benjamin F. Holden
Born Aug. 15, 1856
Died Dec. 8, 1879

Martha J. Johnson
Born 1822
Died 1855
   MOTHER

Thomas Walter
Son of T. L. & M. A. Elam
Born Jan. 14, 1887
Died Feb. 5, 1887

Luleskey B. Manning
March 17, 1864
July 25, 1919

One Stone
W. E. Wilkinson
Mar. 25, 1871

   His Wife
Lavinia Kelzer
Aug. 20, 1865
July 2, 1928

RUTHERFORD COUNTY

WOODFIN CEMETERY   p. 3

Sacred to the memory of
    John Naylor
who departed this life
February the 19th 1855
In the 66th year of his age.

    The wife of John Naylor
is also buried in this cemetery,
no stone located.

    Wade Hampton Naylor and his wife
Hannah McGill Naylor are buried in
this cemetery, (a son of John Naylor)
no stone located.

    John Naylor came to Bedford County,
Tenn. from North Carolina.

TOMBSTONE - INSCRIPTIONS

YOUREE GRAVEYARD
RUTHERFORD COUNTY

Located 12 miles South-East of Murfreesboro, Tenn., on the Murfreesboro and Bradyville Pikes, on farm of O.P. Jernigan, formerly old Youree Place.
Copied by Miss Annie Campbell, Murfreesboro, Tennessee.
March 8, 1937.

Margret M. Caffey, wife of
J. A. M. Caffey,
Born Dec. 7, 1869.
Died Feb. 20, 1891.

J. N. Caffey,
Born Aug. 22, 1823.
Died Dec. 4, 1892.

Sarah Caffey,
Born Feb. 15, 1839.
Died Aug. 27, 1889.

F. A. McKnight,
Born ---, 1835.
Died ---, 1926.
His wife,
Isabella Caffey,
Born ---, 1846.
Died ---, 1921.

Elizabeth Youree, Wife of
F. H. Youree,
Born Sept. 13, 1828.
Died Jan. 16, 1874.

Nancy S. Youree,
Born April 25, 1867.
Died Sept. 23, 1871.

Dorothy Youree,
Born August 6, 1860.
Died June 10, 1863.

W. M. Lowe,
Born Aug. 20, 1797.
Died Oct. 6, 1863.

Mrs. Rody Lowe,
Born Jan. 24, 1795.
Died Jan. 22, 1857.

Charles Lowe,
Born March 1, 1824.
Died Dec. 13, 1831.

Willie Patrick,
Born April 16, 1885.
Died Sept. 18, 1888.

Jonnie Patrick,
Born Jan. 1, 1888.
Died April 28, 1888.

Infant Daughter of
J.M. Patrick,
Born August 31, 1886.
Died Sept. 10, 1886.

Emmet Patrick,
Born Feb. 22, 1884.
Died July 27, 1884.

Erskin Patrick,
Born April 3, 1882.
Died Oct. 17, 1922.

Mary McGill,
Born March 1, 1787.
Died Nov. 19, 1842.

David N. McGill,
Born July 4, 1824.
Died July 18, 1850.

RUTHERFORD COUNTY

LETTERS FROM JOSIAH PHILIPS TO HIS SON DAVID PHILIPS
1793 & 1799

These letters are now owned by Mrs. A. H. McLean, 416 E. Main St.,
Murfreesboro, Tennessee
Copied by Mrs. Sadie McLaurine, Dec. 7, 1938

Josiah Philips, the great, great grandfather of Mrs. McLean, was in the Revolutionary War and a scout at Valley Forge. He lived all his life in Chester Co. Penn. His parents, Joseph & Mary Philips, were from Wales, and came to America in 1755, settling in Pennsylvania.

It was through him that Mrs. McLean joined the D. A. R.

Old Letter, addressed thus,
To David Phillips, living in
Kentucky
By favour of Mr. Paul

Pennsylvania, West Chester County, March 3rd, 1793

My Beloved Son:-

    I take this opportunity of writing a few lines unto you, by Mr. Paul and it is the first chance I have had since you went from us to that far country, it is late at night and my eyes is weaker than when you saw me last, so that I can but write a little out of a great deal, in the first place those of us that Remain alive are in common midling well in health, Blessed be the Lord for Mercys. I hope these lines will come to your hands and find you in a comfortable way in things Spiritual and things Temporal, is the Desire of your loving Father, Amen. I have received but one letter from you since you went into that country, all were very glad to See it, ever Since you saw us have been Exercised with various Providences, in a few days after you went I fell down about nine feet and Broke a Bone in my Right foot. Your Mamy Delivered of a daughter about the same time. We called her name Martha, her breast got sore and at lenth it was lanced. Both of us for a considerable time helpless, this being over, this Winter was a year the Small pox came on Six of our family and our Beloved Daughter died, aged 18 months. in a small intermission your Grandfather took sick and died the 18th day of May 1792 on the 18th of September after your Mamy had a son Born named Isaac, and on the 26th day of December your Grandmother departed this life, all of them Delivered from a place of Sin and sorrow and gone home to Glory as I humbly hope and Beleve, if the Lord in his providence will allow you to come hear, I shall be glad to see you my Son, if it will happen so that you are not Recondiled to live in that Country, it would be my Desire that your kind Uncle would give the money to you to carry to me that I gave him for the land if he be able at the time of your Coming hear. I Refer this matter to you both altogether. I would wish to hear your

RUTHERFORD COUNTY

(Letters from Josiah Philips to his son David Philips 1793 & 1799)
(p. 2)

Sentiments in Regard of your living in that Country, because I do not know what is Best to do with your Brothers John and Josiah, the place that used to belong to your Uncle David I have bought in order to have a little More Room, it would raise my Credit hear very much if I had the patents for them lands for my Conduct in Respect of it is a little uncommon in this Country, therefore if you Desire to live in that place, Desire your Uncle to send me the patents if possible. Give my kind love to your Uncle and Aunt and may the Lord bless you my Son with the knowledge of himself in Christ Jesus. Your Mamy joins with me in the most Tenderest regard and love to you. Farewell, my son, John and Josiah send their love to you and little Josee has not forgot you. farewell and farewell, from your Father,

       Josiah Philips.

* * * * * * * * * * * * * * * * *

    Old Letter, addressed thus:-

    To David Philips, living in
    Friends Care, Bedford County,
    Pennsylvania, pr. Post to be left
    in the Post office in Bedford Town
    thes March 12th 1799.

March 12th 1799, Pennsylvanie,   Township.

Beloved Son- I Recv'd two letters from you one Dated December 28th 1798, Another dated February ye 10th 1799- Both at one time from Hunt Downings office. I got them on the 10th of this Instant. When I opened the last letter I found very Disagreeable News and felt my heart much affected to be informed of the Death of your Beloved wife and my strange Daughter inlaw that I never had seen, or heard of her Being sick. I have had you both on My Mind and My heart, at a throne of Grace Desireing Spiritual Blessings on your conjugal Engagements but I somehow or other did not think of you or your Dear wife dieing so soon. This makes it more affecting to me, for In common I look for Death and Disappointments every day now I know that you are parted and that she is sleeping in the Dust of death and more over gone to the land of forgettings for a season, this is a great favour conferred on us poor Mortals by our Divine parent. By Experience I know that you have met with a Sorrowful Dispensation, but let us Always try to Give up to God in Every thing for he takes Nothing only what he gave, for

RUTHERFORD COUNTY

(Letters from Josiah Philips to his son David Philips   1793 & 1799   p. 3)

death has Reigned from the Beginning and has laid Nations low in the Dust and is the last Enemy of man that Shall be Conquered the voice of Christ to us now living is be ye also Ready. I am exceeding glad to find the language of your letter so full of Resignation to the Divine power and mind of heaven for this is the Exercise of the Spirit of Christ in the heart of Every Christian in a lesser or greater degree. My Beloved Son, you are young and your trials are Increasing and it May be there are Many more before you, Endeavor to look to the Lord for Continued Direction as I have Reason to Believe you have done heretofore, and if the Spirit of Christ Rule in your heart, Remember you live in an Enemys Country, therefore pray for the Sanctifyd use of Every thing the lord pleased to cause you to pass through. So that when you have gone through all the sorrow and Labour of this life, that you may Dwell with Christ for ever   Amen.

You informed me of your Intention to go to Cumberland. May the God of Heaven Direct your Way. Give us the earliest Intelligence of your Welfare and prosperity in Respect of the land there for my Infirmityes of Body are increasing fast and I would wish to Settle my little affairs as to this world Before I lye down in   Graveyard with my Dear Associates once that are gone Before. My apprentices are free and gone. Your brother John Seems to be on the wing of going, your Brother Josiah prospers at the trade finely, so far he is with me at Every Seven day Night and first Day so the Bargain is for I find him in Clothing. I suppose he in writing has told you the particulars. I have been in varys Difficultys and gone through several Dispensations so now I am of the opinion that the End is drawing nigh, Before I close this my letter I mention one thing to you that may be of use when we are far apart that is my Exercise in Respect of the Affairs of our land and Nation, that I am more Disposed to pray that the God of Heaven would guide and Direct our Rulers to make such laws that may Give us pure liberty, than I am to Sign Petitions or Quarrels on the Subject so miserably as we are doing Quarreling instead of praying to God for a Blessing on our land, on our Rulers, I am afraid will be our Ruin,- these few lines Comes with much love from your Father Josiah Philips, Give my kind love to all your friends there, especially the parents of your Beloved wife, that now is not. Your beloved Mamy and all the children that are Capable send their love to you.
To David Philips.   (Signed)
              Josiah Philips.

For other Civil War Records transcribed in

Rutherford County, see

W.P.A. Transcriptions on File in the

Tennessee State Library

"Civil War Records   Vol. 3 (Middle Tennessee)"

RUTHERFORD COUNTY

CIVIL WAR LETTER

PREFACE

JOSIAH G. DUKE TO MRS. REBECCA PHILLIPS

    The following letter is a copy of the original one written by a Confederate soldier to his grandmother. The letter is at present owned by the writer's second cousin, Mrs. A. H. McLean, 416 E. Main St., Murfreesboro, Tenn.
    Josiah G. Duke was a grandson of Josiah and Rebecca Phillips. He was living in Texas at time of Civil War, and enlisted from that State, serving in the 4th. Regiment of the Texas Volunteers, under command of Colonel Hood.

* * * * *

Copied by:
Mrs. Sadie McLaurine,
Murfreesboro, Tennessee,
December 7, 1938.

* * *

RUTHERFORD COUNTY

CIVIL WAR LETTER
JOSIAH G. DUKE TO MRS. REBECCA PHILLIPS

                                            Jourdan Valley Tenesee
                                            Camp Texas, near
                                            Richmond, Virginia.

Dear Grandma.
                After a long while I agane take my pen in hand to write to you. I am well at present and hope you are enjoying the same blessing. When I wrote you last it was a long while ago, some five or six years, and I am ashamed of myself for not writing oftener, and I hope you will pardon me.

    Well when I wrote you last I was at home and had nothing to think of. I had a kind Mother and Father to direct me and take care of me, but it is not so now. I am away from them now and have to take care of myself, but that I can do very well, but it is not like same at home. I had all I wanted and that was plenty, and when my days work was done, I could go home and sit around the fireside with loved ones, but not so now, for I am a soldier and have to live diferent when my days work is over, I can go to my tent and sit down and think of loved ones far away and wish that I could see them, but I can't say when that will be, for I have enlisted for the war and will have to stay till it breaks up, and nobody knows when that will be, but I hope it will not be long before it breaks up.

    I belong to the 4th. Regiment of Texas Volunteers, under the command of Colonel Hood, and we are well pleased with him. He is a Texan himself, and a good soldier and has the appearance of a brave man and that is just what Texans want, is a man that will lead them on to victoria or death, not boasting at all, but I am glad that I can call myself a Texan, for Texan soldiers never knew defeat, that is the reputation we have and we intend to keep it. All we want is to have a fight with the Yankees and show them how bad we can whip them.

    Well grandma, I promised you that when I leave a war that I would come and see you. Well, I am true to my promise if I live, so you may look out for me when the war breaks up, for I am coming.

    Well, I have received four letters from home since I've. been here, and they were all well and doing well and making good crops of cotton and corn.

    I left home on the 30th. of July and camped at Harrisburg, Texas until the 19th. of August, when we started to Virginia we had to walk across Louisiana, and it rained on us all the way. We had to waid all the way except when we were swimming, but we endured it all without a murmer. We arrived at Richmond the 10th. September and we are getting tired of this place, but we will leave before long and go to where we can get a sight at the Yankees, it matters not where that may be. When I left home it was to get a shot at the Yankees, and I won't be satisfied until I have done it, and then I will be willing to go home.

    Well, you must excuse bad writing, for I have no place to write on and it comes unhandy. You must write to ma at home and tell her that you received a letter from me.

    Well, I will stop. I would ask you to write me, but I would not get it, for I don't know when I will be where to receive it.

(Josiah G. Duke to Mrs. Rebecca Phillips, p. 2)

Give my respects to all the folks. No more at present.
I remain your affectionate grandson until death.

                                    Josiah G. Duke.

* * * *

RUTHERFORD COUNTY

CIVIL WAR LETTERS

PREFACE

O. R. HIGHT TO MARY C. HIGHT

The following letters are copies of the original ones written from camp by O. R. Hight, a confederate soldier, who was serving in Captain W. A. Landers' Company, Colonel T. W. Newman's Regiment, to his mother, Mrs. Mary C. Hight. The letters are at present owned by a nephew, J. D. Roberts, of Bradyville Pike, Murfreesboro, Tennessee, who is Register of Rutherford County at the present time.

O. R. Hight enlisted in the war at the age of 18, was wounded in the battle of Murfreesboro, and died near Tullahoma, Tennessee before he could reach his home in Normandy. A sister took his body home and buried the remains in Normandy.

* * * * *

Copied by:
Miss Mabel B. DuBois,
Murfreesboro, Tennessee,
October 10, 1938.

* * *

RUTHERFORD COUNTY

CIVIL WAR LETTERS
O. R. HIGHT TO MARY C. HIGHT

State of Tenn. Camp Trousdale
July the 11, 1861

Dear Mother.

It is with pleasure that I take my pen in hand to rite you a few lines to let you know that I am well at this time, hoping when these lines comes to hand they will find you all well. I received your leter the 8 and was glad to hear from you.

I have nothing of any importance to rite to yo, only we are all very well satisfied. We have as good water here as any in old Bedford. They give a false alarm here this morning about 3 o'clock, and one last sundy morning. John Deen and Sam Blackman is boath well.

We drawed our pay 9 and got $16.50 a peace. Will send you same by the first one that pases. I am afraid to send it in a leter. You rote that Mid Holland refused to let you have any more pervisions. I will rite to him in a day or too about it. I rote him one and sent it by Frank when he come home. They _____ when they come home that Bill Johnson had left him.

I want you to rite to me as soon as you get this and rite all about what the people is a doing, how much wheat Cotner made and others, and rite who has maried sense I left and who is dead.

I had to stand guard last knight and today is rest day with me.

I expect we will stay here a good while. Rite to me as soon as you get this. You rote in your last leter that Ann was a coming home next Monday, rite whether she does or not. I am a going to have my likeness taken and send it home.

We will draw our money the first of next month, which will bee $11. I want you to take care of my watch for me, and doly and drum and mol till I come home. Rite how my corn looks and how all the rest looks. So no more at present. Be shore not to sell. Mayflour time is over now and you can git a horse to do your milling.

Nothing more at present.
Rite to me as soon as you get this.

O. R. Hight
to
Mary C. Hight

* * * * *

RUTHERFORD COUNTY

CIVIL WAR LETTERS
O. R. HIGHT TO MARY C. HIGHT

Aug. 16, 1861.

fridy night

Dear Mother.
    I will rite you a few lines to let you know whare we are. We are at big creek gap and doing well, and I hope that when these few lines come to hand will find you all enjoying thee Same Blessing. I have nothing strange to right to yo all.
    We are now 45 miles from Knoxville. We was ordered from Comberlin Gap day B-fore yesterday on a force march, and when we landed I was very tired. We was ordered from there with the Expectation of a Fight. I don't know how long we will stay here. They was four companys came from Cumberland gap, they was 6 others stayed there. We may stay here, but I don't think we will stay here long. They have got two canons there and the mountain is 16,000 feet high, and they is a man sets up there with a spy glass. I was up there Sundy, me and some of the other boys and got huckleberries. We marched from there in 23 ours, which was 35 miles. We marched all knight.
    They is two Calvalry Companys here and two at Cumberland gap, and they have got brest works there. One regiment can whip 10,000. We can stand up there and see the men drill.
    Well Mother, I want you to rite to me soon, I want to hear from you and I will send you some money when we draw again. We will draw some the first of next month and we will get $22 dolars.
    I want you to take care of your things till I come home, and rite to me and tell Mid Holland to rite to me. I have rote to him three times and have not got any answer. I want him to rite to me without fail, and you two. We may go to Cumberlan gap in a week. Write to me. Back the leters to Col. Newman's regiment, Capt. Lander's Company, and if we leave there before they git there they will folow.
    Well Mother I want you to rite to me and I want you to take care of yourself while I am gone and I will send you some money to buy some wheat with, and you must sow it. Take care of your hogs and my cow and watch, and when I send you money I will send you a nough to git it fixt, and you must have it fixt. I have paid Mat Curtner four dolars that we owed him for mo, and when I send you money you must pay Alfred Huffman one dolar, and it will be all that I owe.
    So no more at present.
    Rite to me.

                                            O. R. Hight to Mary C. Hight.

* * * * *

RUTHERFORD COUNTY

CIVIL WAR LETTERS
O. R. HIGHT TO MARY C. HIGHT

Sept. the 22, 1861

Dear Mother.

  I seat myself this morning to inform you that I am well & hope these few lines may find you all well & dewing well. I resoived your leter yesterday & was glad to here from you & to her that you was all well.
  Mother we are in the State of Kantucky, 14 miles from Cumberland Gap. We come here last Saturday, the 14th. & they put us to throwing up a battery. I worked last Wednesday & that night our company had to go 17 miles to a place by the name of Barbersville to take the place. They was 4 Regts. here & they sent 2 companies of each Regt. had to go & the cavellry. They was about 75 of the calvery & 7 companies of the infantry. They was a rite smart string of us. The cavalry went in front. We never got to fire nery time. The 2 foremost companies ___ all that got to fire of the infantry. The cavalry tore down the pens & charged in on them & fired on them & we all commenst hollowing & they Broke. We got 2 prisners. We killed several of them. We first herd that they was 10 killed then herd they was 28. We can't tell how meny they was killed. They killed one of our men & wonded 3 or 4, but not but one bad. I don't think the men that got shot belonged to the cavelry company.
  We are all tolerable well at this time. I would like to come home and stay awhile with you all.
  Mother I expect we will have a heap of hard fighting here if we stay here. We thought we was a going to have a fight the other morning, but they was most two many of us for them.
  Mother I want to no how mutch fodder has been saved on the place, or whether they has ben enny saved or not, & I want to no how meny hogs you have got & whether you have got my coalt on enny pasture or not.
  Samuel Blackman got a leter from Victory Heard & they was all well. We hav tolerble bad water here. We hav to drink creek water part of the time. They is one spring here, but we cain't get water for all out of it. The water is bad as far as I hav been. I hav wrote all I no that is interesting at the presant, only gave my love & best respecks to all the nabors & write to me as soon as you can & direct your leter to Cumberland Gap, Tenn. threw the cear of W. A. Landers, in Col. T. W. Newman's Regt.

        yours truly,

        O. R. Hight
         to
        Mary C. Hight

* * * * *

RUTHERFORD COUNTY

CIVIL WAR LETTERS
O. R. HIGHT TO MARY C. HIGHT

Tenn. January the 18, 1862.

Dear Mother.

I take my pen in han to inform you that I am well at this time, hoping when these lines comes to hand they will find you all well. I received your letter the other day and was glad to hear from you and to hear that you was all well and doing well.

I have nothing strange to rite at this time. We had a battle on the 19 and got whipt, and had to leave our houses. We went upon fishes Creek and commenst fighting about 8 o'clock. It lasted about 2 ours, when we had to retreat and come back to our brest works and staid there all day and till 10 o'clock in the night. We then crost the river and left there and came down here last sundy and are here yet, but I don't think we will stay here long.

There is several of us agoing back to Knoxville, or to Bowling Green, Kantucky. I think we will go down the river soon. The boats runs up here regular.

Well I will tell you who got kild - George Fuller, Cullin Cribs, John Reding, Tom Jones, John Bromfield, was all that was kild. We are here in the woods without a tent or anything else much. I did not get hurt but there was one on eache side of me shot, John Dwire was one. I shot 14 shoots and then run and come to camps with the rest of the boys that I could find scatard along the road.

Well mother I will send you 10 dolars, and you can do what you please with it. You had beter save some to by potato seed with, for I want you to plant a large patch of both kinds and start a litle crop till I come home. Let Mr. House have what ground he wants and you all put in the rest agin I come home, and then I will do the rest. I will send you 10 dolars, and if you want any let me know and I will send it to you. I want you to rase a big crop of everything this year, not set there and starve. Times is hard but they will be a heap harder and you had beter commense in time. If you kneed money to by any corn or anything else with rite to me and I will send you the money to by it with, and you must all work as soon as grass comes. I want you to put ____ on a good grass lot somwhere if it cost 5 dolars a month, I will buy it.

Well I must bring my leter to a close.

Rite to me as soon as you git this and let me know what you all a doing. Rite all about everything.

O. R. Hight
to
Mary C. Hight

* * * * *

RUTHERFORD COUNTY

CIVIL WAR LETTERS
O. R. HIGHT TO MARY C. HIGHT

Gainsburough
Feb. the 3, 1862.

Dear Mother.

I take my pen in hand to inform you that I am well at this time. I have nothing strange to rite to you at this time.

We are here at Gainsburough on Cumberlan river. We come here last Saturday, but I don't think we will stay here long. I recon you have herd all about the fight that we had last Sunday was two weeks ago. We had to leave our houses. We have drawn more tents. The report is that we kild about 15 hundred of them and that they kild about 3 hundred of our men, I don't know how true it is. They kild general Zollicoffer, and we think that he kild one of their Colonels. We sent a flag of truth back after his body, but they had done sent round to Nashville by railroad. They excepted our flag and let them come in. They have got some of our wounded men prisoners and they say that they may come home as soon as they git able if they will promis not to take up arms agin the North anymore. They say that there is 40,000 of them there at fishing creek. They taken several canons from us, and mules and wagons. When we got done crosing the river we burnt the boat to keep them from giting it, and burnt the Comisary.

Well Mother I will send you 10 dolars to git them rails made with, and if you kneed them you can have them made, and if not, you can do what you please with it. I will send you some more if you kneed it. I sold my watch for 20 dolars, and they paid us 22 dolars.

I want you to make a crop, or start one till I come home, and I will make it. I want you to plant a big crop of potatoes and coton. Let Mr. House have what ground he wants, and you tend the rest. If you will try you can git a horse for its feed. If you havn't got feed a nough rite to me and I will send you money to by it with, if you can git the horse. Times is hard and they will be harder, and you had beter fix for them, and pay your taxes and take care of what stock you have got.

You wrote that old House said that he would do as he pleased when he got there. Let him come I will show him when I come home.

Rite to me as soon as you git this.
No more at present.

O. R. Hight
to
Mary C. Hight

* * * * *

RUTHERFORD COUNTY

CIVIL WAR LETTER
GEN. JOS. E. JOHNSON TO JAMES D. MARKHAM

The following letter is a copy of the original one written at the close of the war by Gen. Jos. E. Johnson to James D. Markham, a confederate soldier. The letter is at present owned by James D. Markham's daughter, Mrs. Sadie McLaurine, Murfreesboro, Tennessee.

Copied by Mrs. Sadie McLaurine, Murfreesboro, Tennessee - September 1938.

                                                Head Quarters
                                                Army of Tennessee
                                                North Carolina.
                                                May 2nd. 1865

Comrade :-

In termination of our official relations, I earnestly exhort you to observe faithfully the obligations of a good and peacefull citizen at your home, as well as you have performed the duties of a thorough soldier in the field. By such a course you will best secure the comfort of your family & kindred and restore tranquility to our Country.

You will return to your home with the admiration of our people, won by the courage & devotion you have displayed in this long war.

I shall always remember with pride the loyal support and generous confidence you have given me - I now part with you with deep regret & bid you farewell, with feelings of candid friendship - & with earnest wishes that you may enjoy hereafter all the enjoyment and prosperity in the world.

                                                Jos. E. Johnson,
                                                General C. S. A.

* * * * *

RUTHERFORD COUNTY

CIVIL WAR RECORD
JAMES D. MARKHAM

The following record was taken from James D. Markham's notation on his Certificate of Membership of United Confederate Veterans, and has General Jos. E. Johnson's letter attached thereto. This certificate is at present owned by James D. Markham's daughter, Mrs. Sadie McLaurine, Murfreesboro, Tennessee.

Copied by Mrs. Sadie McLaurine, Murfreesboro, Tenn. - September 1938.

"Jas. D. Markham served as a "Webb foot Infantry" till wounded by a minnie ball in left knee, Sept. 19th. 1863, in Battle of Chicamauga, Tenn. - furloughed, and got home Saturday Sept. 26th. 1863 - confined to bed three months, & at home 6 months - Returned to Army at Dalton, Ga. - April 9th. 1864 & was again shot in left leg - on Rocky Face Mountain - shell exploded - Transferred to signal corps, and was in same balance of the war - surrendered with Gen'l. Johnston May 2nd. 1865 - near Greensboro, N. C. - was engaged in the following battles: Kinston, N. C., Chicamauga, Tenn., Dalton, Ga., & in Battles of Gen'ls. Bragg, Johnston and Hood."

- - -

His record shows that he entered for service in Confederate States Army in March 16th. 1861, in Capt. John A. (or H.) Avirett, Jr's. Company, which afterwards became Company B. - of the 32nd. and 58th. Regiment, Holtz Claw's Brigade, Army of Tennessee - & during latter part of service was in Hoods' Signal Corps. Lieut. Carey commanding. He was born in Perry Co. Ala. - on 16th. of May 1844.

He was married in 1872 - to Miss Annie Shelton Hayes of Athens, Ala. - where they lived during most of their married life - later moving to Birmingham in 1900 - where he lived till his death in Sept. 1909.

* * * * *

RUTHERFORD COUNTY

CIVIL WAR RECORDS

PREFACE

DIARY OF DR. JAMES B. MURFREE

MURFREE COLLECTION OF LETTERS

    The following records, as shown by the Table of Contents, are copies of the original diary kept by Dr. James B. Murfree of Murfreesboro, a Confederate Soldier, while serving as Surgeon in the Confederate States Army, and letters in his possession, which were written during the Civil War. These papers are owned at the present time by his daughters, Misses Rob and Libby Murfree, of 115 S. Highland Ave., Murfreesboro, Tennessee.
    Dr. Murfree was born and reared in Murfreesboro, and at the time war broke out, in 1861, he was practicing medicine in Murfreesboro, at which time he enlisted in Company I, of the First Tennessee Regiment, and was detailed as Medical Officer from this Company. He was appointed Assistant Surgeon by the State of Tennessee June 9, 1861, commissioned Assistant Surgeon in the Confederate Army, and served in this position until the 6th. of July, 1862, at which time he was appointed Surgeon, and retained that appointment to the close of the war. He, at one time, had charge of the hospital at Knoxville, Tennessee, later one in Emory, Va. He returned to Murfreesboro at close of the war, and practiced medicine there until time of his death, 1912. His son, Dr. Matt B. Murfree, is practicing physician at the present time in Murfreesboro. The town of Murfreesboro was named for his grandfather, Col. Hardy Murfree.
    Hardy Murfree, writer of one of these letters, was a brother of Dr. James B. Murfree.

                                            * * *

Copied by:
Miss Mabel B. DuBois,
Mrs. Sadie McLaurine,
October - 1938.
Murfreesboro, Tenn.   * * *
                        *

RUTHERFORD COUNTY

**CIVIL WAR RECORDS
B. W. AVENT TO DR. JAMES B. MURFREE**

                                        Head Quarters Army Med. Board,
                                                  Knoxville, T.
                                               Augt. 5th. 1861.

Asst. Surgeon James B. Murfree.

Sir -

    You are hereby detailed as Asst. Surgeon to the Military Hospital for the Eastern Division of this State, situated in this City.
    You will immediately report yourself to Surgeon Ramsey for duty.

                                                          Respectfully,

                                                          B. W. Avent,
                                                          Surg. Genl.

                          * * * *
                           *

RUTHERFORD COUNTY

CIVIL WAR LETTERS
E. D. HANCOCK TO DR. JAMES B. MURFREE

Murfreesboro, 22nd. Feb. 1862.

Dr. J. B. Murfree.

Dear Sir.

I dispatch to you this morning in answer to yours.

I have not fully determined whether I will remain here, or go South, but I think I shall remain here, because I am now inclined to the opinion that it is but a question of time about the "wiping out of the rebellion", at least it seems so to me now. Everything is in such a state of confusion here now that it is difficult for a man to think calmly enough to decide anything properly.

John Holmes was taken prisoner and was very sick at the time.

Charles Donoho and D_____ were taken prisoners, but not here.

All well here except some of the negroes I brought from Mississippi.

Cary is a little unwell this evening. I think she is taking the measles. I have one case at home now.

I suppose Anna has written you the latest news from Hal and Hardy.

Johnson's whole army are here, how long they will remain I do not know.

The latest news here from Fort Donelson is that the Federals have gone down the Cumberland with their entire army & gun-boats. There are no Federals or gun-boats at Nashville, and have not been there, & I think will not come there.

My love to Ada, and respects to yourself.

Yours truly & in haste,

E. D. Hancock.

* * * * *

*

RUTHERFORD COUNTY

CIVIL WAR LETTERS
HARDY MURFREE TO DR. JAMES B. MURFREE

Camp Blythe - near
Corinth, Miss.

12th. May /62.

Dear Doc:-

I have just received your letter and hasten to reply. I intended to have written to you soon after the battle, but the uncertainty of the transmission of the mails from this place north, detered me. I would have given you a description of the battle of Shiloh, & would do so now, but we are packing up all of our extra baggage preparatory to a move, where, I cannot tell, though I believe forward. Our extra baggage will be sent to Okaloma, Miss. We are to take nothing except a tent to eight men, one or two blankets, and a few cooking utensils.

We were on the extreme right of the line of battle in Gen'l. Chalmer's Brigade on the night before the battle, and could hear the Yankees drums nearly all night. Early next morning, 6th. April, we were ordered to join General Cheathams division, but on our way there Gen'l. Johnson ordered us (the left wing of our reg't. the right wing not having caught up) to a fort, two or three miles from the battle ground to assist a reg't. of infantry, one of cavalry and a battery of cannons to prevent the enemy from coming in our rear. We remained there till nearly 12 o'clock and then Col. Maney took us to the field of action. We did not get into the battle until about 3 o'clock P. M. When we went in we met two reg'ts. - one an Alabama and the other a La., giving way before the Yankees. We laid down & opened fire on the Yankees, when they stopped, faltered and finally fled. It was a Brigade mostly Missourians and Iowaians. We took a good many prisoners, and killed a good many. We advanced a short distance towards the river (Tenn.) when the enemy's shell from their gun boats prevented us from going any further. Major Field ordered us to get out of the way of the shells, and in doing so, I got lost from the Batallion, and it being nearly dark, I, in company with Jas. Morton and Sol. Hollowell, turned into a Yankee camp, and after regaling ourselves with some crackers, coffee etc. we laid down in a tent and went to sleep. It was one of the camps from which we had driven the Yankees. We drove them from every one of the camps, Got bacon, flour, sweet meats, etc. On the next day, Monday, I was on my own hook, being lost from my battalion. I was lost during the entire day. Got to our camp and with my company that night (Monday). Our company lost one, (killed) Andrew Bass, and several slightly wounded. Dave Sublett was shot behind the shoulder. He was lying down. Tip Hodge was badly stunned by a shell explosion near him. It bursted in a few feet of us. Anderson Jetton was lying the second one from me. A minnie ball passed through the seat of his breeches. We devil him a good deal about the locality of his wound. It was a terribly sublime scene. To hear the roar of the cannon, the rattle of the musketry, were grand, but the sight of the dead & wounded was awful. Men lay thick all around us, wounded in every conceivable way. Some with their heads shot off with cannon balls. Legs & arms

(Hardy Murfree to Dr. James B. Murfree, p. 2)

were torn off a great many men. You could see the thigh bones perfectly.

We have been looking for a big battle here for ten or twelve days. We have had pretty severe skirmishes several times in the last few days. We are expecting it to come off every day. We are strongly fortified. We have a rifle pit for several miles in length. We have several large siege guns & a good many batteries of brass pieces, (4, 6 & 12 pounders). I believe that the Yankees are afraid to come on us.

We have orders to send our extra baggage to Okalona, Miss. From which I argue that we will move on them. If we can whip them and rout them, we will go into Tenn, I hope.

We hear from home occasionally, from men coming from there. Hal and I both escaped unhurt. Hal and Brevard Jetton were both sick, and were sent to Jackson, Miss. They were weakened very much by diarrhoea. They were mending when they left. I hope they will be back in a short time again.

Our company is reduced to a very small number, only 40 or 50, by disease.

Give my love to Ada. Write whenever you can get an opportunity. I will write as often as I can.

Give my love to all at home, when you can write them.

                      Yours affectionately,

                          Hardy Murfree.

* * * * *

RUTHERFORD COUNTY

CIVIL WAR LETTERS
SPECIAL ORDER FROM MAJ. GEN. E. KIRBY SMITH

          Hd. 2nd. Depart E. Tenn.
          Knoxville, Aug. 1, 1862.

Special Order }
 No. 136 }

  Leave of Absence is hereby granted to Asst. Hospital Surgeon, Jas. B. Murfree for four days, at the expiration of which time he will resume his duties at this post.

        By Command of
         Maj. Gen. E. Kirby Smith,
          J. G. B. Elton.

To Asst. Surgeon Jas. B. Murfree
   Genl. Hospital.

    * * * * *
     *

RUTHERFORD COUNTY

CIVIL WAR LETTERS
L. P. Y. TO DR. JAMES B. MURFREE

Rome, Ga. May 5, /63.

Dr. Jas. B. Murfree.

Dear Doc.

I wrote to you from near Spring Hill some time since in reference to getting a position in your hospital, and requested you to reply to me at Columbia. I unexpectedly have found myself in this place and write you this for the purpose of getting an answer from you at this place, as I believe we have a daily mail from Knoxville to this place.

Gen. Forest will probably remain here until next Monday to recruit his horses & men.

Our march in persuit of the yankees, who were aiming for this place, Atlanta ___, is unprecedented in this war for hardships and privations. Our horses hadn't been unsaddled for one week, during which time we didn't average two hours out of the twenty four for rest & sleep. In one instance we traveled forty eight hours without getting out of our saddles, without feeding our horses, or eating ourselves. During the march we had seven regular pitched fights with them, two of which were in the night.

After the second fight all of our command remained back except two regiments, Starnes & Biffles. The yankees surrendered to us about twenty miles from this place, sixteen hundred strong, (mounted infantry) and two pieces of artilery, our force not exceeding five hundred. We scarcely had force sufficient to guard them into town. Forest made them believe he had seven regiments, by that he captured the barbarians and Rome was saved.

The citizens are making arrangements to give us a grand picnic next Saturday.

Write to me by return mail and let me know what the chances are for a position in your hospital. If you couldn't succeed in getting me a regular position you could probably get me a detail position until I could get posted up & make other arrangements. I wouldn't like to go before an examining board right away. You know it requires very little time for a man to become rusty in medicine if he turns his attention entirely from it, as I have done for the past twelve months. I would like to get a commission for several reasons. My means of support are swept away by this war & I will have to rely upon my own individual exertions after the war is over & of course I would prefer the practice of medicine to anything else. I would prefer the position of assistant surgeon, or surgeon in Cavalry, to any other in the army, but I see very little prospects of getting such a place, as there are no vacancies that I know of.

If you should effect the arrangements that I speak of I could not go immediately from this place. I would be compelled to go to Courtland, North Ala. and from there to Chattanooga.

Suppose you come down to Rome next Saturday, it's only a short trip.

Your Friend as Ever,
* * * * *
L. P. Y.

RUTHERFORD COUNTY

CIVIL WAR RECORD
DIARY OF DR. JAS. B. MURFREE

Monday Sept. 7, 1863.

An order came for us to march. We had since we left Knoxville been impressed with the belief that we were falling back to a more advantageous point, and that we would entrap the enemy, but for the last day or two it began to become evident that we were retreating from Tenn. and the idea was not relished by the soldiers.

At nine o'clock we commenced to march and after marching all night we came to Graysville in Georgia, at about 8 o'clock.

Tuesday - September 8, 1863.

Here we encamped, had our horses shod, wagons repaired &C. Our camp being on the Chickamauga river we had a nice bath, but our clothes all being very dirty, washing was not so pleasant, so we had to put on dirty clothes again.

Wednesday - Sept. 9th. 1863.

Moved this morning at daylight, whole army moving at 9 o'clock, reached Ringold, having <u>mined</u> the road. Found Ringold quite a nice little town, but almost a deserted village. Moved on towards Rock spring, which point we reached about 3 o'clock P. M. the travel was a very disagreeable one, as the roads were very dusty, the weather hot and dry. Gen'l. Buckner's whole corp being on the march with all of their supply, Bagge &C. Wagons stretching out for miles caused a perfect cloud of dust. At Rock spring we encamped, our baggage wagon not getting up until late at night.

Thursday - Sept. 10th. 1863.

Left Rock Spring at about 12o'clock M. Marched through a perfect cloud of dust in advance of the army to McLemore's Cave, when we encamped, having to do without supper &C, to sleep on the ground without covering, as our wagon did not come until quite late.

Friday - September 11th. 1863.

This morning we awaked and arose from our hard pallet, but with a better breakfast than our last supper (our wagons have come up in the night), were ready for the days action. This morning I met with my old friend, Dr. Jno. S. Fletcher, Buckner's corp, the evening he joined Hindman's Division. Hindman being the senior Maj. General, assumed command. Hindman's Division the day before were drawn up in line of battle for several hours. It was generally rumored in camp that we were to have a battle today. The order was given for the march to commence today at daylight for the purpose of attacking the enemy, but the march did not move until 7 or 8 o'clk. A. M. The line of march was first.
   Stewart Division
   Preston's Division
   Hindman's Division
with a battery in rear of each brigade. The ambulances of whole command

with the infirmary corp following the whole command. Early in the day skirmishing with the enemy commenced, which kept up for several hours, when our artillery opened upon the enemy and our whole line was advanced, the enemy retiring, which failed to bring on a general engagement. The result of the fight was 7 or 8 wounded on our side, while 8 of the enemy were found on the battlefield, their wounded we had no means of estimating. At dark the enemy having entirely disappeared, our line of march was taken for trench. Dug Gap in Bird Mountain. We marched until 2 o'clock at night, when halted and found a resting place as best we could. I, with several others, crawled into a pile of straw and slept until daylight.

Saturday - Sept. 12, 1863.
As daylight dawned, the voice of Dr. Jennings rang in my ear "get up" - "get up" or you will be left behind. It was with great reluctance that I crawled out of my bed of straw. We were soon on the march, but our progress was slow, as the road was crowded with wagons. Very early in the morning we came to the Pigeon Mountain, where we detained several hours waiting the wagons to cross. We crossed at Dug Gap. I was sent forward to Lafayette to make preparation for the sick of the command. By rapid riding I soon made Lafayette, and after seeing Dr. Flewellan, Gen'l. Bragg's Med. Director, returned to meet my comrades at the outskirts of the town. We went into camp and remained there until sunrise.

Sunday - September 13th. '63.
When the whole command moved out on the road to Chattanooga, expecting to meet the enemy. After marching five or six miles, halted and fed our stock. Cannonading was distinctly heard and some thought that we would have hot work, but I suppose that there was no need for our command , and we were marched back to Lafayette and encamped.

Monday - September 14th. '63.
Today was passed in camp very quietly, nothing of interest occurring. Our camp was close to a little _____ that was used as a corp Hospital.

Tuesday - September 15th. 1863.
Another day quietly passed in camp at Lafayette. Lafayette was once a nice little country town in Walker County, Georgia, but now it is almost desolated & nothing of interest or attraction about it.

Wednesday - September 16th. '63.
Today I am twenty eight years old. Upon this epoch many pages might be written, but a soldier's life is such as to do away with all the fanciful and imaginary dissertations upon life and time and come down to a matter of fact way of thinking and doing. Today I received an order to report to Surg. S. H. Stout, Med. Director of Hospitals, for assignment to duty in the Hospitals of Buckner's corp, visited friends in the 1st. and 18th. Tenn. Regt. Was with my Brother, Lt. Hardy Murfree at his camp. Night came on and the sadness of parting with my associates weighted upon my spirits and I regretted to have to part with them. Had it not have been for the prospect of seeing my wife I would have protested against the order, but deeming it my first

(Diary of Dr. Jas. B. Murfree, p. 3)

duty to look after the interest of my ____ above all others, I obeyed the orders, stating to the Medical Director that if a Battle was imminent I did not want to leave until it was over.

Thursday - Sept. 17, 1863.
Arose before daylight, got breakfast, bid farewell to loved friends and before the golden sun had cast its rays over the rural village, Dr. Hilliard, Capt. Williams & myself were on the road to Resaca. After a ____ journey we reached Resaca late in the evening, but learning that we could not get transportation for our horses we determined to go to Calhoun, Ga. which point we reached late in the night, and failing to get quarters in a house had to lie on the ground with nothing but a light shawl to cover with. A slight rain fell on us.

Friday - September 18, 1863.
Left our wagon and horses to be carried through the country, we got on the cars and went to Marietta, which point we reached about 3 o'clk. in the afternoon. Found Marietta to be a very nice little city. Reported to Surg. Stout and was ordered to re-open the Asylum Hospital at Dalton, Ga., also ordered to go in search of Hospitals that had been shipped from Virginia remained in Marietta that night.

Saturday - September 19th. 1863.
Left Marietta early in the morning, went to Atlanta and remained there until 7 o'clock in the evening.

Sunday - September 20th. 1863.
Reached Augusta this morning about sunrise, stopped at the Southern States Hotel, but learning where my wife was boarding, left and went to see her. Spent the day very happy with my wife and babe and other friends and relations. It was a great joy to be once more with ____ I love so much. Found that they were both very well and comfortably situated. Attended funeral service in the Episcopal Church in the afternoon, afterwards walked about the city with my wife.

Monday - September 21, 1863.
Spent today in Augusta, found it a most delightful city and saw but little external evidence that we were engaged in a most extensive war. The high price of goods was the most striking evidence of the war. Augusta is one of the prettiest cities I ever visited, probably a prettier place than Philadelphia. In the afternoon rode out with my wife and others to the Sand Hills near Augusta. In the evening attended the Theatre with my wife. Learning that night that a heavy engagement had occurred between our army and the enemy near the Chickamauga River, in Northern Georgia, I determined to go immediately to my new post of duty near the front. Made diligent search for my Hospital stores, but failed to find them.

Tuesday - September 22.
Left Augusta about sunrise, after bidding an affectionate farewell to my wife. Traveled all day in the cars, saw nothing of particular interest on the road except Stone Mountain. Distance from Augusta to Atlanta is 171 miles. Reached Atlanta just before dark, found there

several thousand federal prisoners who had been captured at the late battle on the Chickamauga, changed cars at Atlanta and started for Dalton, which place I reached next morning about 2 o'clock.

Wednesday - September 23.
Found Dalton a quiet little town with some attempt at splendor. It is the most incomplete town I ever saw. Found the Hospital I was to take charge of without any supplies whatever, 5 or 6 trains of cars loaded with wounded soldiers who were suffering for the want of attention were daily passing. The demands for food and medical attention were constantly being made upon the Hospital, but alas we were but little prepared to meet such demands. But we met the demands as best we could and through the kindness of the ladies (who furnished us with bandages & rags) were enabled to dress the wounds, and by taxing our cooks to the utmost were enabled to give them some food.

Thursday - September 24.
Today passed as the day before, in trying to do something, but without the means to do anything. Oh the heart rending feeling to see my own fellow soldiers who have braved their breasts to the storms of shell & shot, suffering for attention and not be able to relieve them.

Friday - September 25.
Another day of discomforture. Wrote to my wife, as I do every day. Wounded from the Battle field still pass, and our means of ministering to their wants are still meagre.

Saturday - September 26.
Spent today quietly in the discharge of my duties.

Sunday - September 27th.
Having so many duties to attend this day did not attend church as I would like to have done. Many and many a sabbath day has passed since I have listened to the preaching of the word of God. I have not heard a sermon preached since I left Knoxville.

Monday - September 28th.
Another quiet day. I find Dalton by no means a pleasant place. I have made application to a great many of the citizens for board for my family, who I am very anxious to have with me.

Tuesday - September 29th.
I have made since I have been in this place an invariable duty to write to my wife every day and have not failed to write on any day yet. I almost daily receive a letter from her, but occasionally she fails to write, and then I feel very uneasy in regard to her welfare. Today passed quietly by.

Wednesday - September 30th.
Still at Dalton, and very unpleasantly situated, but soldiers ought not to complain.

Thursday - October 1st.

(Diary of Dr. Jas. B. Murfree, p. 5)

Today passed without anything of moment or interest occurring. Dr. Hilliard, the Post Surgeon, is quite sick. Getting the Hospital in better condition.

Friday - October 2, 1863.
Nothing of interest has occurred today.

Saturday - October 3rd.
Today we were all made glad by the arrival of Dr. Slack, my Hospital Steward, with Hospital stores which were brought from Knoxville around through Virginia and South Carolina.

Sunday - October 4th. 1863.
Amputated the thigh of a soldier wounded in the knee joint at the battle of Chickamauga. Patient stood the operation well.

Monday - October 5th.
Was much gratified at being able (by the arrival of supplies) to better provide the wounded. The day passed quietly off.

Tuesday - October 6th. 1863.
Another day is numbered with the past. How rapidly time is fleeting away, and what little improvement we make of it.

Wednesday - October 7th. 1863.
Still another day has passed quietly by.

Thursday - October 8th. 1863.
Today nothing of interest has occurred. The streets are afloat with rumors.

Friday - October 9th. 1863.
Today was one of unusual interest on account of receiving a telegram from my wife, stating that Mrs. Valentine (her everyday companion) was going to leave Augusta for Griffin, Ga.

Saturday - October 10, 1863.
Another quiet day.

Sunday - October 11th. 1863.
Another Sabbath day has passed and I failed to attend divine worship. Have been much troubled about finding a house to live in. Having utterly failed to secure boarding anywhere. I started D. H. Tolley to Augusta after my wife this morning.

Monday - October 12th. 1863.
Nothing of interest occurred today.

Tuesday - October 13th. 1863.
Secured board for a few days for family at Dr. Alston's. Expect my wife to reach here tomorrow.

* * * * *

RUTHERFORD COUNTY

CIVIL WAR LETTERS
S. MOORE TO DR. JAMES B. MURFREE

                                                Confederate States of
                                                      America -
                                        Surgeon General's Office,
                                             Oct. 18th 1864.

Sir -
     You are informed that the condition of the Hospital under your charge, as reported by Medical Inspector, I. H. Morton, in his report of Oct. 6th. 1864, is deemed very satisfactory.

                                            Very Respectfully,
                                                Your obt. Serv't.

                                                    S. Moore
                                            Surgeon General, C. S. A.

Surgeon
James B. Murfree, in charge,
Emory Hospital, Emory, Va.

                                  * * * * *

RUTHERFORD COUNTY

CIVIL WAR RECORDS
GENERAL ORDER FROM GEN'L. R. E. LEE

Headquarters - Army of Va.

April 10th. 1865.

Gen'l. orders } of No. 9

After five years of arduous service, marked by unsurpassed courage and fortitude, the army of No. Va. has been compelled to yield to overwhelming numbers & resources. I need not tell the brave survivors of so many hard fought battles, who have remained steadfast & true to the last, that I have consented to this result, not from any distrust of them, but feeling that valor and devotion would accomplish nothing that would compensate for the losses that have attended the continuance of the contest. I determined to avoid the useless sacrifice of those whose past services have endeared them to their countrymen.

By the term of the agreement, Officers & men can return to their homes and remain until exchanged.

You will take with you the satisfaction that proceeds from the consciousness of duty faithfully performed, and I earnestly pray that a Merciful God will extend to you his mercy and protection.

With an unceasing admiration for your constancy and devotion to your Country, and a grateful remembrance of your kind and generous consideration for myself, I bid you an affectionate farewell.

(Signed)

R. E. Lee -
Gen'l. - Army of Va.

* * * * *

RUTHERFORD COUNTY

CIVIL WAR LETTERS
WM. MORROW TO MAJ. GEN. STONEMAN

Knoxville, Tenn.

July 15, 1865.

Sir:-

I am requested by Dr. Jas. B. Murfree, who has been in charge of the Confederate Hospital at Emory, to make application for a passport and transportation for himself & family (four persons in all), from Bristol, Tenn. to this place.

He has been detained at Emory by the serious illness of his wife. If possible, he desires to avoid detention at Greenville or the Plains, and come to this point to take the required oath.

If possible to grant his requests, the courtesy will be properly appreciated.

Will you please be so kind as to inform me of your decision in the matter.

Very respectfully,

Wm. Morrow.

A. A. G. Dept. Hd. 2nd.,
Knoxville, Tenn.

* * * * *

On the back of this letter is the following notation -

"No passport required. Comd'g. officers at Jonesboro, or Greenville is authorized to grant transportation in this case.
By command of -
Maj. Gen. Stoneman.

* * * * *

RUTHERFORD COUNTY

CIVIL WAR LETTERS
MAJ. GEN. MORROW TO DR. JAMES B. MURFREE

Hd. 2nd. Morrows Post
End of his wife's apron strings,
Knoxville, Tenn.

July 28, 1865.

Reply returned to Dr. J. B. Murfree through forty eight different channels.

As the circumstances which called this communication forth have ceased to exist, this paper and all these indorsements will be filed. It will serve, it is earnestly hoped at the Hd. 2nd. as a perpetual reminder of the generosity of that government (in furnishing transportation for yourself and family), which you were so anxious to break up. Thus it is, that the best government God ever saw, treats its enemies for acts of unkindness, returning kindness.

Go then, erring rebel, and teach your numerous children as they grow old enough to understand to revere this government, just as though it had not stole their daddy's horses, et cetera. Let them gaze in wonder at that Great Eagle, which has swallowed some million of negroes, an indefinite amount in untold weight of silver, plates, spoons, forks, etc. to say nothing of thousands of silk dresses & every article found in the rebellious states, of value at the North, the bird that has done all this without producing a single unpleasant symptom.

By command of -
Maj. Gen'l. Wm. Morrow.
A. A. G.

* * * * *

The above letter was attached
to Maj. Gen. Stoneman's reply
to Maj. Gen. Morrow's letter.

RUTHERFORD COUNTY

CIVIL WAR RECORDS

PREFACE

SKETCH OF ROBERT MARTIN RUCKER

ROBERT MARTIN RUCKER TO MRS. SAMUEL R. RUCKER

    The following records are copies of the original letters written from camp and prison by Robert M. Rucker, a Confederate Soldier, to his mother, also a record of the maneuverings of his Company during the war. These papers are at present owned by his daughter Rosalind, Mrs. John M. Pickard, Sr., who lives at the old homestead, on Route # 3, Murfreesboro, Tennessee.
    Robert Martin Rucker was the son of Samuel Reed and Mattie Bedford Martin Rucker. He enlisted in the service in May 1861, serving in Co. A., 2nd. Tennessee Regiment of Polk's Brigade, was transferred to Patrick R. Cleburne's Brigade of the Army of Tennessee, in February 1862.

* * * * *

Copied by:
Mrs. Sadie McLaurine,
Murfreesboro, Tennessee,
September - 1938.

* * *

*

RUTHERFORD COUNTY

CIVIL WAR RECORDS
SKETCH OF ROBERT MARTIN RUCKER

Robert Martin Rucker was born Dec. 3, 1830, entered in the service of the Civil War in May 1861, serving in Co. A., 2nd. Tennessee Regiment, Polk's Brigade, Cleburn Division, Hardee's Corps. He was married on July 24, 1867, to Mrs. A. L. Cowan. Spent his entire life in the house, standing today, on the road from Lascassas to Walter Hill, where his daughter, Mrs. Pickard now lives. Mrs. Rosalind Pickard and all her brothers and sisters were born in this house, which is 108 years old, still in a livable condition, and a lovely old place. He died in his 78th. year, on September 22, 1908.

The following record was attached to the letters copied from Mrs. Pickard's collection: (concerning his Company)
"Entered the Confederate Army at Lynchburg, Va. in May 1861, was sent to Acqua Creek & remained on duty till July 15, 1861, when it was placed in Holmes' Brigade & participated in the first battle of Bull Run, or Manassas, on July 21, 1861.

In Feby. 1862 was transferred to the Army of Tennessee & placed in Patrick R. Cleburn's Brigade, and anticipated in the following engagements:-

    Seige on Pittsburg Landing - April 6, 7, 1862
    Seige of Cumberland Gap - Aug. 20, 27, 1862
    Richmond, Ky. - Aug. 31, 1862
    Seige of Covington, Ky. - Sept. 17-23, 1862
    Perryville, Ky. - October 8, 1862
    Stones River, Tenn. - December 31, 1862
    Chicamauga, Ga. - Sept. 19-20, 1863
    Ringgold, Ga. - Nov. 26, 1863
    Gen. Johnson's Campaign - from Dalton to Atlanta,
        April to July 1864
    Resacca, Ga. - May 14-15, 1864
    Peachtree Creek - July 20, 1864
    Atlanta, Ga. - July 22, 1864
    Jonesboro, Ga. - Aug. 31, 1864
    Franklin, Tenn. - Nov. 30, 1864
    Nashville, Tenn. - Dec. 16, 1864
    Bentonville, N. C. - March 21, 1865
    Surrendered, - April 17, 1865"

* * * * *
*

RUTHERFORD COUNTY

CIVIL WAR LETTERS
ROBERT MARTIN RUCKER TO MRS. SAMUEL R. RUCKER

Smithfield Station,
near Raleigh, N. C.
March 13th. 1865.

Mrs. Samuel R. Rucker -

Dear Mother:-

It has now been just three months since I left what I once could call "home". I feel truly gartified that I was once more permitted to visit it again, though only a few short days, and when again, if ever, I'll be permitted the same privilege, time only can determine. Perhaps not again till this cruel war is over, (if I'm so fortunate as to be spared) when that will be, no human can tell.

I left Mr. Edmondson's Sunday morning, next after leaving your house & had quite a heavy walk of it to the Tennessee river, where I caught up with my command, then we walked from there to Tupelo, Miss. I bought a furlough while at this place, of 25 days length, and went down to Uncle Jack Rucker's & Mr. Richard Ledbetters, had a very good time, both of their families were well. They have plenty to eat. I stayed there some fourteen days, when I started back to my command, which had in the meantime gone to S. C.

It has been only a few days since I caught up with my command at Chester, S. C.

We are now in the old North State. There are but eight of my old Company left, my old mess are all gone, so you can see I am alone. West Rucker did not report back, neither did Furgerson or Edmondson. However, the two last I have not heard of since I left old Rutherford. Perhaps they did not come out at all. West has gone to Cavalry with Carter's Co. B. J. Hill com'd.

Tell Sophie as I passed through Macon, Ga. I tried to get to see Mr. Betty. I laid over a day for that purpose, but was disappointed at last. He was away, had gone up to Jonesboro to press in some negroes and did not return before I left. I regret so much that I missed seeing him. He was well and hearty, I understand.

I am expecting a "Flag of Truce", from you now every day. I am so anxious to hear from home, not having heard a syllable since I left your house, you may well imagine my anxiety. Do write me whether you have gotten a safe guard or not & whether Capt. Fleming & Lizzie are living with you, if so, you will need none. Write me how you are getting along etc.

I have not seen any of the boys of the 18th. or 25th. since I came out of Tenn., except Charley Baird. I saw him the other day. He is well and hearty. I would like to hear what became of Pink Edmondson. I miss him so much.

Remember me kindly to all of my good neighbors, especially Mr. Matthews, Gardners, Subletts and Alfords. My love to Uncle Ben, Cousin Bettie & Sophie and the rest of our kin.

Oh! write me about Wm. Rucker - what became of him? I have never heard. My respects to Mrs. Mitchell.

Affectionately, your son
R. M. Rucker.

* * * * *

RUTHERFORD COUNTY

CIVIL WAR LETTERS
ROBERT MARTIN RUCKER TO MRS. SAMUEL R. RUCKER

                                        Point Lookout Prison,
                                              Maryland,
                                           Apr. 4th. 1865.

Mrs. Samuel R. Rucker -

My Dear Mother:-
    You will doubtless be surprised to hear of my being in prison, but such is the fate of war, sometimes. I was captured on the 22nd. of last month, I and two others of my Brigade, near Goldsboro, North Carolina, two days after the fight at Bentonville. I was in the engagement on the 19th. & escaped unhurt, truly the Almighty has answered the prayers of my dear Mother and other dear loved ones at home for my safety so far. I was captured on the morning of the 22nd. on pickett. My command fell back from their line of breastworks and failed to notify me of their leaving, and next morning was captured. I have been treated very kindly since my capture. I was carried to Newburn, N. C. and there put on board of a vessel and brought by way of Fortress Monroe up to this prison on the Chesapeake Bay. Just arrived yesterday. I am pretty much alone here. No Tennesseans, but very few, none that I know, however.

    Palmers Brigade was in the fight on the nineteenth, but I have not been able to learn definitely who of our neighbors boys were hurt. I understood that Lieut. Sam Smith was wounded, though not dangerously. Charley Baird was in the fight, but I think was not hurt. Ed Mathews was not there, was with the wagon train, which had not come up with the command at the time of battle. This is what I understood from one of the 32nd. Tenn. of the Brigade, but for the truth of this information I cannot vouch. Mark Saunders, of the 20th. Tenn. was wounded severely in the arm, but not dangerous. Bally Murphey, of my Co. was wounded slightly. All the other boys of my old Co. escaped unhurt, there are but eight of them left. Lieut. Henderson, Howard, three Murphy boys, Ben Cosby, Elisha Saga and myself. I mention this for the benefit of their friends near Murfreesboro. None of the 20th. were hurt but Saunders. The first Tenn. was not in that fight. Their Brig. had not come up.

    Mother, I do not expect you have heard a word from me since our army left Tennessee last winter. I wrote three different letters to you by "Flagg of Truce" since I left, but have not heard a word in answer from you, or any of my friends in Tennessee. Do write immediately. I am so anxious to hear from you.

    I spent two weeks of furlough at Uncle Jack Ruckers and Mr. Ledbetters, very pleasantly, last winter. When I left, their families were both well. Sally Thompson was gay and lively as a cricket.

    West R. is with Bells Brig. Cav. I never have learned what became of Pinkney E. or Miles Furgerson. They were left in Tennessee.

    Mother, you know you are a good, true & loyal woman to the Federal Government and I have been a Rebel soldier for four years, but my faith now, & has been for some time very much shaken in our ultimate success, and Tennessee, Middle Tenn; old Rutherford that gave me birth - God Bless her & her people. All I hold to as dearest on earth - my good old Mother, my affectionate relatives, & my kindest and best of neighbors, are all

(Robert Martin Rucker to Mrs. Samuel R. Rucker, p. 2)

there. They are my people. They are my friends, but I am a stranger in the Southern States proper, no friends but my comrades that I have been with for four long years, and they have fallen one by one until each one thinks it is his time next.

I hope this "cruel war" will soon be over. I feel conscious that I have at all times endeavored to discharge my duty, & I am certain that there are thousands of others who for the sake of their precious carcasses and love of this filthy Lucre, have not done theirs. So, I am getting sick & tired of other people's duty, who are just as competent to try to do theirs as I am my own. But, we are told "that all things happen for the good of man", but enough of this.

I have just been interrupted by shaking hands with Catesby Edmondson, who with the rest of his company (all captured), just came into this prison. He is well & sends his respects. Was captured a few days ago at Richmond. Don't send me anything yet, for I do not know whether I will remain at this prison, or be sent somewhere else. I will know in a few days & write you again.

        Your affectionate son

         R. M. Rucker.

P. S.
  I am in fine health.

* * * * *

RUTHERFORD COUNTY

CIVIL WAR LETTERS

PREFACE

R. H. TAYLOR TO NORA TAYLOR

    The following letters are copies of the original ones written by R. H. Taylor, a Confederate soldier, to his sister, Nora Taylor Campbell, and a part of a letter written to his Mother. The letters are at the present time owned by his niece, Miss Annie Campbell, 226 N. Walnut St., Murfreesboro, Tenn.
    R. H. Taylor was killed at Franklin in 1864. His home was in Versailles, Tennessee. He served as a private in the 20th Tennessee Regiment C.S.A.

* * * * *
*

Copied by:
Miss Mabel DuBois,
Murfreesboro, Tenn.
October 24, 1938.

* * * * *
*

RUTHERFORD COUNTY

CIVIL WAR LETTERS
R. H. TAYLOR TO NORA TAYLOR

Camp Trousdale,
June 30th. '61.

Dear Sister.

I seat myself this evening to answer the letter which I received the evening after I started my last letter. I would have waited a day or two before I wrote to Pa if I had have expected a letter so soon. It reached me about four days sooner than I expected it would.

I am still in good health, and hope by prudent conduct to continue so. If you get this letter before Mother starts those things that I wrote for, tell her to wait awhile, as I expect to get home in a week or two. Tell Ned to stay at home until I come, as there will be as good a chance to get in our Company then as now, tell him that a week or two will make but little difference anyway. I want him to be sure to wait untill I see him as I knew better what to do than he does.

Our officers are getting tighter and tighter. The 43 art. of war was read to us the other evening, which says that if a sentinel be caught sleeping on duty death shall be his portion, provided ten balls can kill him, that's right tight when there is no enemy about, but now is as good a time to train the boys as they will ever have.

There is seven of our boys in the Hospital now with the measles, but five of them will be able to go home in a few days, the other two has just been carried there; and several more will have to go there in a few days.

Well Nora, I have received about 7 or 8 letters since I left home and have written about the same. Not but one of my letters met with bad luck, I guess, as I have never received any answer to it. Perhaps you dont know anything about it. I wrote a letter to Lizzie, or at least it answered in the place of one, and haven't received any answer. I just want you to find out whether she received it or not.

We have had a very good rain here since I wrote last, and I think that it will rain more soon. I'm going to write a letter to Sallie Wilson, and send it in the same envelope.

Nora, I don't feel much like writing this evening. I stood guard last night, slept this morning and am drowsy this evening.

We did not drill last Sunday, nor today, but I guess we will go out on dress parade this evening. I wish you could be here and see us this evening. I'm certain that you would admire the sublimity of the scene.

Tell Asea howdy, and that I'm coming home before long.
Give my love to all and share a portion yourself.

R. H. Taylor.

* * * * *
*

RUTHERFORD COUNTY

CIVIL WAR LETTERS
R. H. TAYLOR TO NORA TAYLOR

Miss Nora Taylor.

Dear Sister -

    As you write to me every opportunity so very promptly, I guess as how I had better write you a few lines, although I have nearly exhausted my vocabulary writing to Ma. So you will excuse me if I don't write a real fluent letter. It is with us somewhat like it was with the boys while they were at Bowlinggreen, Ky., but I'll bet a fifty cents individual shin plaster that you don't know whats in my letters before you read them. The monotony of camp is only broken by the General reviews and drills that we have, and they have become so frequent that a person mearly thinking of it would think that they had become monotonous, but that is a mistake, there is something new for the eye and mind to feast upon at every review. A person with any soul could not help enjoying the grandeure of the scene that is presented to them at every review.

    Our reviews are always graced by the presence of some nice, important ladies, and be assured that their presence tends to liven up the wayworn soldier, by causing him to remember the beautiful sweetheart, or wife that they left behind. Oh: It does my very soul good when I see a real beautiful young lady, who appears to be as pure and spotless as an angel, and to know that some who are equally as nice sympathize with me in the hardships and dangers which I have to undergo, and even pray that I may be among the number that is permitted to come out safe, and return home to enjoy the peace and liberty which is so hard for us to gain in company and sweet communion with those we love. Tis such thoughts as these that keeps the soldiers from being low spirited, it has been proven that where men harbour continually feelings of anger and revenge, that their mental faculties soon become impared, and soon the physical man fails, then he is gone by the board.

    Well, in turning over my paper I've managed to get it rong end upwards, but you must look over such mistakes.

    Nora I'll not say anything about the army, as there is nothing new. If the yanks come here we will give them what they have been needing a long time.

    I'm a great mind to send about half dozzen other letters down there which would have been stiled April fools; but as I have no surity of them getting there I'll not send them. I hardly suppose the girls would appreciate them anyway, as they are so low spirited, tell them to stir up and not give way to trifles.

    One of my Mississippi sweethearts married lately. She doubtless did well.

    Give my respects to all the girls. Write every opportunity, and give me all the news of the day.

    It is time to get supper so good by.

                                                R. H. T.

* * * * *

RUTHERFORD COUNTY

CIVIL WAR LETTERS
R. H. TAYLOR TO NORA TAYLOR

Nora you must send us some gurty purchy buttons if you can, let them be as thick as possible.

Dear Nora -

The horn has just sounded for preaching and generally attend, but as I have the implement for writing I'll write you a few lines anyway, for I could not think of writing to home without saying a few words to you.

I have just dined heartily on cornbread and dumplings of the same, grits we had for breakfast, and if we have good luck we will have more for breakfast tomorrow morning; that is, if the oven don't turn over and spill them all in the fire. I guess you would know them better by the name of choped hominy. When we first came in the army we would have grumbled mightily at the rashions we get; but now we only laugh at the scanty rashions and bless full rashions, some of the boys say that in another year we can live on half we get at present. Some of the boys say that if ever we gain our independence that we may thank the cow race for it.

Well Nora, we have been haveing a good time here for a long time, and it would even be interesting to you, that is the grand reviews, drills, sham fights and the maneuvering of the troops in every way imagenable. On those occasions the generals spirt round - - - - - - - - -
- - - - - - - (part of letter missing) - - - - - - - - - - - - - - - -

* * * * *

- - - - - - - and who I will ever love and respect. The respect that I have for those friends will cause me to stay in the army when all else would fail.

Ma, you must write to us, even if you have to write by flag of truce, a letter from you would animate my very soul, no one knows how much good a letter does until they are deprived of them for awhile. I am going to send this by Capt. Gray, perhaps you can send me an answer by him.

Give my love and kindest wishes to Pap and all the children also to all enquiring friends if there be any. If you write by flag of truce you can't write much, but if you can send one by hand write me all the news.

Dock Wilson is at Atlanta on post duty.
Minos Jordan is in fine health, the Faris boys are both well.
Dink is on furlough, and in fact all the boys are in good health.
Tenn. Manier and Frank Nance is off at the Hospital.
I'll close as I guess you are tired of reading -

I remain as ever your son,

R. H. Taylor.

* * * * *

RUTHERFORD COUNTY

CIVIL WAR RECORDS

PREFACE

ARTICLE ON COLONEL C. D. VENABLE

    The following record is a copy of an article written by Richard Ransom, regarding Col. C. D. Venable. This paper was found among some old papers belonging to Richard Ransom, who lived at Murfreesboro, Tennessee prior to his death on February 4, 1903. The paper belongs to Mr. Ellis Ransom, 531 E. Lytle St., Murfreesboro, Tennessee, who is a great nephew of Richard Ransom.
    Colonel C. D. Venable was a Confederate soldier, his home being in Henry County, Tennessee, to which county he was returning for recruits when he sickened and died at the village of Versailles, Tennessee in December 1862.

* * * * *

Copied by:
Sadie M. McLaurine,
Murfreesboro, Tennessee,
May 29, 1939.

* * *
*

RUTHERFORD COUNTY

COL. C. D. VENABLE, C. S. A.

"The resting place of this deceased soldier and Confederate Officer is probably not known by many of his own Regiment, comrades nor friends, and believing that those of them now living would like to know, induces me to write this short sketch concerning his death & burial.

While General Bragg's Army was camped at Murfreesboro, Tenn., in December 1862 Col. Venable, together with about a half dozen officers, including one Surgeon, left the Army under orders to go to West Tennessee to get up recruits for their command, Col. Venable's home being in Henry County Tennessee.

They proceeded the first day, which was Saturday in the Christmas week of 1862, to Versailles, a village 12 miles S. west of Murfreesboro, where they stopped at the residence of my mother, for the night. Col. Venable complained of not feeling well and was suddenly taken worse, and by ten o'clock that night, he was a corpse.

The next day he was buried by his comrades, assisted by members of my mother's family and some neighbors, and was buried in my mother's burying ground, and which has since been adopted by her as a family burying ground.

I believe he was the first to be buried there, (some negroes being buried near), but since then she has had the lot enclosed by a red cedar plank and post fence, and neatly painted, which now contains besides the grave of Col. Venable, those of three of her children and three of her grandchildren. She has now growing in the enclosure Magnolias, evergreens and several varieties of rose bushes & flowers of several kinds, which she is still able to cultivate, water and fertilize, though she is in her 81st year.

There is, at the head of Col. Venable's grave, a stone slab with the inscription "Col. C. D. Venable, 5th Tenn." placed there by Mr. B. B. Taylor of the neighborhood, who had kinsmen in Colonel Venable's Regiment from Henry County.

I knew Col. Venable personally, being a member of the 24th Tenn. Regiment Infantry, brigaded with his Regiment, and knew that he was a gallant officer, and popular with the soldiers of Strahl's Brigade. His friends may be assured that his last resting place is neatly ornamented & well enclosed, I, having visited the spot last week. Aug. 14, 1890."

"Richard Ransom."

(NOTE: We visited this cemetery in May 1939, and it is beautifully kept. The roses and other flowers are all blooming. We saw Col. Venable's grave, and have it listed, also inscription on his grave.
- Sadie McLaurine)

ABBOTT, Gertrude, 33
ABBOTT, O. H. P., 148
ABBOTT, O. H. P., 149
ABSTON, Miss, 68
ADAMS, Eva May, 57
ADAMS, Susan A., 44
ADCOCK, J. T., 145
AGEE, Elder H. F., 155
AGEE, N. P., 155
AGEE, Ruth, 155
AGEE, Tennie, 155
AKIN, Henrietta E., 11
AKIN, Wm. E., 11
ALEXANDER, John D., 1
ALEXANDER, Mary R., 1
ALEXANDER, Mary R., 2
ALFORD, Mr., 190
ALSTON, Dr., 183
AMATE?, Edwin, 50
AMATE?, Susan Ann, 50
ANDERSON, N. E. (f), 47
ANDREWS, Betty, 64
ANDREWS, Patty, 64
ANDREWS, Richard, 64
ANDREWS, Sally, 64
ANDREWS, Wm., 64
ARNOLD, Ed (Capt.), 126
ARNOLD, Harriet, 126
ARNOLD, Harriett N., 126
ARNOLD, John F., 131
ARNOLD, John F., 133
ARNOLD, Wm. F., 131
ARNOLD, Wm. F., 133
ARRINGTON, Angeline Avondale, 26
ARRINGTON, Thomas J., 26
AVANT, Nancy, 3
AVANT, Nancy, 6
AVENT, B. W., 173
AVIRETT, Annie Shelton, 171
AVIRETT, John A. (H.?) jr., 171
BAIRD, Abigail, 123
BAIRD, Abigal, 2
BAIRD, Abigal Martin, 1
BAIRD, Adam, 123
BAIRD, Amanda Virginia, 2
BAIRD, Bennettie Patillo, 126
BAIRD, Charley, 190
BAIRD, Charley, 191
BAIRD, Chas. Beady, 2
BAIRD, Elener, 1
BAIRD, Elizabeth Eliza, 1
BAIRD, Fanny Henderson, 1
BAIRD, Fanny Henderson, 1
BAIRD, Hugh P., 132
BAIRD, J. P. (m), 126
BAIRD, J. R., 126
BAIRD, Jame Pinkney, 1
BAIRD, James Pinkny, 2
BAIRD, Jas. Pinkney, 126
BAIRD, Josiah M., 1
BAIRD, Josiah Martin, 1
BAIRD, Josiah Martin, 2
BAIRD, Lemuel M., 2
BAIRD, Lemuel Moore, 1
BAIRD, Lemuel P., 1
BAIRD, Mary R., 1
BAIRD, Mary Rebeena, 1
BAIRD, Mary T., 126
BAIRD, Sara A., 126

BAIRD, Victoria, 132
BAIRD, Violet Henderson, 2
BAIRD, W. D. (m), 126
BAIRD, Wm., 126
BAIRD, Wm. D., 1
BAIRD, Wm. D., 123
BAIRD, Wm. D., 2
BAIRD, Wm. D. Franklin, 1
BAIRD, Wm. D. Franklin, 2
BAIRD, Wm. Dinwiddie, 1
BAIRD, Wm. Dinwiddie jr., 2
BAIRD?, Anthony, 1
BAIRD?, Eliza, 1
BAIRD?, Harriette, 1
BAIRD?, Julia, 1
BAIRD?, Levi, 1
BAIRD?, Lucinda, 1
BAIRD?, Mary, 1
BAIRD?, Matilda, 1
BAIRD?, Sarah, 1
BAKER, Bray (m), 69
BAKER, Elizabeth, 68
BAKER, Elizabeth, 69
BAKER, George (Sir), 69
BAKER, Henry, 69
BAKER, Henry, 69
BAKER, Hinton J., 112
BAKER, Katy, 69
BAKER, Lawrence, 69
BAKER, Nannie, 112
BAKER, Sallie, 23
BAKER, Simmons, 69
BAKER, Wm., 69
BALLARD, Susanna, 68
BANKS, Alexander, 63
BANKS, Ben, 63
BANKS, Hardy, 63
BANKS, Hardy, 64
BANKS, James, 63
BANKS, Martha, 64
BANKS, Patty, 63
BANKS, Polly, 63
BARFIELD, Road, 3
BARLOW, Benj. D., 144
BARLOW, Fanny M. G., 144
BARNES?, Susan, 86
BARRHAM, Sarah, 34
BARROW, Mrs., 63
BARTON, Sallie Elizabeth, 23
BASS, Ambrose, 3
BASS, Ambrose, 5
BASS, Ambrose, 6
BASS, Andrew, 175
BASS, Andrew, 3
BASS, Andrew, 5
BASS, Andrew, 6
BASS, Ann, 3
BASS, Ann, 5
BASS, Arthur, 87
BASS, Ben Jordan, 5
BASS, Ben Jourdon, 3
BASS, Benjamin, 5
BASS, Bessie, 87
BASS, Charlotte Amelia, 6
BASS, Charlotte Amelia, 87
BASS, Eliiza (Lida) Howse, 87
BASS, Eliza, 3
BASS, Eliza, 5
BASS, Eliza, 6
BASS, Eliza Catherine Ann, 5

BASS, Eliza Catherine Ann, 5
BASS, Frances, 3
BASS, Frances, 5
BASS, Frances, 6
BASS, Fred, 3
BASS, Fred, 5
BASS, George, 3
BASS, George, 5
BASS, George, 6
BASS, Hartwell, 3
BASS, Hartwell, 5
BASS, Hartwell Jordan, 6
BASS, Hartwell Jordan, 87
BASS, Hartwell Jordon, 3
BASS, Hartwell P., 151
BASS, Hartwell P., 87
BASS, Hartwell Polk, 3
BASS, Hartwell Polk, 6
BASS, Henry, 3
BASS, James, 3
BASS, James, 5
BASS, James, 6
BASS, Jennie S., 151
BASS, Jennie S., 151
BASS, John James, 3
BASS, John James, 5
BASS, John James, 5
BASS, Lida Howse, 3
BASS, Lida Howse, 6
BASS, Malinda, 6
BASS, Martha, 3
BASS, Martha, 5
BASS, Martha Sarah, 5
BASS, Martha Sarah Hix, 3
BASS, Mary, 3
BASS, Mary, 5
BASS, Mary, 5
BASS, Mary, 5
BASS, Mary, 6
BASS, Mary Ann, 3
BASS, Mary Ann, 6
BASS, Mary Anna, 5
BASS, Mary Yeargan, 87
BASS, Mary Yeargen, 6
BASS, Masry Yeargan, 3
BASS, Miss Lanier?, 5
BASS, Nancy, 3
BASS, Nancy, 5
BASS, Nancy, 6
BASS, Nathan, 3
BASS, Nathan, 5
BASS, Rebecca, 6
BASS, Robert, 3
BASS, Robert, 5
BASS, Robert, 6
BASS, Ruth, 6
BASS, Sarah, 3
BASS, Sarah, 5
BASS, Sarah, 6
BASS, Sarah, 6
BASS, Sarah Jane Meriwether, 6
BASS, Temperance, 5
BASS, Temperance Jordon, 3
BASS, Thomas, 3
BASS, Thomas, 5
BASS, Thomas, 6
BASS, Wm., 3
BASS, Wm., 5
BASS, Wm., 6
BASS, Wyatt, 3
BASS, Wyatt, 5

BASS, benjamin, 3
BASS?, Charltes, 6
BASS?, Lida, 6
BATEY, Ann, 5
BATEY, Benjamin, 81
BATEY, G. C. (m), 37
BATEY, Lucy Lorena, 37
BATEY, Luisa, 86
BATEY, Martha, 3
BATEY, Martha, 5
BATEY, Tabitha, 81
BATEY, Wm., 3
BATEY, Wm., 5
BATEY?, Christopher, 88
BATT, Polly, 43
BATTLE, A. (Gen.), 149
BATTLE, Adelaide, 87
BATTLE, Allen, 87
BATTLE, Elizabeth, 87
BATTLE, Jennie, 87
BATTLE, L. H., 88
BATTLE, Lucian, 87
BATTLE, Rebecca Frusanna, 87
BATTLE, Robert, 87
BATTLE, Sarah M., 149
BATTLE, Sarah M., 81
BEARD, Richard (Capt.), 134
BEASLEY, E. Addie, 141
BEASLEY, Lillie Mae, 76
BEESLEY, Bettie, 111
BEESLEY, Cascendro?, 111
BEESLEY, Charles A., 111
BEESLEY, Christopher, 111
BEESLEY, John, 111
BEESLEY, Lillian Orlean, 111
BEESLEY, Mary Sue, 57
BEESLEY, Mollie L., 111
BEESLEY, N. W., 111
BEESLEY, Rachel, 111
BEESLEY, S., 111
BEESLEY, daughter, 111
BELL, C. W. (Capt.), 77
BELL, Catherine, 77
BELL, Fannie, 68
BELL, Fannie Dickinson, 68
BELL, Henry Frazier, 133
BELL, John, 64
BELL, John, 67
BELL, John (Hon.), 68
BELL, John jr., 68
BELL, Mary, 68
BELL, Sarah Louisa, 67
BEMBURY, Dr., 60
BEMBURY, Lavinia, 60
BENSON, Nannie, 46
BETHEL, Elizabeth Buchanan, 26
BETHEL, Hall (Rev.), 26
BETHEL, Mary Ann Judson, 26
BETHEL, Mollie, 25
BETTS, Sally, 103
BILLINGS, Kate, 72
BINFORD, Baker L., 7
BINFORD, Elizabeth K., 7
BINFORD, Henry L. S., 7
BINFORD, J. M. L., 7
BINFORD, James H. L., 7
BINFORD, James H. L., 8
BINFORD, Jas. W., 7
BINFORD, John P., 7
BINFORD, John P., 8

BINFORD, Joseph, 7
BINFORD, Lucy B., 7
BINFORD, Maria W., 7
BINFORD, Nacy F., 7
BINFORD, Nancy, 7
BINFORD, Peter E. T., 7
BINFORD, Sarah A. E., 7
BINFORD, Susan S. C., 7
BINFORD, Thos. A., 7
BINGHAM, Chas., 155
BLACHMAN, Alfred W., 6
BLACK, Catharine W., 112
BLACK, Eliza P., 112
BLACK, Fanny, 112
BLACK, Fanny J., 112
BLACK, Nannie, 112
BLACK, Nannie L., 112
BLACK, Samuel P., 112
BLACK, Samuel P. sr., 112
BLACK, Samuel P. sr., 112
BLACK, Thomas C. M.D., 112
BLACKMAN, Alfred W., 3
BLACKMAN, Anne, 34
BLACKMAN, ____, 3
BLACKMAN, ____, 5
BLAKE, Admiral, 69
BLAKE, Blanch, 28
BLAKE, Blanche, 35
BLAKE, G. E. (m), 28
BLAKE, George E., 35
BLAKE, Gladys, 35
BLAKE, Wm. M., 35
BLANCH FAMILY, ____, 9
BLANCHE, Alfred E., 9
BLANCHE, Caroline M., 9
BLANCHE, Caroline M., 9
BLANCHE, E. A. (m), 9
BLANCHE, Elizabeth A., 9
BLANCHE, Emily, 9
BLANCHE, Ezekiel, 9
BLANCHE, Ezekiel (Rev., Lt. Col.), 9
BLANCHE, James B., 9
BLANCHE, John, 9
BLANCHE, Lucy K., 9
BLANCHE, Lucy K., 9
BLANCHE, Margaret H., 9
BLANCHE, Margaret H., 9
BLANCHE, Mary C., 9
BLANCHE, Mildred, 9
BLANCHE, Mildred Cook, 9
BLANCHE, Nancy Taylor, 9
BLANCHE, Polly, 9
BLANCHE, Polly B., 9
BLANCHE, Rebecca, 9
BLANCHE, Rebecca M., 9
BLANCHE, Sally White, 9
BLANCHE, Samuel, 9
BLANCHE, Samuel White, 9
BLANCHE, W. H., 9
BLANCHE, Wm. H., 9
BLINKHORN, Elizabeth, 33
BLINKHORN, ____ (m), 33
BOCK, Adam, 130
BOCK, Adam, 9
BOCK, Estelle, 9
BOCK, George, 9
BOCK, John, 9
BOCK, M. LaDelle (Mrs.), 9
BOCK, Margaret J. (Miss), 9
BOCK, Margaret Jordan, 9

BOCK, Virginia, 130
BODDIE, Charles, 68
BODDIE, Susan, 68
BOND, Chloe, 143
BOND, Sara, 90
BOND, Sarah, 89
BONNER, Mar. Fannie, 28
BONNER, Miss, 35
BOOKER, Effoid D., 54
BOOKER, Eliza L., 54
BOOKER, Musadora Alice, 54
BOOTH, Edwin, 106
BOOTH, Katy, 69
BORING, Amon, 130
BORING, Nancy, 130
BOWLES, Sarah Elizabeth, 57
BOWMAN, Bettie, 68
BOWMAN, Maj., 68
BOYERS, Mrs., 63
BRADLEY, John, 50
BRADLEY, John (Major), 113
BRADLEY, John (Maj.), 119
BRADLEY, Molly, 50
BRADLEY, Sarah, 50
BRADY, Susan G, 142
BRADY, W. T. (m), 142
BRICKELL, Ann, 60
BRICKELL, Bathsheba, 60
BRICKELL, Bathsheba, 61
BRICKELL, Benjamin, 60
BRICKELL, Betsy, 60
BRICKELL, Betsy, 61
BRICKELL, Betsy, 61
BRICKELL, Betsy, 62
BRICKELL, James Noailles, 61
BRICKELL, John, 61
BRICKELL, Johnathan, 60
BRICKELL, Joseph, 60
BRICKELL, Lavinia, 60
BRICKELL, Lavinia, 61
BRICKELL, Marina, 60
BRICKELL, Martha, 60
BRICKELL, Martha, 61
BRICKELL, Matthias, 61
BRICKELL, Matthias (Lt. Col.), 60
BRICKELL, Matthias (Rev.), 60
BRICKELL, Nancy, 60
BRICKELL, Nancy, 60
BRICKELL, Nancy, 62
BRICKELL, Rachiel, 60
BRICKELL, Rachiel, 61
BRICKELL, Rebecca, 60
BRICKELL, Rebecca, 62
BRICKELL, Robert, 61
BRICKELL, Sallie, 63
BRICKELL, Sally, 60
BRICKELL, Sally, 64
BRICKELL, Thomas, 61
BRICKELL, Thomas, 61
BRICKELL, Thomas Noilles, 60
BRICKELL, Wm., 60
BRICKELL, Wm., 60
BRIDGES, Henry, 10
BRIDGES, Nancy Mulherin, 10
BRIGHT, John, 68
BRIGHT, Priscilla, 68
BRITT, Mr., 63
BRITT, Sally, 63
BROCK, James, 120

BROCK, James (Dr.), 120
BROCK, Lula, 120
BROCK, Martha, 120
BROCK, Martha, 120
BROMFIELD, John, 169
BROWN, Mary, 68
BROWN, Robert S. (Lieut.), 135
BROWN, Tom, 20
BROWN, Tom, 54
BRUMBACH, Frank P., 11
BRUMBACH, Mary James, 11
BUCHANAN, Alexander, 10
BUCHANAN, Alexander, 10
BUCHANAN, Alexander, 11
BUCHANAN, Alexander B., 11
BUCHANAN, Charley B., 10
BUCHANAN, Edw. M. (f), 11
BUCHANAN, Elizabeth, 10
BUCHANAN, Elizabeth, 11
BUCHANAN, Family, 10
BUCHANAN, George, 10
BUCHANAN, George A., 11
BUCHANAN, George A., 11
BUCHANAN, Henrietta E., 11
BUCHANAN, Henrietta M., 11
BUCHANAN, Henry R., 10
BUCHANAN, Ida B., 11
BUCHANAN, Ida B., 11
BUCHANAN, James, 10
BUCHANAN, James B., 10
BUCHANAN, Jane, 10
BUCHANAN, Jane T., 10
BUCHANAN, Jane T.?, 10
BUCHANAN, Jane Trindell, 10
BUCHANAN, Jane Trindell, 34
BUCHANAN, Jno., 11
BUCHANAN, John (1st), 10
BUCHANAN, John (2nd), 10
BUCHANAN, John D., 11
BUCHANAN, John II, 10
BUCHANAN, John III, 10
BUCHANAN, John P., 10
BUCHANAN, John R., 10
BUCHANAN, Katie McKay, 11
BUCHANAN, Lena B., 11
BUCHANAN, Letty, 10
BUCHANAN, Louella M., 11
BUCHANAN, Margaret, 10
BUCHANAN, Margaret, 11
BUCHANAN, Margaret O., 11
BUCHANAN, Martha, 10
BUCHANAN, Mary, 10
BUCHANAN, Mary Ann, 10
BUCHANAN, Mary James, 11
BUCHANAN, Mary Ridley, 11
BUCHANAN, Missie, 11
BUCHANAN, Moses R., 10
BUCHANAN, Nancy B., 10
BUCHANAN, Nancy Mulherin, 10
BUCHANAN, Richard G., 10
BUCHANAN, Richard G., 11
BUCHANAN, Sally, 10
BUCHANAN, Samuel, 10
BUCHANAN, Sarah, 10
BUCHANAN, Sarah, 10
BUCHANAN, Sarah B., 10
BUCHANAN, Sarah V., 10
BUCHANAN, T. A., 11
BUCHANAN, Wm., 10

BUCHANAN, Wm. Y., 11
BUCHANAN, family, 29
BUREY, Peggy, 20
BURGE, Martha, 5
BURGE, Mr., 3
BURGE, Mr., 5
BURGESS, Mr., 68
BURGESS, Priscilla, 68
BURK, M. Annie, 70
BURNETT, Wm., 119
BURNETT, Wm. (Pvt.), 119
BURNS, Marina, 61
BURTON, Frank (Col.), 64
BURTON, Lavinia Bembury, 60
BURTON, Lavinia Bembury, 64
BUSH, Mary, 56
BUSH, Perseville (m), 56
BUSH, ____ (m), 56
BUTLER, Ann L., 12
BUTLER, Ann Laura, 12
BUTLER, Bettie O., 12
BUTLER, Bettie Olivia, 12
BUTLER, Dennis S., 114
BUTLER, Dennis S., 12
BUTLER, Dennis S., 13
BUTLER, Henry W., 114
BUTLER, Henry W., 13
BUTLER, Henry Warren, 12
BUTLER, I. W. (m), 114
BUTLER, Isaac W., 13
BUTLER, Isaac Watson, 12
BUTLER, Isadora, 12
BUTLER, James K. P., 114
BUTLER, James K. P., 12
BUTLER, James K. P., 13
BUTLER, Joe E., 114
BUTLER, John S., 12
BUTLER, John Samuel, 12
BUTLER, Josiah E., 13
BUTLER, Josiah Edmonson, 12
BUTLER, Lewis, 114
BUTLER, Lucy K., 12
BUTLER, Lucy Katherine, 12
BUTLER, Mary, 78
BUTLER, Mary Ann, 12
BUTLER, Nancy E., 114
BUTLER, Nancy E., 12
BUTLER, Nancy E., 13
BUTLER, Solomon Satterwhite, 12
BUTLER, Thomas Overton, 12
BUTLER, W. S. (m), 12
BUTLER, Warner, 114
BUTLER, Warner L., 13
BUTLER, Warner Lewis, 12
BUTLER, Wm. R., 12
BUTLER, Wm. Reuben, 12
BUTLER, Wm. Reuben, 13
BUTLER, Wm. S., 114
BUTLER, Wm. S., 13
BUTLER, Wm. Smith, 12
BYRN, Sarah C., 127
BYRN, Wm. B., 127
CABLE, Mary E., 54
CABLE, Thos. M., 54
CAFFEY, Isabella, 157
CAFFEY, J. A. M. (m), 157
CAFFEY, J. N., 157
CAFFEY, Margret M., 157
CAFFEY, Sarah, 157
CALLAWAY, Frances, 104

CALLAWAY, Frances, 104
CALLAWAY, Frances Walton, 103
CALLAWAY, George, 103
CALLAWAY, Rances, 105
CALLAWAY, Richard, 104
CALLAWAY, Richard, 105
CAMBER, Dorothy, 105
CAMPBELL, Alice Elizabeth, 29
CAMPBELL, Annie, 193
CAMPBELL, Annie E., 30
CAMPBELL, Annie E., 95
CAMPBELL, Annie E., 97
CAMPBELL, Annie L., 115
CAMPBELL, Archibald, 14
CAMPBELL, Camilla T., 14
CAMPBELL, David, 116
CAMPBELL, David S., 115
CAMPBELL, David S., 14
CAMPBELL, David S., 15
CAMPBELL, Eleanor, 115
CAMPBELL, Eleanora Taylor, 116
CAMPBELL, Elisabeth M., 14
CAMPBELL, Elvira Eagleton, 116
CAMPBELL, Elvira Eagleton, 25
CAMPBELL, Elvira H., 14
CAMPBELL, Elvira H., 15
CAMPBELL, Elvira Hamilton, 25
CAMPBELL, G. E. (m), 35
CAMPBELL, Geo. E., 29
CAMPBELL, George Ewing, 15
CAMPBELL, H. Curry, 29
CAMPBELL, Harry Elam, 116
CAMPBELL, John A., 116
CAMPBELL, John A., 14
CAMPBELL, John A., 15
CAMPBELL, Josiah, 116
CAMPBELL, Josiah, 14
CAMPBELL, Margaret Cora, 14
CAMPBELL, Margaret Cora, 15
CAMPBELL, Martha, 14
CAMPBELL, Mary M., 14
CAMPBELL, Nancy, 14
CAMPBELL, Nancy E., 114
CAMPBELL, Nancy E., 12
CAMPBELL, Nancy E., 12
CAMPBELL, Nancy E., 35
CAMPBELL, Nancy Elizabeth, 29
CAMPBELL, Nancy Mann, 115
CAMPBELL, Nancy Mann, 14
CAMPBELL, Nancy Mann, 14
CAMPBELL, Nettie Sumpter, 116
CAMPBELL, Samuel, 115
CAMPBELL, Samuel, 14
CAMPBELL, Samuel, 25
CAMPBELL, Samuel III, 116
CAMPBELL, Samuel jr., 115
CAMPBELL, Samuel jr., 116
CAMPBELL, Samuel jr., 14
CAMPBELL, Samuel jr., 15
CAMPBELL, Samuel sr., 115
CAMPBELL, Samuel sr., 14

CAMPBELL, Sarah, 80
CAMPBELL, Vira Bell, 116
CAMPBELL, Virginia B., 14
CAMPBELL, Wm. E., 115
CAMPBELL, Wm. E., 116
CAMPBELL, Wm. Eagleton, 15
CANNON, Adeline, 68
CANNON, Clement, 43
CANNON, Gov., 68
CANNON, Susan, 43
CANTRELL, Dorsey, 144
CARLTON, Alice, 118
CARLTON, Benagea, 117
CARLTON, Bettie, 18
CARLTON, Bettie, 18
CARLTON, Bettie (Mrs.), 19
CARLTON, Beula May, 17
CARLTON, Blake, 16
CARLTON, Blake, 16
CARLTON, Blake, 17
CARLTON, Charles B., 118
CARLTON, Christopher G., 117
CARLTON, Cora, 18
CARLTON, David Walker, 118
CARLTON, David Walker, 18
CARLTON, David Walker, 19
CARLTON, F. Elam, 118
CARLTON, F. M., 118
CARLTON, F. M., 19
CARLTON, F. M. (Mrs.), 118
CARLTON, F. M. (m), 18
CARLTON, Francis, 18
CARLTON, Francis Elam, 18
CARLTON, Francis Marion, 18
CARLTON, Frank, 18
CARLTON, Frank Elam, 18
CARLTON, Frank Elam, 19
CARLTON, Hannah, 117
CARLTON, Hannah (Walker), 18
CARLTON, Henry Frazicr, 117
CARLTON, Herbert, 118
CARLTON, Ira Ernest, 17
CARLTON, Irvin Lee, 17
CARLTON, J. M., 17
CARLTON, J. M. (m), 16
CARLTON, J. N., 16
CARLTON, James F., 17
CARLTON, James M., 16
CARLTON, John N., 16
CARLTON, Julia A. F., 16
CARLTON, Julia Ann F., 16
CARLTON, Kinion, 118
CARLTON, Kinion, 18
CARLTON, Kinion (m), 117
CARLTON, Kirby G., 117
CARLTON, Kirby Gordon, 17
CARLTON, Leila E., 118
CARLTON, Leila Estelle, 17
CARLTON, Lizzie, 16
CARLTON, Lucinda Elizabeth, 118
CARLTON, Lula Estella, 17
CARLTON, M. B., 17
CARLTON, M. B. (m), 117
CARLTON, M. B. (m), 118
CARLTON, M. B. (m), 16
CARLTON, Margaret, 117
CARLTON, Margaret, 118
CARLTON, Margaret E., 16

CARLTON, Margaret E., 16
CARLTON, Margaret L., 117
CARLTON, Martha Ann, 117
CARLTON, Martha M., 118
CARLTON, Martha M., 17
CARLTON, Mary, 117
CARLTON, Mary, 16
CARLTON, Mary (Mrs.), 17
CARLTON, Mary Anna, 18
CARLTON, Mary Annah, 18
CARLTON, Mary Annah, 18
CARLTON, Mary J., 117
CARLTON, Mary Jane, 16
CARLTON, Mary Walker, 16
CARLTON, Mary Walker, 17
CARLTON, Minerva Elizabeth Taylor, 18
CARLTON, Minos B. (Mrs.), 16
CARLTON, Minos B. sr., 17
CARLTON, Minus B., 17
CARLTON, Nanie V., 16
CARLTON, Nannie Vera, 17
CARLTON, Richard W., 17
CARLTON, Robert, 118
CARLTON, Robert Taylor, 18
CARLTON, Robert Taylor, 19
CARLTON, S. A. R., 17
CARLTON, Samuel Herbert, 18
CARLTON, Samuel Herbert, 19
CARLTON, Sarah J., 16
CARLTON, Sarah J., 17
CARLTON, Tabitha, 117
CARLTON, Tabitha, 118
CARLTON, Tabitha, 16
CARLTON, Tabitha E. (Nance), 17
CARLTON, Tennessee, 118
CARLTON, Thomas F., 17
CARLTON, Willis M., 118
CARLTON, Wm., 117
CARLTON, Wm., 17
CARLTON, Wm. Blake, 117
CARLTON, Wm. J., 16
CARLTON, Wm. J., 16
CARLTON, Wm. J., 16
CARMAN, Elizabeth, 21
CARMAN, Hanner, 21
CARMAN, Lanny, 21
CARMAN, Polly, 21
CARMAN, Wm., 21
CARNAHAN, Semmus (f), 46
CARROLL, Wm., 65
CAWTHON, A. M. (m), 121
CAWTHON, Eva, 75
CAWTHON, James, 121
CAWTHON, Rhoda V., 121
CAWTHON, Richard C., 121
CAWTHON, Sallie, 121
CHADWICK, Mattie V., 112
CHATTANOOGA, ____, 3
CHILDRESS, John Whitsitt (Judge), 134
CHRISTIAN, Sarah, 3
CHRISTIAN, Sarah, 6
CHRISTOPHER, Mary, 70
CIMMONS, B. Samuel, 20
CIMMONS, Edward, 20
CIMMONS, Edward, 20
CIMMONS, Edward, 21
CIMMONS, Elender, 21
CIMMONS, Iby, 21

CIMMONS, Jane, 21
CIMMONS, John, 21
CIMMONS, Nancy, 21
CIMMONS, Nellie, 20
CIMMONS, Prissy, 21
CIMMONS, Robert, 20
CIMMONS, Sally, 21
CIMMONS, Thomas, 20
CLARK, Absolum, 73
CLARK, Carroll, 73
CLARK, Carroll sr., 73
CLARK, Eliza, 43
CLARK, Elizabeth, 73
CLARK, Elvira, 73
CLARK, Euphemia, 72
CLARK, Euphemia, 73
CLARK, Gilliam, 73
CLARK, Isiah, 73
CLARK, James, 73
CLARK, Margaret, 73
CLARK, Nancy, 62
CLARK, Polly, 34
CLARK, Sarah, 73
CLARK, Theresa, 73
CLARK, Wm., 73
CLAW, Holtz, 171
CLAY, Henry, 106
CLAY, Jonathan, 96
CLAYTON, H. H. (Dr.), 133
CLAYTON, James (Capt.), 133
CLEBURNE, Patrick R., 188
CLEBURNE, Patrick R., 189
CLOUD, Jas., 34
CLOUD, Sarah Jane, 34
CLYNE, Christen (m), 20
CLYNE, Katherine, 20
CLYNE, Margaret, 20
CLYNE, Mary, 20
COCK, E. G., 130
COCK, Edmond G., 130
COCK, Emily H., 130
COCK, James M., 130
COLEMAN, Billy Boots, 147
COLEMAN, Ellen, 112
COLEMAN, Fanny J., 112
COLEMAN, Mary Eliza, 112
COLEMAN, Sally N., 112
COLEMAN, W. P., 112
COLEMAN, Walter P., 112
COLEMAN, Walter Preston M.D., 112
COLLIER, Eliza L. McFadden, 22
COLLIER, James M., 22
COLLIER, James M., 22
COLLIER, Martha, 130
COMER, Mary McClaren, 90
COMPTON, Claud, 134
COMPTON, Porter E., 133
COOK, Eliza, 68
COOK, Gen., 68
COOK, Mark, 61
COOK, Mildred, 9
COOK, Mildred, 9
COOK, Nancy, 61
COOPER, Sarah, 87
CORBELL, Alice L., 54
CORBELL, Eliza L., 54
CORBELL, Eliza L., 54
CORBELL, Hampton jr., 54
CORBELL, J. P. H., 55

CORBELL, John Preston Hampton, 54
CORBELL, Mary E. (Mrs.), 55
CORBELL, Mary Elizabeth, 54
CORBELL, Nancy Jane, 54
CORBELL, Oston jr., 55
CORBELL, Thomas M., 54
CORBELL, Thos. I. W., 54
CORBELL, Wm., 55
CORBELL, Wm. P. H., 55
CORBELL, Wm. Pleasant Henderson, 54
COSBY, A. G., 129
COSBY, Ben, 191
COSBY, C. B., 129
COSBY, Sarah, 129
COUTNEY, Miss, 3
COUTNEY, Miss, 5
COVINGTON, E., 145
COVINGTON, Elizabeth, 145
COVINGTON, Jane D., 138
COVINGTON, Jane D., 138
COVINGTON, Jesse, 138
COVINGTON, John, 138
COVINGTON, John, 138
COVINGTON, Julia Ann, 138
COVINGTON, M. L., 145
COVINGTON, Marquis Lafayett, 138
COVINGTON, Sue A., 42
COVINGTON, Susan A., 140
COWEN, A. L. (f), 79
CRADDOCK, Charles Egbert, 63
CRADDOCK, Chas. Egbert, 134
CRAWFORD, Elizabeth, 53
CRIBS, Cullin, 169
CROCKETT, Granville, 86
CROCKETT, M. J. (f), 151
CROCKETT, Sarah, 86
CRYER, George, 63
CRYER, Hardy, 63
CRYER, James, 63
CRYER, John, 63
CRYER, John, 63
CRYER, Johnny, 63
CRYER, Polly, 63
CRYER, Sam, 63
CRYER, Sarah, 63
CURRIN, Jonathan, 123
CUSTER, Cora, 28
DANCE, Letitia, 148
DANCE, Letitia, 149
DANIEL, Cassie, 46
DANIEL, Duna Josephine, 44
DANIEL, Edmund Lawrence Gardiner, 44
DANIEL, Emma Caroline, 44
DANIEL, Florence Leona, 44
DANIEL, Hibernia B., 44
DANIEL, M. E., 44
DANIEL, Martha, 46
DANIEL, Mary Louise, 44
DANIEL, Nancy Josephine, 44
DANIEL, Wm. Eddins, 44
DAVIDSON, Artilla Jane, 86
DAVIDSON, B. H. (Dr.), 86
DAVIDSON, B. H. (Dr.), 88
DAVIS, Ard P., 121
DAVIS, Nancy, 61
DAVIS, Ralph, 3

DAVIS, Ralph, 6
DAVIS, Ralph jr., 3
DAVIS, Ralph jr., 6
DAVIS, Sadie, 32
DAVIS, Virginia M., 6
DEMENT, Abner, 23
DEMENT, David, 23
DEMENT, David, 23
DEMENT, David jr., 23
DEMENT, John, 23
DEMENT, John, 23
DEMENT, Lucinda, 23
DENUGENT, Gilbert, 74
DICK, M.D. of TX, 6
DICKINSON, Benjamin, 67
DICKINSON, David, 125
DICKINSON, David, 66
DICKINSON, David, 67
DICKINSON, David (Esq.), 58
DICKINSON, David W., 125
DICKINSON, David W., 65
DICKINSON, David W., 65
DICKINSON, David Wm., 66
DICKINSON, David Wm., 67
DICKINSON, Eliza J., 67
DICKINSON, F. Priscilla, 65
DICKINSON, Fanny, 67
DICKINSON, Fanny N., 125
DICKINSON, Fanny N., 64
DICKINSON, Fanny Noailles, 58
DICKINSON, Fanny Priscilla, 67
DICKINSON, Hardy, 67
DICKINSON, James, 67
DICKINSON, John, 66
DICKINSON, Joseph, 60
DICKINSON, Lavinia, 60
DICKINSON, Lavinia, 67
DICKINSON, Luke, 67
DICKINSON, Margaret, 60
DICKINSON, Martha Elizabeth, 67
DICKINSON, Mary, 67
DICKINSON, Matthias, 60
DICKINSON, Mr., 62
DICKINSON, Nancy, 62
DICKINSON, Priscilla, 67
DICKINSON, Priscilla, 68
DICKINSON, Rachiel, 60
DICKINSON, Rebeckah, 66
DICKINSON, Sallie Brickell, 125
DICKINSON, Sally Louise, 64
DICKINSON, Sarah, 67
DICKINSON, Sarah Louisa, 67
DICKINSON, Wm. Dickinson, 67
DICKINSON CEMETERY, , 125
DICKONSON, David, 68
DICKONSON, Sallie, 68
DICON, Malinda, 3
DICON, Malinda (of MS), 6
DICUS, Anna F., 136
DILLON, C. D. (Rev.), 134
DIXON, Charlotte, 110
DODSON, Minerva Jordan, 141
DOLLIN, Anthony, 33
DOLLIN, Jane, 33
DONOHO, Charles, 174

DOSIER, Malissa P., 90
DOUGLAS, Ellen, 112
DOUGLASS, Dewitt Clinton, 68
DOUGLASS, Martha Ann, 68
DRAKE, Dr., 62
DRAKE, Mr., 62
DRAKE, Nancy, 62
DRAKE, Octavia Lavert, 62
DRAPER, W. M. (Mrs.), 39
DRAPER, W. M. (Mrs.), 7
DROMGOOLE, Joh E., 9
DROMGOOLE, John E., 9
DROMGOOLE, Lucy K., 9
DROMGOOLE, Rebecca M., 9
DROMGOOLE, Rebecca Mildred Blanch, 128
DROMGOOLE, Will Allen, 128
DROMGOOLE, Will Allen (author), 9
DRUMWRIGHT, Lizzie, 16
DUKE, Josiah G., 161
DUKE, Josiah G., 162
DUKE, Josiah G., 163
DUNEHOO, Mr., 68
DUNEHOO, Virginia, 68
DUNSTAN, Capt., 64
DUNSTAN, Sally, 64
DUNSTAN, Wm. Hardy, 64
DURHAM, Margaret, 73
EAGLETON, Adele, 26
EAGLETON, Alexander, 24
EAGLETON, Angeline Avondale, 26
EAGLETON, Angeline Avondale, 26
EAGLETON, Bethel, 26
EAGLETON, David, 24
EAGLETON, David, 24
EAGLETON, David, 24
EAGLETON, Elijah (Rev.), 24
EAGLETON, Eliza McEwen, 25
EAGLETON, Eliza McEwen, 25
EAGLETON, Eliza McEwen, 25
EAGLETON, Elvie, 26
EAGLETON, Elvie, 26
EAGLETON, Elvira, 116
EAGLETON, Elvira, 26
EAGLETON, Elvira H., 15
EAGLETON, Elvira Hamilton, 24
EAGLETON, Elvira Hamilton, 25
EAGLETON, George, 26
EAGLETON, George Ewing, 25
EAGLETON, George Ewing, 25
EAGLETON, George Ewing (Rev.), 25
EAGLETON, Isaac Anderson, 24
EAGLETON, Isaac Anderson, 25
EAGLETON, Isabella, 24
EAGLETON, James, 24
EAGLETON, James M. (Dr.), 25
EAGLETON, James M. (M.D.), 25
EAGLETON, Jean (f), 24
EAGLETON, John, 24
EAGLETON, John A., 25
EAGLETON, John Alexander, 25

EAGLETON, John Alexander, 25
EAGLETON, John Alexander, 26
EAGLETON, Johnnie, 26
EAGLETON, Margaret, 115
EAGLETON, Margaret, 24
EAGLETON, Margaret, 25
EAGLETON, Margaret Angeline, 116
EAGLETON, Margaret Angeline, 24
EAGLETON, Margaret Angeline, 25
EAGLETON, Margaret Angeline, 25
EAGLETON, Margaret Elizabeth, 26
EAGLETON, Margaret Elizabeth, 26
EAGLETON, Margaret Ewing, 116
EAGLETON, Margaret Ewing, 24
EAGLETON, Margaret Ewing, 26
EAGLETON, Margaret Ewing (Mrs.), 25
EAGLETON, Mary, 24
EAGLETON, Mary A., 25
EAGLETON, Mary A., 25
EAGLETON, Mary Ann Judson, 26
EAGLETON, Mary Ethlina, 25
EAGLETON, Mattie, 26
EAGLETON, Mollie, 25
EAGLETON, Mollie, 26
EAGLETON, Newton Walker, 26
EAGLETON, Robert, 24
EAGLETON, Samuel, 26
EAGLETON, Samuel Ewing, 24
EAGLETON, Samuel Ewing, 25
EAGLETON, Wm. (Rev.), 115
EAGLETON, Wm. (Rev.), 116
EAGLETON, Wm. (Rev.), 15
EAGLETON, Wm. (Rev.), 24
EAGLETON, Wm. (Rev.), 25
EAGLETON, Wm. (Rev., D.D.), 25
EAGLETON, Wm. (Rev., D.D.), 26
EAGLETON, Wm. Clark, 24
EAGLETON, Wm. Clark, 25
EAGLETON, Wm. Clark, 25
EAGLETON, Wm. L., 26
EAGLETON, Wm. Lemuel, 26
EASTER, John, 128
EATON, David, 126
EATON, Esther M., 126
EATON, John, 126
EATON, Joseph, 126
EATON, Joseph H., 126
EAVES, Robert, 28
EAVES, Robert, 35
EAVES, Susan, 28
EAVES, Susan, 35
EAVES, W. H. (m), 28
EAVES, Wm., 28
EAVES, Wm., 35

EAVES, Wm. H., 35
EDMONDSON, Mr., 190
EDMONDSON, Pink, 190
EDWARD, Jarman (Mrs.), 108
EDWARDS, Amanda C., 27
EDWARDS, Amanda C., 28
EDWARDS, Amanda C., 34
EDWARDS, Andrew H., 154
EDWARDS, Ann, 28
EDWARDS, Ann, 34
EDWARDS, Ann, 35
EDWARDS, Anna, 28
EDWARDS, Arthur, 29
EDWARDS, Arthur M., 27
EDWARDS, Arthur Owen, 34
EDWARDS, Arthur Owen (Capt.), 28
EDWARDS, Bettie, 28
EDWARDS, Bettie, 28
EDWARDS, Betty, 34
EDWARDS, Blanch A., 154
EDWARDS, Catherine W., 27
EDWARDS, Cora, 28
EDWARDS, Ed. D. (m), 28
EDWARDS, George, 28
EDWARDS, George W., 34
EDWARDS, George W., 35
EDWARDS, George W. (Capt.), 28
EDWARDS, James A., 27
EDWARDS, James A., 27
EDWARDS, James A., 29
EDWARDS, Jane, 28
EDWARDS, Jane M., 27
EDWARDS, Jarman (Mrs.), 113
EDWARDS, Jarman (Mrs.), 40
EDWARDS, Jarman (Mrs.), 49
EDWARDS, Jarman (Mrs.), 50
EDWARDS, Jas. A., 34
EDWARDS, Jas. K. P., 34
EDWARDS, Jas. K. Polk, 28
EDWARDS, Jennie, 35
EDWARDS, John, 29
EDWARDS, Judith, 27
EDWARDS, Judith M., 27
EDWARDS, Judith M., 34
EDWARDS, Judith W., 27
EDWARDS, Louisa W., 27
EDWARDS, Mamie Goetz, 28
EDWARDS, Nancy, 27
EDWARDS, Nancy, 35
EDWARDS, Nancy T., 27
EDWARDS, Nancy T., 27
EDWARDS, Nancy T., 28
EDWARDS, Nancy T., 34
EDWARDS, Nannie J., 154
EDWARDS, Owen, 27
EDWARDS, Owen, 28
EDWARDS, Owen, 29
EDWARDS, Owen H., 27
EDWARDS, Sallie Hickman, 27
EDWARDS, Sarah M., 27
EDWARDS, Susan, 28
EDWARDS, Susan Ann, 27
EDWARDS, Susan Ann, 27
EDWARDS, Susan Ann, 34
EDWARDS, Susan Ann, 35
EDWARDS, Susie, 28
EDWARDS, Thomas, 29
EDWARDS, Wm. C. (Capt.), 27
ELAM, Daniel, 30

ELAM, Edward, 30
ELAM, Jane, 30
ELAM, M. A., 155
ELAM, Nancy, 144
ELAM, T. L., 155
ELAM, Thomas Walter, 155
ELLIOTT, J. H. (m), 130
ELLIOTT, Mary, 33
ELLIOTT, Nannie G., 130
ELLIOTT, Sallie B. Henry, 130
ELLIOTT, Wm., 130
ELWOOD, Sarah, 33
ELWOOD, Wm., 33
ERSKINE, Bettie, 68
ERSKINE, Miss, 68
ERSKINE, Samuel?, 68
ESTELLE, Mrs., 62
EVERETT, Elizabeth, 10
EVERETT, Thos. H., 10
EVERGREEN CEMETERY, 129
EWING, Edwin (Hon.), 130
EWING, Jane Caroline, 130
EWING, Margaret, 115
EWING, Margaret, 25
EWING, Orville, 134
FARRIS, C. B., 136
FARRIS, C. B. (m), 136
FARRIS, Charles Blackman, 136
FARRIS, Charlie Rough, 136
FARRIS, John Wesley, 136
FARRIS, Margaret T., 136
FARRIS, Mary J., 136
FATHERA, E. B., 31
FATHERA, Ebenezer Bester, 31
FATHERA, James C., 31
FATHERA, James C., 31
FATHERA, James Willson, 31
FATHERA, James Willson, 31
FATHERA, John Randolph, 31
FATHERA, Martha, 31
FATHERA, Mary, 31
FATHERA, Matilda, 31
FATHERA, Matilda Pace, 31
FATHERA, Wm. Landrom, 31
FAUST, Susan, 61
FERGUS, Edw. M. (f), 11
FERGUSSON, Adam, 32
FERGUSSON, Adam, 32
FERGUSSON, Charles Marshall, 32
FERGUSSON, Duncan, 32
FERGUSSON, Frank Kerby (Gen.), 32
FERGUSSON, Hester Ann, 32
FERGUSSON, Isabella, 32
FERGUSSON, Linton Stephens, 32
FERGUSSON, Marina Carita, 32
FERGUSSON, Medora Catherine, 32
FERGUSSON, Nina, 32
FERGUSSON, Nina Minora, 32
FERGUSSON, Ruskin, 32
FERGUSSON, Sadie, 32
FERGUSSON, Sterling Price, 32
FERGUSSON, Willard Hampden, 32
FERGUSSON, Wm. Wallace, 32
FIGURES, Elizabeth, 69
FIGURES, Mr., 69

FINNEY, Mary, 63
FINNEY, Thomas, 63
FISHER, A. B., 80
FITTS, Emily, 9
FLEMING, Capt., 190
FLETCHER, Ann, 120
FLETCHER, Frances Clay, 37
FLETCHER, Granderson, 120
FLETCHER, Jane, 86
FLETCHER, Jeremiah, 37
FLETCHER, Jim, 86
FLETCHER, Jno. S. (Dr.), 179
FLETCHER, Martha C., 120
FLETCHER, Nancy White, 37
FLETCHER, Nancy White, 38
FLEWELLAN, Dr., 180
FLOYD, Mahala (col. servant), 116
FOLEY, Lt., NC Rev. Troops, 143
FOREST, Gen., 28
FOUTE, Mary Ethlina, 25
FRANCE, Mary E., 54
FRANKLIN, Tenn., 3
FRAZIER, Bettie, 68
FRAZIER, Henry, 68
FRAZIER, W. R., 136
FREAS, Mary F., 127
FREAS, Samuel H., 135
FREAS, Samuel H. (Dr.), 127
FROST, Ruth, 3
FROST, Ruth, 6
FULLER, E. W. (m), 28
FULLER, E. W. (m), 35
FULLER, E. W. jr., 35
FULLER, Elline, 35
FULLER, George, 169
FULLER, Jane, 28
FULLER?, Elizabeth, 35
FURGERSON, Miles, 191
FURGERSON, Pinkney E., 191
GAINES, John Wesley (Hon.), 95
GAINES, Maria Frances Wait, 95
GALLAWAY, L. G. (m), 125
GALLAWAY, Martha, 125
GANAWAY, John, 121
GANAWAY, Mary W. R., 121
GANNAWAY, Burrell, 137
GANNAWAY, Burwell, 141
GANNAWAY, Fanny M. L. E., 137
GARDINER, Caroline Matilda, 44
GARDINER, Caroline Matilda Thear?, 44
GARDINER, Edmund Laurence, 44
GARDINER, Hibernia Booker, 44
GARDINER, John Fletcher, 44
GARDINER, John Richerson Love, 44
GARDINER, Mary G., 44
GARDINER, Samuel Ephraigon, 44
GARDINER, Samuel G., 44
GARDINER, Samuel George, 44
GARDINER, Susan A., 44
GARDINER, Susan E., 44

GARDNER, Mary Gillum, 43
GARDNER, Mr., 190
GARDNER, Samuel George, 43
GARNER, Mary Lewis, 77
GENTRY, Camilla, 87
GENTRY, Virginia B. C., 14
GEORGE, Jane, 140
GEORGE, Rachel Anna, 42
GIBSON, Elizabeth, 50
GIBSON, Robert M., 50
GILES COUNTY, _____, 3
GILLESPIE, Eleanor M., 144
GILLIAM, Martha Woodson, 144
GILLIAM, Wm., 144
GILMORE, John D., 155
GILMORE, Mary Luvenia, 155
GLENN, Sarah, 110
GLOVER, Betsy, 43
GLOVER, Lancaster, 43
GODWIN, Ann, 62
GODWIN, Betsy, 62
GODWIN, Eliza, 62
GODWIN, Mr., 62
GOLIGHTLY, Shemuel M., 123
GOODMAN, Rebecca, 9
GOODWIN, Anne, 33
GOODWIN, Anne, 34
GOODWIN, Barbara, 33
GOODWIN, Blanche, 33
GOODWIN, E. (f), 33
GOODWIN, Elizabeth, 33
GOODWIN, Elizabeth, 33
GOODWIN, Elizabeth, 33
GOODWIN, George, 10
GOODWIN, George, 34
GOODWIN, George jr., 34
GOODWIN, Gertrude, 33
GOODWIN, Henry, 33
GOODWIN, James, 33
GOODWIN, James, 33
GOODWIN, Jane, 33
GOODWIN, Jane, 34
GOODWIN, Jane Hazlewood, 33
GOODWIN, Jane T.?, 10
GOODWIN, Jane Trindell, 34
GOODWIN, Jesse, 34
GOODWIN, John, 33
GOODWIN, John, 33
GOODWIN, John, 33
GOODWIN, John, 33
GOODWIN, John, 34
GOODWIN, John Lamb, 34
GOODWIN, Levina, 34
GOODWIN, Martha, 33
GOODWIN, Mary, 33
GOODWIN, Mathew, 33
GOODWIN, Mathew, 33
GOODWIN, Morton, 33
GOODWIN, Nancy, 34
GOODWIN, Nancy, 34
GOODWIN, Peter jr., 33
GOODWIN, Peter sr., 33
GOODWIN, Peter, 3rd, 33
GOODWIN, Polly, 34
GOODWIN, Polly Clark, 34
GOODWIN, Rachel, 33
GOODWIN, Rachel, 33
GOODWIN, Rebecca, 33
GOODWIN, Robert, 33

GOODWIN, Robert, 33
GOODWIN, Robert, 33
GOODWIN, Sarah, 33
GOODWIN, Sarah, 33
GOODWIN, Sarah, 34
GOODWIN, Sarah, 36
GOODWIN, Sarah Jane, 34
GOODWIN, Sarah Webb, 34
GOODWIN, Susan Ann, 27
GOODWIN, Susan Ann, 27
GOODWIN, Susan Ann, 34
GOODWIN, Susanna, 33
GOODWIN, Suzanna, 33
GOODWIN, Tabitha, 34
GOODWIN, Wm. W., 34
GRANTLAND, Eliza J., 125
GRANTLAND ESTATE, , 125
GRAY, Capt., 196
GRAY, Miss, 27
GREEN, Mary A., 25
GREER, Isaac, 34
GREER, Nancy, 34
GREER, Tabitha, 34
GREGORY, Margaret, 60
GRIGG, A. P. (m), 46
GRIGG, Rhoda I., 46
GRIGG, Rhoda Lowe, 46
GRIGG, S. C. (Dr.), 46
GRUNDY, Felix (Hon.), 63
GTANTLAND?, Eliza J., 67
HALE, Bettie, 154
HALE, E. H., 154
HALE, E. H. J., 154
HALE, Elizabeth, 139
HALE, Elizabeth, 42
HALE, J. Harley, 154
HALE, John W., 154
HALE, M. E., 154
HALE, Nannie, 154
HALE, S. J. (f), 154
HALE, wife of John W., 154
HALL, Ella M., 46
HALL, J. D. (Dr.), 46
HALL, Joe P., 11
HALL, Margaret O., 11
HALL, Mollie L., 111
HALL, Mr., 86
HALL, Sarah, 86
HAMLET, Eliza, 95
HANCOCK, E. D., 174
HARDEMAN, Mary Moore Hilliard, 60
HARDEMAN, Wm., 62
HARDEMAN, Wm., 64
HARDIMAN, Dolly, 46
HARDING, Giles Scales jr., 132
HARDING, Hallie B., 11
HARDING, Lorena Peck Ransom, 132
HARDING, W. B., 11
HARE, Benjamin, 66
HARE, Bryan, 66
HARE, Elizabeth, 66
HARE, Grace, 66
HARE, Jesse, 66
HARE, John, 66
HARE, John, 67
HARE, John Lawrence, 66
HARE, Lucresy, 66
HARE, Luke, 66
HARE, Mary, 66

HARE, Moses, 66
HARE, Penelope, 66
HARE, Priscilla, 66
HARE, Priscilla, 67
HARE, Sarah, 66
HARE, Sarah, 67
HARLAN, J. J., 115
HARRIS, Elizabeth, 80
HARRISON, Carter B., 133
HARTMAN, Alonzo Baoom, 11
HARTMAN, Amelia Claire, 11
HARTMAN, Catherine Bateman, 11
HARTMAN, Florence, 11
HARTMAN, Hallie B., 11
HARTMAN, Helen Margaret, 11
HARTMAN, Ida B., 11
HARTMAN, Ida Blanche, 11
HARTMAN, Jno. B., 11
HARTMAN, Jno. B., 11
HARTMAN, John B., 11
HARTMAN, Katie McKay, 11
HARTMAN, Louella M., 11
HARTMAN, Maggie Maud, 11
HARTMAN, Mai, 11
HARTMAN, Mary E., 11
HARTMAN, Paul H. (Mrs.), 10
HARTMAN, Paul Hays, 11
HARTMAN, Wm. P., 11
HARWELL, Nancy, 27
HAWAY, Jas., 20
HAYES, Annie Shelton, 171
HAYES, Emma Tatum (Mrs.), 91
HAYES, Emma Tatum (Mrs.), 93
HAYES, Mary M., 94
HAYNES, Ann Trabue, 37
HAYNES, Ann Trabue, 38
HAYNES, Benjamin I., 111
HAYNES, Bill (col. slave), 37
HAYNES, C. C. (m), 138
HAYNES, Elvira Ann, 37
HAYNES, Elvira Ann, 37
HAYNES, Elvira F., 37
HAYNES, Elvira Frances, 37
HAYNES, Hyram H., 138
HAYNES, I. J. C., 37
HAYNES, I. J. C., 38
HAYNES, I. J. C. (m), 37
HAYNES, I. W., 38
HAYNES, Ivy J. C., 37
HAYNES, Ivy J. C., 37
HAYNES, Ivy J. C., 37
HAYNES, Ivy W., 37
HAYNES, J. A., 138
HAYNES, Julia A., 37
HAYNES, Julia Ann, 138
HAYNES, Julia Ann, 138
HAYNES, Loretta White, 37
HAYNES, Loretta White, 38
HAYNES, Lucy Lorena, 37
HAYNES, Lucy Lorena, 37
HAYNES, M. I., 37
HAYNES, Martha Alice, 38
HAYNES, Martha Allas, 37
HAYNES, Mary Itilla, 37
HAYNES, Mary Itilla, 52
HAYNES, Missie, 11
HAYNES, Sophia, 37

HAYNES, Sophia, 77
HAYNES, W. A., 138
HAYNES, W. A. (m), 138
HAYNES, W. A. (m), 138
HAYNES, W. R. (Mrs.), 77
HAYNES, W. R. (m), 37
HAYNES, Wm. Airchaball?, 138
HAYNES, Wm. Rufus, 37
HAYNES, Wm. Rufus, 77
HAYNES?, Frances Clay, 37
HAYS, Edward T., 93
HAYS, Mary M., 93
HAZARD, Hester Ann, 32
HAZARD, Lot, 32
HAZLEWOOD, Jane, 33
HENDERSON, Amanda H., 39
HENDERSON, Dewitt, 39
HENDERSON, Elizabeth Eliza, 1
HENDERSON, Eugene, 39
HENDERSON, G. T. (Rev.), 120
HENDERSON, G. T. (Rev.), 77
HENDERSON, Greenville T., 120
HENDERSON, James F., 39
HENDERSON, Jane E., 39
HENDERSON, Logan, 39
HENDERSON, Lt., 191
HENDERSON, Margaret E., 39
HENDERSON, Margaret Elizabeth, 26
HENDERSON, Margaret Enoch, 39
HENDERSON, Margaret J., 39
HENDERSON, Matilda, 120
HENDERSON, Melville C., 120
HENDERSON, Samuel S., 26
HENDERSON, Violet, 39
HENRY, Nannie G., 130
HENRY, Sallie B., 130
HENSON, Bessie Olivia, 76
HENSON, Samuel A., 76
HEROD, Zona, 92
HICKMAN, Sallie, 27
HICKS, Isaac M., 126
HICKS, Sarah P., 127
HIGHT, Mary C., 164
HIGHT, Mary C., 165
HIGHT, Mary C., 166
HIGHT, Mary C., 167
HIGHT, Mary C., 169
HIGHT, O. R., 164
HIGHT, O. R., 165
HIGHT, O. R., 166
HIGHT, O. R., 167
HIGHT, O. R., 169
HILL, Alice E., 70
HILL, Ann, 61
HILL, B. J., 190
HILL, Clemmie, 23
HILL, Dr., 61
HILL, Lavinia, 61
HILL, Nancy, 61
HILL, Natt, 61
HILL, Thomas M., 130
HILL, Wm. Henry, 130
HILLIARD, Dr., 181
HILLIARD, Dr., 183
HILLIARD, Isaac, 124
HILLIARD, Isaac, 64

HILLIARD, Isaac (Mrs.), 64
HILLIARD, John, 33
HILLIARD, Lavinia H., 124
HILLIARD, Mary Moore, 64
HILLIARD, Sarah, 33
HIX, Martha Sarah, 3
HIX, Martha Sarah, 5
HIX, Mr., 3
HIX, Mr., 5
HIX, Pocahontas, 5
HODGE, Samuel H. (Maj.), 121
HODSHIRE, Mamie Goetz, 28
HOGAN, Jane, 10
HOLDEN, Benjamin F., 155
HOLDEN, John F., 136
HOLDER, Horace L., 117
HOLLIS, Lester (f), 46
HOLLOWELL, Sol., 175
HOLLOWELL, Wat J., 111
HOLMES, Chas. Wade, 3
HOLMES, Chas. Wade, 6
HOLMES, Earnest M. (Dr.), 134
HOLMES, Eva, 6
HOLMES, John, 174
HOLMES, Lida Howse, 6
HOLMES, Virginia M., 3
HOLMES, Virginia M., 6
HOLMES, Wm. Mimms, 6
HOLMES, Wm. Mimms, 3
HOOD, Col., 161
HOOVER, Josie (f), 46
HORD, Benj. McCulloch, 133
HORTON, Ann M., 35
HORTON, Blanche M., 35
HORTON, Elizabeth, 35
HORTON, Georgia, 35
HORTON, J. E., 35
HORTON, Jas. E., 28
HORTON, Jas. E., 35
HORTON, Jennie, 35
HORTON, Robert E., 35
HORTON, Robt. E., 35
HORTON, Susan, 28
HORTON, Susan Ann, 35
HOUSE, G. A., 110
HOUSE, Louisa Jane, 110
HOUSE, M. A., 110
HOUSE, Mary Ann, 110
HOUSE, Mr., 169
HOUSE, Wm. George, 110
HOWARD, A. L., 136
HOWARD, T. H., 136
HOWARD, infant son, 136
HOWSE, Eliza Catherine Ann, 3
HOWSE, Eliza Catherine Ann, 5
HUFF, Gertrude, 87
HUGHES, Isaac, 103
HUGHES, Isaac, 105
HUGHES, Martha, 103
HUGHES, Sally, 103
HUGHES, Sally, 105
HUNT, Benjamin M., 40
HUNT, Eliza F., 40
HUNT, Hallie, 108
HUNT, Hallie, 40
HUNT, Hallie, 49
HUNT, Hallie, 50
HUNT, James W., 40

HUNT, James W., 40
HUNT, Jeremiah, 40
HUNT, Jeremiah, 40
HUNT, John P., 40
HUNT, Martha Ann Burgis, 40
HUNT, Mary Susan, 40
HUNT, Mattie C., 40
HUNT, Nancy G., 40
HUNT, Sallie, 40
HUNT, Sallie S. (Taylor), 40
HUNT, Samuel G., 40
HUNT, Sarah Elizabeth, 40
HUNT, Simeon, 40
HUNT, Thomas J., 40
HUNT, Wm. J., 40
HYDE, B. H. (Mrs.), 53
HYDE, H. B., 3
HYDE, H. B. (Mrs.), 5
HYDE, H. B. (Mrs.), 86
HYDE, Hartwell Blount, 3
HYDE, Hartwell Blount, 6
HYDE, Mary Yeargen, 6
IRVING, Washington, 106
IVIE, Pattie Jeanette, 56
IVIE, Thos. W., 56
IVY, Thos. W. jr., 56
IVY, Thos. W. sr., 56
JACKSON, Anna George (Mrs.), 42
JACKSON, Annie George, 140
JACKSON, Carmine, 139
JACKSON, Cora, 18
JACKSON, Elizabeth, 139
JACKSON, Elizabeth, 42
JACKSON, Elizabeth W., 139
JACKSON, Elizabeth W., 42
JACKSON, Emlyann V., 139
JACKSON, F. M., 145
JACKSON, F. M. (Capt.), 140
JACKSON, Francis (1st), 42
JACKSON, Francis (2nd), 42
JACKSON, Francis III, 42
JACKSON, Francis jr., 139
JACKSON, Francis sr., 139
JACKSON, Grover, 140
JACKSON, J. A., 139
JACKSON, Jasper, 139
JACKSON, John C., 145
JACKSON, John C., 145
JACKSON, John Childress (Capt.), 145
JACKSON, John G., 139
JACKSON, Judith, 139
JACKSON, Loyola S., 139
JACKSON, Lucinda Elizabeth, 118
JACKSON, Marion, 118
JACKSON, Mary A., 139
JACKSON, Mary B., 139
JACKSON, Mary J., 139
JACKSON, Mary Jane, 145
JACKSON, Mary L. E., 139
JACKSON, Oceana B., 139
JACKSON, Rachel Anna, 42
JACKSON, Sue A., 42
JACKSON, Sue Adalade, 145
JACKSON, Susan A., 140
JACKSON, T. N., 139
JACKSON, Valera, 140
JACKSON, W. J., 139
JACKSON, Williams Lafayette, 145
JACKSON, Willis, 117
JACKSON, infant child, 140
JACOBS, Elizabeth D., 46
JAMISON, Bettie Julia, 56
JAMISON, Charles Moore, 56
JAMISON, Idalette, 56
JAMISON, J. H. sr., 56
JAMISON, J. H. sr., 56
JAMISON, James H. jr., 56
JAMISON, John W. (Rev.), 134
JAMISON, Pattie Jeanette, 56
JAMISON, Sarah Dorsey, 56
JEFFERSON, Thomas, 103
JERNIGAN, O. P., 157
JETTON, Anderson, 175
JETTON, Brevard, 176
JETTON, Hal, 176
JOHNSON, Andrew, 73
JOHNSON, Anna, 139
JOHNSON, Henry C., 141
JOHNSON, Henry Phelps, 63
JOHNSON, James, 73
JOHNSON, Jos. E. (Gen.), 170
JOHNSON, Jos. E. (Gen.), 171
JOHNSON, Joshua M., 141
JOHNSON, Maggie, 35
JOHNSON, Martha J., 155
JOHNSON, Minerva Jordan, 141
JOHNSON, W. T. (m), 139
JOHNSTON, Mai, 11
JOHNSTON, Margaret E., 39
JONES, Amma, 70
JONES, Amos (Dr.), 9
JONES, Caroline M., 9
JONES, Eliza L., 55
JONES, Eunice, 61
JONES, Isaac (Dr.), 61
JONES, Lavinia, 61
JONES, Lizzie, 72
JONES, Mary, 56
JONES, Nancy, 60
JONES, Nannie, 61
JONES, Tom, 169
JONES, ____ (m), 56
JORDAN, Ben (Mrs.), 23
JORDAN, E. W., 141
JORDAN, Eliza Green, 90
JORDAN, James F., 90
JORDAN, John A. (Mrs.), 137
JORDAN, John A. (Mrs.), 141
JORDAN, Leland, 126
JORDAN, Letitia Perkins, 126
JORDAN, M. C., 137
JORDAN, M. C., 141
JORDAN, M. C., 141
JORDAN, Margaret Blanche, 9
JORDAN, Margaret Caroline, 9
JORDAN, Margaret H., 9
JORDAN, Martha J., 141
JORDAN, Minos, 196
JORDAN, Robt. L., 141
JORDAN, Sophia, 120
JORDAN, Starnes, 141
JORDAN, Stephen, 9
JORDAN, Stephen A., 9
JORDAN, Temperance, 5
JORDAN, Thomas, 120
JORDAN, Virginia, 130
JORDON, Temperance, 3
KEEBLE, Edward (Hon.), 68
KEEBLE, Mary, 68
KEEBLE, Richard H., 135
KEELE, Richard, 119
KELLY, Dr., 60
KELLY, Rachiel, 60
KELTON, Mary F., 46
KELTON, Rachel, 46
KELTON, Thos., 46
KELZER, Lavinia, 155
KENNEDY, Margaret, 10
KERBY, Frank, 32
KERBY, Medora Catherine, 32
KEYSER, Catherine, 120
KEYSER, Chas., 120
KEYSER, Matilda, 120
KIMBRO, Hannah, 50
KIMMONS?, Wm., 20
KING, John M. (Dr.), 122
KING, Julia Ann, 56
KING, Mary, 56
KING, Sarah M., 27
KING, ____ (m), 27
KING?, H. A. J., 88
KIRBY, Julia Milton, 94
KIRK, Elener White, 1
KNIGHT, Bettie O., 12
KNIGHT, Eliza McEwen, 25
KNIGHT, Eliza McEwen, 25
KNIGHT, James M., 114
KNIGHT, James M. (Mrs.), 114
KNIGHT, Jas. M., 12
KNIGHT, L. W. (Dr.), 25
KNIGHT, Lucian Lamar, 106
KNIGHT, Martha (Patty), 103
KNIGHT, Murfree, 61
KNIGHT, Nancy, 61
KNIGHT, Woodson, 103
KNOSTMAN, John (Esq.), 58
KNOSTMAN, Louise, 58
KNOTT, A. B. (m), 34
KNOTT, Amanda, 34
LANDERS, W. A., 167
LANDERS, W. A. (Capt.), 164
LANIER, Sarah, 87
LANNIER, Miss, 3
LANNIER, Miss, 5
LAUGHLAND, Samuel, 3
LAUGHLAND, Samuel, 5
LAURANCE, Judith W., 27
LAURANCE, ____ (m), 27
LAWRENCE, Edmund, 87
LAWRENCE, J. Dink, 151
LAWRENCE, Mary A., 87
LAYNE, Susie, 70
LEACH, James I., 82
LEACH, John, 82
LEACH, Thomas, 82
LEACH, Winefred, 82
LEACH, Wm., 82
LEATH, Mary J., 109
LEATHERMAN, Kate, 1
LEDBETTER, Mr., 191
LEDBETTER, Wm., 129
LEDBETTER, Wm. (Capt.), 133
LEDBETTERS, Richard, 190
LEE, R. E. (Gen.), 185
LEGRAND, Nancy, 7
LEGRAND, Nancy S., 7
LEINAU, Daiel, 124
LEINAU, Eliza, 124
LEINAU, Lavinia, 124
LEIPER, John, 124
LEIPER, John (Mrs.), 12
LEMON, Mr., 62
LEMON, Nancy, 62
LEPARD, Matthias, 121
LEVERT, Henry (Dr.), 106
LEVERT, Octavia, 106
LEWIS, Betty, 53
LEWIS, Fielding (Col.), 53
LEWIS, Frances, 53
LEWIS, Jane, 53
LEWIS, Jane Meriwether, 53
LEWIS, Jane Meriwether, 86
LEWIS, Jane Meriwether, 87
LEWIS, Lucy, 53
LEWIS, Meriwether, 53
LEWIS, Robert, 53
LEWIS, Robert (Col.), 53
LEWIS, Wm., 53
LILLARD, John (Mrs.), 113
LILLARD, Mordecai, 142
LILLARD, Mordicae, 133
LITTON, Lorena, 75
LOCKE, Betsy, 43
LOCKE, Charles, 43
LOCKE, Charles Coppage, 43
LOCKE, Eliza, 43
LOCKE, Elizabeth, 43
LOCKE, Gardiner Batte, 43
LOCKE, Gardner Batte, 43
LOCKE, Gilly, 43
LOCKE, John West, 43
LOCKE, Joseph, 43
LOCKE, Judith Mayse, 43
LOCKE, Mary G., 44
LOCKE, Mary G., 44
LOCKE, Mary Gilliam, 43
LOCKE, Mary Jane, 43
LOCKE, Nancy Berchet, 43
LOCKE, Patsey Jones, 43
LOCKE, Polly, 43
LOCKE, Susan, 43
LOCKE, Thomas Batte, 43
LOE, John Richardson, 43
LOFTIN, John A., 118
LOFTIN, Martha M., 118
LOFTON, Catherine W., 27
LOFTON, Martha M., 17
LOFTON, Thomas, 27
LONGFELLOW, Henry W., 106
LOUISIANA, ____, 3
LOVE, C. T., 11
LOVE, Elizabeth, 11
LOVE, John Richerson, 44
LOVEJOY, Loyola S., 139
LOWE, Alfred G., 46
LOWE, Cassie, 46
LOWE, Charles, 157
LOWE, David C., 46
LOWE, Elizabeth D., 46
LOWE, Ella M., 46
LOWE, Hettie T., 46
LOWE, James W., 115
LOWE, Jas. Y.?, 46
LOWE, Jimmie, 46
LOWE, Joseph A., 46
LOWE, Josie (f), 46
LOWE, Lester (f), 46
LOWE, Martha, 46

LOWE, Martha J., 46
LOWE, Martha J., 46
LOWE, Mary F., 46
LOWE, Mollie, 46
LOWE, Nannie, 46
LOWE, Nannie S., 46
LOWE, Nicholas P., 46
LOWE, Rachel, 46
LOWE, Rhoda, 46
LOWE, Rhoda I., 46
LOWE, Rody, 157
LOWE, Semmus (f), 46
LOWE, W. M., 157
LOWE, W. S., 46
LOWE, Wm., 46
LOWE, Wm., 46
LOWE, Wm. E., 46
LYTLE, Wm. (Capt.) DAR Chapter, 119
LYTLE, Wm. H. (Dr.), 135
MACKAIN, James, 104
MACKAIN, Polly, 104
MALONE, Mackie (Miss), 148
MANEY, Adeline, 68
MANEY, David, 68
MANEY, Eliza, 68
MANEY, Elizabeth, 64
MANEY, Elizabeth, 68
MANEY, Elizabeth, 68
MANEY, Elizabeth, 69
MANEY, Elizabeth Mary, 58
MANEY, Elizabeth Meredith, 68
MANEY, Fannie, 68
MANEY, Fannie, 68
MANEY, Fannie Dickinson, 68
MANEY, Henry, 68
MANEY, Henry, 68
MANEY, Henry, 68
MANEY, James, 58
MANEY, James (Dr.), 122
MANEY, James (Dr.), 64
MANEY, James 1st, 68
MANEY, James 2nd, 68
MANEY, James 3rd, 68
MANEY, James II, 69
MANEY, James III, 68
MANEY, James IV, 68
MANEY, James V, 68
MANEY, John, 68
MANEY, Lawrence, 68
MANEY, Louis, 68
MANEY, Margaret, 68
MANEY, Martha, 68
MANEY, Martha Ann, 68
MANEY, Martha L. A. C., 64
MANEY, Mary, 58
MANEY, Mary, 68
MANEY, Mary, 68
MANEY, Mary Roberts, 69
MANEY, Meredith, 68
MANEY, Priscilla, 68
MANEY, Sallie, 68
MANEY, Sally Hardy, 64
MANEY, Susan, 68
MANEY, Susan, 68
MANEY, Susanna, 68
MANEY, Thomas, 68
MANEY, Thomas, 68
MANEY, Virginia, 68
MANEY, Wm., 68

MANEY, Wm., 68
MANEY, Wm. (Maj.), 64
MANIER, Tenn., 196
MANN, Nancy, 115
MANNING, Luleskey B., 155
MARKHAM, James D., 170
MARKHAM, James D., 171
MARKHAM, Sadie, 170
MARR, George, 27
MARR, Susan, 27
MARR, Susanna Perkin, 27
MARTIN, Abigail, 1
MARTIN, Abigal, 1
MARTIN, Elizabeth, 23
MARTIN, Mary, 23
MARTIN, Mattie Bedford, 79
MARTIN, Mattie Bedford, 79
MARTIN, Obiadiah, 23
MARY, ____, 3
MATHEWS, Cephas T., 26
MATHEWS, Ed, 191
MATHEWS, Elvie, 26
MATTHEWS, Mr., 190
MAXWELL, W. J., 138
MCADOO, B. H., 47
MCADOO, B. H., 48
MCADOO, B. H. (m), 47
MCADOO, Darthula A., 47
MCADOO, E. T., 47
MCADOO, E. T., 47
MCADOO, Eda P., 47
MCADOO, Eva D., 47
MCADOO, Flora O., 47
MCADOO, Lockey C., 47
MCADOO, Margaret A., 47
MCADOO, Mary E., 47
MCADOO, N. E. (f), 47
MCADOO, Nancy T., 47
MCADOO, Robert Hodgie, 47
MCADOO, Samuel P., 47
MCADOO, Sary F., 47
MCADOO, Solon H., 47
MCADOO, Sophia H., 47
MCADOO, Virginia, 47
MCADOO, Virginia H., 47
MCADOO?, Ann Eliza N., 93
MCALLISTER, Clara L., 72
MCALLISTER, Daniel sr., 72
MCALLISTER, Elizabeth (Mrs.), 72
MCCLAIN, Joe M., 135
MCCLANAHAN, Caroline M., 50
MCCLANAHAN, Cassandey?, 50
MCCLANAHAN, Cassandra, 50
MCCLANAHAN, Cornealy Jane, 49
MCCLANAHAN, Elijah, 49
MCCLANAHAN, Elizabeth, 50
MCCLANAHAN, Hannah, 50
MCCLANAHAN, Harriett H., 50
MCCLANAHAN, Harriett Newell, 50
MCCLANAHAN, James R., 50
MCCLANAHAN, James Roulston, 50
MCCLANAHAN, James T., 49
MCCLANAHAN, Jane, 50
MCCLANAHAN, Jane, 50

MCCLANAHAN, John B., 50
MCCLANAHAN, John Bradley, 50
MCCLANAHAN, Lockey W., 50
MCCLANAHAN, M., 50
MCCLANAHAN, Mary B., 107
MCCLANAHAN, Mary B., 50
MCCLANAHAN, Mary B., 50
MCCLANAHAN, Matilda, 50
MCCLANAHAN, Matilda, 51
MCCLANAHAN, Matthew, 49
MCCLANAHAN, Matthew, 50
MCCLANAHAN, Robert, 49
MCCLANAHAN, Samuel, 50
MCCLANAHAN, Samuel, 50
MCCLANAHAN, Samuel, 50
MCCLANAHAN, Samuel (Maj.), 119
MCCLANAHAN, Sarah, 50
MCCLANAHAN, Sarah Ann, 49
MCCLANAHAN, Sarah Matildy, 50
MCCLANAHAN, Sintha H., 49
MCCLARAN, Jas. Lee, 76
MCCLARAN, Nannie R., 76
MCCLAREN, Lee (Mrs.), 75
MCCOLLOUGH, D. S. (m), 141
MCCOLLOUGH, Martha J., 141
MCCRANE, Bertha, 76
MCCULLOUGH, James, 134
MCDONALD, George W. sr., 109
MCDONALD, Isabella, 109
MCDONALD, Isabella Ward, 109
MCDONALD, Jennie, 109
MCDONALD, M. B. (Miss), 109
MCDONALD, Martha J., 92
MCEWEN, James Alexander, 89
MCEWEN, Martha B., 89
MCEWEN, Nancy Eleanor, 89
MCFADDEN, Anna, 22
MCFADDEN, Anna, 37
MCFADDEN, Anna, 52
MCFADDEN, Bettie, 52
MCFADDEN, Caroline, 52
MCFADDEN, Eliza, 52
MCFADDEN, Eliza L. (Mrs.), 22
MCFADDEN, Elvie, 135
MCFADDEN, G. S., 37
MCFADDEN, Guy, 52
MCFADDEN, Hallie (f), 52
MCFADDEN, Henry, 52
MCFADDEN, Itatla (Mrs.), 37
MCFADDEN, James, 52
MCFADDEN, Jennie, 52
MCFADDEN, John, 52
MCFADDEN, Lou, 52
MCFADDEN, Mary Itilla, 52
MCFADDEN, Nancy, 52
MCFADDEN, Samuel, 52
MCFADDEN, Samuel Guy, 52
MCFADDEN, Sarah, 52
MCFADDEN, Sophia, 22
MCFADDEN, Sophia, 37

MCFADDEN, Sophia, 52
MCFADDEN, Susan, 52
MCFADDEN, Wm. R., 52
MCFARLIN, Emily C., 120
MCGAUGHEY, Abner, 34
MCGAUGHEY, Levina, 34
MCGILL, David N., 157
MCGILL, Mary, 157
MCGOWAN, Harper H., 43
MCGOWAN, Lucy A., 142
MCGOWAN, Lucy H., 142
MCGOWAN, Nancy, 43
MCGOWAN, Patsey Jones, 43
MCGOWAN, Thomas, 43
MCGOWAN, Thos. H., 142
MCKINLEY, John, 124
MCKINLEY, John, 124
MCKINLEY, Rebecca, 124
MCKINLEY, Sarah, 129
MCKINLEY, Susan R., 124
MCKNIGHT, F. A., 157
MCKNIGHT, Isabella, 157
MCLAURINE, Sadie, 170
MCLEAN, A. H. (Mrs.), 158
MCLEAN, A. H. (Mrs.), 161
MCLEAN, A. H. (Mrs.), 43
MCLEAN, Florence, 151
MCMINNVILLE, ____, 3
MCNABB, Isabella, 32
MCRAE, Ann E., 70
MCRAE, Francis R., 71
MCRAE, Wm., 71
MEREDITH, Mr., 69
MERIWETHER, David, 53
MERIWETHER, Elizabeth, 53
MERIWETHER, Jane, 53
MERIWETHER, Lucy, 53
MERIWETHER, Nicholas, 53
MILES, B. M. (m), 143
MILES, C. M. (m), 143
MILES, E. V., 143
MILES, Elizabeth V., 143
MILES, F. W., 143
MILES, F. W., 143
MILES, Lida, 3
MILES, Lida, 6
MILES, Mary Ida, 143
MILES, Nancy W., 143
MILES, Sallie, 143
MILES, Thomas sr., 143
MILES GRAVEYARD, , 143
MILLIGHAN, Lavinia, 61
MILLIGHAN, Rev., 61
MINOR, Mary, 87
MISSISSIPPI, ____, 3
MITCHELL, Elizabeth, 54
MITCHELL, G. C. (m), 137
MITCHELL, Joab, 54
MITCHELL, Louisa, 54
MITCHELL, Mark, 54
MITCHELL, Mary, 54
MITCHELL, Pleasant H., 54
MITCHELL, Sarah E. W., 137
MITCHELL, Thomas C., 54
MITCHELL, Wm., 54
MOLLEY, N. F., 153
MOLLOY, Dan E., 144
MOLLOY, Elizabeth, 144
MOLLOY, Fannie M., 144
MOLLOY, Ferdinand (Maj.), 135

MOLLOY, G. D. (Dr.), 144
MOLLOY, John, 144
MOLLOY, John L., 144
MOLLOY, Judith L., 144
MOLLOY, Lucius N. B., 144
MOLLOY, Martha Woodson, 144
MOLLOY, Nancy, 144
MOLLOY, Nancy, 144
MOLLOY, Wm., 144
MOODY, Lavinia, 61
MOODY, Matilda, 61
MOORE, Bessie King, 57
MOORE, Bettie Julia, 56
MOORE, Bettie Julia, 56
MOORE, Blanche Virginia, 57
MOORE, Caroline Penelopia, 56
MOORE, Carroline P., 56
MOORE, Charles Wm., 57
MOORE, Chas. Hardie, 57
MOORE, Chas. W., 56
MOORE, Chas. W., 56
MOORE, Chas. Wm., 56
MOORE, Elizabeth, 33
MOORE, Elizabeth V., 143
MOORE, Eva May, 57
MOORE, Ezekiel, 56
MOORE, Fanny, 103
MOORE, Gabriel, 56
MOORE, Gilly, 43
MOORE, Hardie Holmes, 56
MOORE, Hardy Henry, 56
MOORE, James Ezekiel, 56
MOORE, James Henrbert, 57
MOORE, James Henry, 56
MOORE, James Herbert (Mrs.), 56
MOORE, Jane, 50
MOORE, John Beesley, 57
MOORE, Julia Ann, 56
MOORE, Julian Caldwell, 57
MOORE, Marina, 61
MOORE, Mary, 56
MOORE, Mary, 63
MOORE, Mary Elizabeth, 57
MOORE, Mary Sue, 57
MOORE, Mildred Anna, 57
MOORE, Mrs., 103
MOORE, Pattie Jeanette, 56
MOORE, Phemia, 73
MOORE, Pheraby Jane, 56
MOORE, S., 184
MOORE, Sarah Elizabeth, 57
MOORE, Thomas, 56
MOORE, Thos. Jefferson, 57
MOORE, Thos. McClure, 56
MOORE, Wm. Chas., 56
MOORE, Wm. Henry, 57
MOORIS, Cyril, 57
MOORIS, Mary Elizabeth, 57
MORGAN, Alex F., 35
MORGAN, Alex. F., 28
MORGAN, Arthur, 35
MORGAN, Arthur L., 28
MORGAN, Blanch, 28
MORGAN, Blanche, 35
MORGAN, Nancy, 35
MORGAN, Nancy T., 27
MORGAN, Nancy T., 28
MORGAN, Susan, 28

MORGAN, Susan, 35
MORGAN, Thomas C., 35
MORGAN, Thos. C., 28
MORGAN, W. C., 28
MORGAN, W. C. (m), 27
MORGAN, Wm. C., 35
MORGAN, Wm. S., 35
MORROW, Maj. Gen., 187
MORROW, Wm., 186
MORTON, Amanda, 34
MORTON, Amanda, 35
MORTON, Amanda C., 27
MORTON, Amanda C., 28
MORTON, Amanda C., 36
MORTON, George A., 35
MORTON, George Arthur, 29
MORTON, Hugh, 103
MORTON, I. H., 184
MORTON, Jacob, 34
MORTON, Jacob, 35
MORTON, Jacob, 36
MORTON, Jacob J., 27
MORTON, Jacob J., 28
MORTON, Jas., 175
MORTON, John W. (Dr.), 36
MORTON, Judith, 27
MORTON, Judith, 29
MORTON, Margaret A., 35
MORTON, Margaret Ann, 29
MORTON, Nancy E., 35
MORTON, Nancy Elizabeth (Bettie), 29
MORTON, Oliver T., 35
MORTON, Oliver Thomas, 29
MORTON, Sarah, 36
MORTON, Sarah, 80
MORTON, Susanna E., 35
MORTON, Susanna Edwards, 29
MORTON, Susannah, 103
MORTON, Wm. Jacob, 29
MORTON, Wm. Jacob, 35
MORTON, _____ (m), 103
MOSBY, Edward, 104
MOSBY, Patty, 104
MULHERIN, James, 10
MULHERIN, Nancy B., 10
MULLINS, Emmet, 11
MULLINS, Katie McKay, 11
MURFREE, Agnes, 61
MURFREE, Annie M., 127
MURFREE, Betsy, 61
MURFREE, Bettie, 68
MURFREE, Daniel, 61
MURFREE, Elizabeth, 64
MURFREE, Elizabeth Maney, 58
MURFREE, Elizabeth Mary, 58
MURFREE, Elizabeth Mary, 58
MURFREE, Elizabeth Mary, 58
MURFREE, Elizabeth Meredith, 68
MURFREE, F. Priscilla Dickinson, 65
MURFREE, Fanny, 58
MURFREE, Fanny N. D., 58
MURFREE, Fanny N. D., 65
MURFREE, Fanny N. D., 66
MURFREE, Fanny N. D., 68
MURFREE, Fanny N. D. (Miss), 60
MURFREE, Fanny Noailles, 64

MURFREE, Fanny Noailles, 67
MURFREE, Fanny Priscilla, 58
MURFREE, Fanny Priscilla Dickinson, 59
MURFREE, Hardy, 127
MURFREE, Hardy, 175
MURFREE, Hardy, 63
MURFREE, Hardy, 64
MURFREE, Hardy, 64
MURFREE, Hardy, 67
MURFREE, Hardy (Col.), 172
MURFREE, Hardy (Col.), 58
MURFREE, Hardy (Col.), 61
MURFREE, Hardy (Col.), 61
MURFREE, Henry, 61
MURFREE, James, 61
MURFREE, James, 61
MURFREE, James, 63
MURFREE, James B., 175
MURFREE, James B. (Dr.), 172
MURFREE, James B. (Dr.), 172
MURFREE, James B. (Dr.), 173
MURFREE, James B. (Dr.), 174
MURFREE, James B. (Dr.), 178
MURFREE, James B. (Dr.), 179
MURFREE, James B. (Dr.), 184
MURFREE, James B. (Dr.), 187
MURFREE, James Brickle (Dr.), 134
MURFREE, Jas. B., 177
MURFREE, Jas. B. (Dr.), 186
MURFREE, Jonathan, 61
MURFREE, Joseph, 61
MURFREE, Lavinia Bembury, 64
MURFREE, Lemuella, 61
MURFREE, Libby, 172
MURFREE, Louise, 58
MURFREE, M. B., 127
MURFREE, Martha, 68
MURFREE, Martha Long Ann Croakley, 64
MURFREE, Mary, 61
MURFREE, Mary, 63
MURFREE, Mary, 64
MURFREE, Mary Ann., 127
MURFREE, Mary Moore, 63
MURFREE, Mary Moore, 64
MURFREE, Mary Moore, 64
MURFREE, Mary Noailles, 134
MURFREE, Mary Noailles, 63
MURFREE, Mary Noailles, 59
MURFREE, Mary Roberts, 134
MURFREE, Matt, 61
MURFREE, Matt (Dr.), 134
MURFREE, Matt B. (Dr.), 172
MURFREE, Matthias B., 134
MURFREE, Matthias B., 64
MURFREE, Matthias Breckell, 64
MURFREE, Medora, 61
MURFREE, Priscilla, 134
MURFREE, Priscilla, 68
MURFREE, Rachiel Dickinson, 64
MURFREE, Rob, 172
MURFREE, Sallie, 61
MURFREE, Sallie, 68
MURFREE, Sallie Brickell, 125
MURFREE, Sally, 58
MURFREE, Sally Brichell, 58

MURFREE, Sally Brickell, 67
MURFREE, Sally Hardy, 64
MURFREE, Sarah, 63
MURFREE, Susan, 61
MURFREE, Wm., 61
MURFREE, Wm., 61
MURFREE, Wm., 63
MURFREE, Wm. H., 127
MURFREE, Wm. H., 58
MURFREE, Wm. H., 59
MURFREE, Wm. H., 61
MURFREE, Wm. H., 68
MURFREE, Wm. Hardy, 58
MURFREE, Wm. Hardy, 58
MURFREE, Wm. Hardy, 64
MURFREE, Wm. Hardy, 67
MURFREE, Wm. L., 58
MURFREE, Wm. Law, 134
MURFREE, Wm. Law, 58
MURFREE, Wm. Law, 59
MURFREE, Wm. Law, 67
MURFREE, Wm. Law (Esq.), 58
MURFREE, Wm. Law jr., 58
MURFREE, Wm. Law jr., 59
MURFREE, no name (f), 64
MURFREE, no name (m), 64
MURFREESBORO, Tennessee, 3
MURPHEY, Bally, 191
MURPHY, Louisa W., 27
MURPHY, Martha, 10
MURPHY, _____ (m), 27
NANCE, Frank, 196
NANCE, Tabitha, 16
NASHVILLE, Tennessee, 3
NAYLOR, Hannah McGill, 156
NAYLOR, John, 156
NAYLOR, Wade Hampton, 156
NAYLOR, wife of John, 156
NEILSON, Sally Hudson, 129
NELSON, Nancy T., 27
NEW, Charles B., 93
NEW, Martha C., 93
NEWMAN, T. W. (Col.), 164
NEWMAN, T. W. (Col.), 167
NEWSOM, A. G. (m), 70
NEWSOM, Albert G., 70
NEWSOM, Albert G., 71
NEWSOM, Alice E., 70
NEWSOM, Alice E., 71
NEWSOM, Amma, 70
NEWSOM, Amma Jones, 71
NEWSOM, Ann E., 70
NEWSOM, Ann E., 70
NEWSOM, Ann E., 71
NEWSOM, Balaam, 71
NEWSOM, Balaam (m), 70
NEWSOM, Balaam R., 71
NEWSOM, Eliza P., 71
NEWSOM, Francis P., 71
NEWSOM, J. K. (m), 70
NEWSOM, J. K. (m), 71
NEWSOM, James K., 70
NEWSOM, James K., 71
NEWSOM, Laura A., 71
NEWSOM, M. Annie, 70
NEWSOM, Mary, 70
NEWSOM, Mary C., 71
NEWSOM, Maud Louise, 71
NEWSOM, Mollie, 71

NEWSOM, Nancy, 71
NEWSOM, Roy S., 70
NEWSOM, Samuel G., 71
NEWSOM, Susie, 70
NEWSOM, Susie, 71
NEWSOM, Susie Layne, 71
NEWSOM, Thomas B., 71
NEWSOM, Tillie McGuire, 71
NEWSOM, W. S., 70
NEWSOM, W. S., 71
NEWSOM, Willie, 71
NEWSOM, Wm. S., 70
NOAILLES, Fanny, 125
NOAILLES, Rachiel, 60
NOLAND, Alice Elizabeth, 29
NOLAND, Alice Louise, 29
NOLAND, J. Hubert (Rev.), 29
NOLAND, James Hubert, 29
NORMA, Henry H. (Gen.), 135
NORTHCUT, Harris B., 127
NORVEL, Ann, 28
NORVEL, ancestors (Welsh), 29
NORVELL, Ann, 34
NORVELL, Ann, 35
NUGENT, Americus T., 72
NUGENT, Charles R., 72
NUGENT, D. D. (m), 72
NUGENT, D. D. jr., 72
NUGENT, Daniel Clive, 74
NUGENT, David D. sr., 72
NUGENT, David Dickson, 73
NUGENT, David Ralston, 72
NUGENT, Euphemia, 72
NUGENT, Euphemia, 73
NUGENT, Henry C., 72
NUGENT, Henry C., 72
NUGENT, J. S. (m), 72
NUGENT, James Billings, 72
NUGENT, James S., 72
NUGENT, Jas. S., 72
NUGENT, Jas. S., 73
NUGENT, John H., 72
NUGENT, Kate, 72
NUGENT, Lizzie, 72
NUGENT, Louisa A., 72
NUGENT, Louisa Ann, 72
NUGENT, Louise, 72
NUGENT, Louise A., 72
NUGENT, Maggie (Marguerite), 72
NUGENT, Margaret May, 72
NUGENT, Mary E., 72
NUGENT, Nina, 72
NUGENT, Orville, 72
NUGENT, Orville C., 72
NUGENT, Orville Clark jr., 72
NUGENT, Wm. H., 72
OCALLATHAN, Edward, 121
OCALLATHAN, Frances, 121
OCALLATHAN, W. A., 121
OLIPHANT, Edmund Gardiner, 45
OLIPHANT, George Presly, 45
OLIPHANT, James Crenshaw, 45
OLIPHANT, James Madison, 44
OLIPHANT, Martha Narcissa, 45
OLIPHANT, Mary Harriet, 45
OLIPHANT, Sarah Ann, 45
OLIPHANT, Susan Matilda, 45

OLIPHANT, Thomas Jefferson, 45
OSBORNE, Elizabeth, 33
OSBORNE, John, 33
OSBORNE, Virginia, 47
OVERTON, Raleigh, 155
OWEN, Chas. L., 151
OWEN, Irene Frances, 151
OWEN, Lena B., 11
PACE, Matilda, 31
PALMER, Gen'l Joseph B., 133
PALMER, Matt, 62
PALMER, Mr., 62
PALMER, Rebecca, 62
PARKER, Mrs., 63
PARKS, Dr., 68
PARKS, Margaret, 68
PARMON, Florence, 11
PARROTT, T. U., 133
PATILLO, Benjamin B., 107
PATILLO, Bennettie, 126
PATILLO, Nancy E., 107
PATRICK, Emmet, 157
PATRICK, Erskin, 157
PATRICK, J. M., 157
PATRICK, Jonnie, 157
PATRICK, Willie, 157
PATRICK, infant daughter, 157
PATTERSON, A. J., 75
PATTERSON, Annie, 75
PATTERSON, Bertha, 76
PATTERSON, Bessie Olivia, 75
PATTERSON, Bessie Olivia, 76
PATTERSON, Eva, 75
PATTERSON, F. E., 75
PATTERSON, Finis E., 75
PATTERSON, Frank R., 75
PATTERSON, Frank R., 76
PATTERSON, James B., 75
PATTERSON, James Bates, 75
PATTERSON, Lillie Mae, 76
PATTERSON, Lorena, 75
PATTERSON, Margaret, 11
PATTERSON, Margaret, 11
PATTERSON, Martha P., 75
PATTERSON, Martha Polemia, 75
PATTERSON, Nancy, 87
PATTERSON, Nannie R., 75
PATTERSON, Nannie R., 76
PATTERSON, Olivia J., 75
PATTERSON, S. A. R., 16
PATTERSON, Samuel A., 75
PATTERSON, Samuel A., 76
PATTERSON, Wm. O., 75
PATTERSON, Wm. Osborne, 75
PATTERSON, infant (f), 75
PAUL, Mr., 158
PECK, Temperance Amanda, 132
PENN, Wm., 104
PETTUS, Mary Alice, 90
PETTUS, Mary Alice Spain, 90
PETTUS, Samuel Leland, 90
PHILIPS, David, 158
PHILIPS, David, 159
PHILIPS, David, 160
PHILIPS, John, 159
PHILIPS, Joseph, 158
PHILIPS, Josiah, 158

PHILIPS, Josiah, 159
PHILIPS, Josiah, 160
PHILIPS, Mary, 158
PHILIPS?, Josee, 159
PHILLIPS, Ida Blanche, 11
PHILLIPS, J. B., 11
PHILLIPS, John Houston, 83
PHILLIPS, Rebecca, 161
PHILLIPS, Rebecca, 161
PHILLIPS, Rebecca, 162
PHILLIPS, Rebecca, 163
PHILLIPS, Susan Roberty, 83
PICKARD, John M. sr. (Mrs.), 188
PICKARD, John M. sr. (Mrs.), 79
PICKARD, Rosalind, 189
PIGGOTT, Gertrude, 33
PIGGOTT, John, 33
PIPKIN, Mrs., 63
PITTS, Fountain E. (Mrs.), 63
PLUMMER, Rhoda, 46
POCAHONTAS, ____, 3
POLK, James K., 113
PORRY?, Blanche, 33
PORTER, Rachel, 33
POSEY, Hallie (f), 52
POTTS, Mary A., 25
PRATER, Mollie, 46
PRESCOTT, Mary Jane, 43
PRYER, Betty, 34
PRYOR, Bettie, 28
PUGH, Sally, 64
QUAYLE, Amanda, 34
QUAYLE, Amanda, 35
QUAYLE, Amanda C., 27
QUAYLE, Amanda C., 28
QUAYLE, Amanda C., 36
QUAYLE, Judith Kathryn, 35
QUAYLE, Kathryn, 27
QUAYLE, Kathryn, 28
QUAYLE, Kathryn, 29
QUAYLE, Kathryn, 33
QUAYLE, Kathryn, 36
QUAYLE, Maggie, 35
QUAYLE, Thomas B., 35
QUAYLE, Thomas B., 36
QUAYLE, Thos. B., 27
QUAYLE, Thos. B., 28
QUAYLE, Thos. B., 34
QUAYLE, Thos. Johnson, 35
QUAYLE, Thos. M., 28
QUAYLE, Thos. M., 35
RANKIN, James Porter (Rev.), 121
RANKIN, Olivia J., 75
RANSOM, Alfred, 145
RANSOM, Bob (P.C.M.D.), 4
RANSOM, D. D., 6
RANSOM, Dick M.D., 4
RANSOM, E. R., 145
RANSOM, Ellen R., 145
RANSOM, Ellis, 145
RANSOM, Frances, 6
RANSOM, J. J. (D.D.), 4
RANSOM, Lutie A., 145
RANSOM, Medicus (Dr.), 132
RANSOM, Medicus (Dr.), 134
RANSOM, Richard, 197
RANSOM, Richard P., 6
RANSOM, W. S., 145

RANSOM, Willis, 145
RANSOM, Willis Snell, 145
RAY, A. T. (f), 120
RAY, John C., 120
RAY, Mary I., 120
RAY, Wm. C., 120
REAB, George Walton, 106
READY, C. H., 146
READY, Charles, 134
READY, Charles sr. (Col.), 146
READY, Lucinda, 146
READY, Mary, 146
REDING, John, 169
REED, Mattie Bedford Martin, 188
REED, Samuel, 188
REEVES, Addie, 77
REEVES, Catherine, 77
REEVES, Catherine Shields, 77
REEVES, Charles, 77
REEVES, Daniel L., 77
REEVES, Daniel Leinau, 77
REEVES, Daniel Lineau, 78
REEVES, Emma (Mrs.), 31
REEVES, Levi W., 77
REEVES, Lewis G., 77
REEVES, Lewis Green, 77
REEVES, Mary Butler, 77
REEVES, Mary Butler, 78
REEVES, Mary Lewis, 77
REEVES, Mary Sophia, 77
REEVES, Moses Guinn, 77
REEVES, Sophia, 37
REEVES, Sophia, 77
REID, B. F. (m), 151
REID, Benjamin, 87
REID, Benjamin Franklin, 151
REID, Mary Ann Elizabeth, 87
REID, Mary E., 151
REID, Mollie Sims, 151
RICHARDSON, Blanche Virginia, 57
RICHARDSON, James T., 81
RICHARDSON, Mary, 4
RICHARDSON, Mary, 5
RIDLEY, Bromfield, 129
RIDLEY, Mary, 10
RIDLEY, Rebecca T., 129
RIDLEY, Sally, 10
RIDLEY, Sarah, 10
RIDLEY, Virginia Rebecca, 129
ROBERTS, J. D., 164
ROBERTS, Jonathan, 64
ROBERTS, Letty, 10
ROBERTS, Mary, 64
ROBERTS, Mary, 68
ROBERTS, Nancy, 64
ROGERS, Mary C., 9
ROLLINS, Marina, 61
ROLLINS, Marina, 61
ROLLINS, Matilda, 61
ROLPH, John, 4
ROLPH, John, 5
ROLPH, Pocahontas, 5
ROOKER, Jenninos, 147
ROOKER, Nannie D., 147
ROOKER, Wm. M., 147
ROSE, Mildred Anna, 57
ROULSTONE, L. D. (m), 155
ROULSTONE, Mary Elizabeth, 155

RUCKER, A. L. (f), 79
RUCKER, Ben, 4
RUCKER, Ben, 5
RUCKER, Jack, 190
RUCKER, Jack, 191
RUCKER, Mattie Bedford, 79
RUCKER, Mattie Bedford Martin, 188
RUCKER, Robert M., 79
RUCKER, Robert Martin, 188
RUCKER, Robert Martin, 188
RUCKER, Robert Martin, 189
RUCKER, Robert Martin, 190
RUCKER, Robert Martin, 191
RUCKER, Robert Martin, 192
RUCKER, Rossie, 79
RUCKER, Samuel R., 79
RUCKER, Samuel R. (Mrs.), 188
RUCKER, Samuel R. (Mrs.), 190
RUCKER, Samuel R. (Mrs.), 191
RUCKER, Samuel R. (Mrs.), 192
RUCKER, Samuel Reed, 79
RUCKER, Temperance Jordan, 5
RUCKER, Wm., 190
RUFUS, Adele, 26
RUFUS, Wm., 26
RUSSELL, Jane Trindell, 10
RUSSWORM, Sallie, 143
RUTHERFORD COUNTY, Tennessee, 4
RUTLAND, Miss, 61
SACKWELL, Elizabeth, 20
SACKWELL, Frankey, 20
SACKWELL, Nancy, 20
SACKWELL, Pruciller, 21
SACKWELL, Robert, 21
SACKWELL, Thomas, 20
SAGA, Elisha, 191
SAGE, Elvira F., 37
SAGE, J. W. (m), 37
SANDERS, Mattie, 26
SATTERWHITE, Lucy K., 12
SATTERWHITE, Soloon, 12
SAUNDERS, Mark, 191
SAURIE, Mrs., 63
SAURIE, Wm. (Rev.), 63
SAXON, Marina, 61
SCOTT, Elizabeth, 103
SCOTT, Elizabeth, 73
SEARCY, Anderson, 149
SEARCY, Anderson, 80
SEARCY, Anderson, 81
SEARCY, Ann, 80
SEARCY, Ann, 81
SEARCY, Catherine Morton, 80
SEARCY, Elizabeth, 80
SEARCY, Elizabeth, 81
SEARCY, Elizabeth T., 148
SEARCY, Fayette, 149
SEARCY, Isham G., 80
SEARCY, Isham G., 81
SEARCY, James Morton, 80
SEARCY, James Morton, 81
SEARCY, John, 80
SEARCY, John W., 148
SEARCY, John W., 80
SEARCY, John W., 81
SEARCY, Judy, 80
SEARCY, Lafayette, 80
SEARCY, Lafayette, 81
SEARCY, Lucy W., 80
SEARCY, Lucy W., 81
SEARCY, R. M. (Lt.), 122
SEARCY, Robert, 149
SEARCY, Robert M., 81
SEARCY, Robert W., 80
SEARCY, Sarah, 80
SEARCY, Sarah M., 148
SEARCY, Sarah M., 149
SEARCY, Sarah M., 80
SEARCY, Sarah M., 81
SEARCY, Sm. W. (Col.), 148
SEARCY, Tabitha, 80
SEARCY, W. W. (Col.), 149
SEARCY, Wm. W., 80
SEARCY, Wm. W., 81
SEARCY, Wm. W., 81
SEARCY, Wm. W. (Col.), 148
SELLARS, Mary E., 47
SHAW, Christopher Columbus, 77
SHAW, Christopher Columbus, 78
SHAW, Mary, 78
SHAW, Mary Butler, 77
SHAW, Mary Butler, 78
SHAW, Susanna, 96
SHEPHERD, Bettie, 92
SHEPHERD, Bettie (Mrs.), 92
SHEPHERD, John, 92
SHERRELL, Fanny Ward, 109
SHIELDS, Catherine, 77
SHILCUTT, Henrietta M., 11
SHILCUTT, Thos. A., 11
SHORT, Anderson, 82
SHORT, Ann Roberty, 82
SHORT, Ashkenas?, 83
SHORT, Elizabeth, 82
SHORT, Frances, 83
SHORT, Franklin Cheatham, 83
SHORT, Jas. H., 82
SHORT, John, 82
SHORT, John Houston, 83
SHORT, Juliet, 83
SHORT, Mahala Elizabeth, 83
SHORT, Martha, 82
SHORT, Mary, 82
SHORT, Mattie Lee, 83
SHORT, Patrick, 82
SHORT, Presley Alexander, 83
SHORT, Robert Lee, 83
SHORT, S. D. (Mrs.), 83
SHORT, S. D. (Mrs.), 89
SHORT, Samuel W., 82
SHORT, Sarah Eleanor, 90
SHORT, Sarah Lizette, 83
SHORT, Spencer Dillon, 83
SHORT, Spencer Dillon, 90
SHORT, Susan Roberty, 83
SHORT, Virginia Parthena, 83
SHORT, Willie Elizabeth, 83
SHORT, Winefred, 82
SHORT, Wm., 82
SHORT, Wm., 83
SIMS, Alexander Mansfield, 87
SIMS, Alexander Mansfield, 88
SIMS, Artilla Jane, 86
SIMS, Bessie, 87
SIMS, Camilla, 87
SIMS, Camilla, 87
SIMS, Charles Yancy, 86
SIMS, Charlotte, 86
SIMS, Charlotte Amelia, 4
SIMS, Charlotte Amelia, 6
SIMS, Charlotte Amelia, 87
SIMS, Charlotte Amelia, 87
SIMS, Clinton, 88
SIMS, Dewitt, 87
SIMS, Edmund Bartlett, 87
SIMS, Edmund Bartlett, 87
SIMS, Edward H., 151
SIMS, Elizabeth Jamison, 86
SIMS, Elizabeth Kennon, 86
SIMS, Elizabeth Kennon, 86
SIMS, Fruzelle, 88
SIMS, Gertrude, 87
SIMS, H. P. (m), 151
SIMS, James Ganaway, 86
SIMS, Jane, 86
SIMS, Jane M., 151
SIMS, Jane M., 151
SIMS, Jane Meriwether, 53
SIMS, Jane Meriwether, 86
SIMS, Jane Meriwether Lewis, 87
SIMS, Jeffie, 87
SIMS, Jennie S., 151
SIMS, John, 86
SIMS, John Lewis, 86
SIMS, Joseph, 86
SIMS, Leonard, 86
SIMS, Leonard, 87
SIMS, Leonard (family) - Original Index, 84
SIMS, Leonard H., 86
SIMS, Leonard H. jr., 86
SIMS, Leonard Jo. C., 151
SIMS, Leonard M., 150
SIMS, Leonard Mansfield, 87
SIMS, Leonard Mansfield, 87
SIMS, Lewis, 151
SIMS, Lewis S., 87
SIMS, Lewis Swepson, 87
SIMS, Lucy, 88
SIMS, Luisa, 86
SIMS, M. S., 151
SIMS, Maggie Bart, 87
SIMS, Mai, 88
SIMS, Martha B., 89
SIMS, Martha B., 89
SIMS, Martha Frances, 150
SIMS, Martha Frances, 86
SIMS, Mary, 104
SIMS, Mary, 87
SIMS, Mary Ann, 12
SIMS, Mary Ann Elizabeth, 87
SIMS, Mary Ann Elizabeth, 87
SIMS, Mary E., 151
SIMS, Mary S., 150
SIMS, Mary S., 86
SIMS, Mary S. Yeargan, 87
SIMS, Mary Yeargan, 87
SIMS, Nancy, 87
SIMS, Nicholas Howard, 87
SIMS, Nicholas Howell, 87
SIMS, Rebecca Frusanna, 87
SIMS, Rebecca Frusanna, 87
SIMS, Robert L., 150
SIMS, Robert Y., 86
SIMS, Roxana J., 86
SIMS, Sarah, 86
SIMS, Sarah, 86
SIMS, Sarah, 87
SIMS, Sarah Jane, 150
SIMS, Sarah Jane, 87
SIMS, Sarah Jane, 87
SIMS, Sarah Jane, 87
SIMS, Sarah Jane Meriwether, 4
SIMS, Sarah Jane Meriwether, 6
SIMS, Sarah Jane Meriwether, 87
SIMS, Sarah Louisa, 150
SIMS, Sarah Louisa, 86
SIMS, Sumner, 87
SIMS, Susan Barnes, 86
SIMS, Susan Frances, 87
SIMS, Susie, 87
SIMS, Swepson, 151
SIMS, Swepson, 53
SIMS, Swepson (Dr.), 150
SIMS, Swepson (Dr.), 151
SIMS, Swepson (Dr.), 87
SIMS, Sweptson (Dr.), 86
SIMS, T., 151
SIMS, Thomas, 150
SIMS, Thomas, 150
SIMS, Thomas, 151
SIMS, Thomas, 86
SIMS, Thomas, 87
SIMS, Thomas C., 86
SIMS, Thomas Hilary, 87
SIMS, Thomas Hilary, 88
SIMS, Wm. Batey, 86
SIMS, Wm. S., 86
SIMS, infant, 87
SIMS, infant, 88
SIMS, infant son, 150
SIMS ESTATE, , 150
SKETCHLEY, Harriett, 64
SLAVE OF B H MCADOO, Albert, 48
SLAVE OF B H MCADOO, Allen Talor, 48
SLAVE OF B H MCADOO, California, 48
SLAVE OF B H MCADOO, Cambia, 48
SLAVE OF B H MCADOO, Caroline, 48
SLAVE OF B H MCADOO, Clary, 48
SLAVE OF B H MCADOO, Dealia, 48
SLAVE OF B H MCADOO, Dean, 48
SLAVE OF B H MCADOO, Edmond, 48
SLAVE OF B H MCADOO, Elvira, 48
SLAVE OF B H MCADOO, Ephraim, 48
SLAVE OF B H MCADOO, Geo. Tilor, 48
SLAVE OF B H MCADOO, Green, 48
SLAVE OF B H MCADOO, Hannah, 48
SLAVE OF B H MCADOO, Harriet, 48

SLAVE OF B H MCADOO, Hebrew, 48
SLAVE OF B H MCADOO, Henry, 48
SLAVE OF B H MCADOO, Isham, 48
SLAVE OF B H MCADOO, Jane, 48
SLAVE OF B H MCADOO, Jas., 48
SLAVE OF B H MCADOO, Joseph, 48
SLAVE OF B H MCADOO, Liza, 48
SLAVE OF B H MCADOO, Louisa, 48
SLAVE OF B H MCADOO, Lucinda, 48
SLAVE OF B H MCADOO, Lucy, 48
SLAVE OF B H MCADOO, Major Nelson, 48
SLAVE OF B H MCADOO, Manerva, 48
SLAVE OF B H MCADOO, Margaret, 48
SLAVE OF B H MCADOO, Martha, 48
SLAVE OF B H MCADOO, Mary, 48
SLAVE OF B H MCADOO, Matilda F., 48
SLAVE OF B H MCADOO, Nancy, 48
SLAVE OF B H MCADOO, Noah, 48
SLAVE OF B H MCADOO, Pegay, 48
SLAVE OF B H MCADOO, Porter, 48
SLAVE OF B H MCADOO, Rachel, 48
SLAVE OF B H MCADOO, Robt., 48
SLAVE OF B H MCADOO, Sam, 48
SLAVE OF B H MCADOO, Thomas, 48
SLAVE OF B H MCADOO, Vica, 48
SLETCHLEY, Martha, 64
SMART, Mary, 5
SMART, Mr., 4
SMART, Mr., 5
SMITH, Alma, 150
SMITH, Artemesia M., 121
SMITH, Benjamin, 120
SMITH, Betsy, 61
SMITH, Clifford G., 151
SMITH, E. Kirby (Maj. Gen.), 177
SMITH, Elizabeth, 151
SMITH, Elizabeth Kennon, 86
SMITH, Emma B., 151
SMITH, Eugene M., 151
SMITH, Florence, 151
SMITH, Frances, 4
SMITH, Granville Ewing, 133
SMITH, H. P. (m), 121
SMITH, Hodge McAdoo (Mrs.), 47
SMITH, Howard, 150
SMITH, Isabella, 121
SMITH, Isadora, 12
SMITH, J. Addiso (D.D.), 134
SMITH, J. Addison (D.D.), 128
SMITH, Jackson, 10
SMITH, James S., 121
SMITH, John, 34
SMITH, John, 86
SMITH, Judyann, 120
SMITH, Katie K., 150
SMITH, Lucian, 151
SMITH, M. LaDelle, 9
SMITH, Nancy, 34
SMITH, Nancy, 5
SMITH, Nancy Mulherin, 10
SMITH, Nicholas P., 61
SMITH, Obadiah, 142
SMITH, Payton Randolph, 4
SMITH, Payton Randolph, 5
SMITH, Robert, 119
SMITH, Robert A., 151
SMITH, Rosia A. B., 121
SMITH, S. B. (Dr.), 142
SMITH, Sam, 191
SMITH, Sam G., 65
SMITH, Samuel H., 142
SMITH, Shirwood W., 121
SMITH, Temperance Jordan, 5
SMITH, Tom, 4
SMITH, Tom, 5
SMITH, Wm. (Sgt.), 119
SMOTHERMAN, James B., 117
SMOTHERMAN, Margaret E., 16
SMOTHERMAN, P. B., 117
SMOTHERMAN, Robert M., 118
SMOTHERMAN, Robert M., 16
SMOTHERMAN, T. S., 136
SMOTHERMAN, Tommie L., 136
SNELL, Felix, 150
SNELL, James H., 110
SNELL, L. J., 110
SNELL, Lucy, 88
SNELL, Mary A. L., 110
SNELL, Sarah Jane, 87
SNELL, W. T. (Mr.), 110
SORSBURG, Henry, 63
SORSBURG, Sarah, 63
SPAIN, D. S., 147
SPAIN, David Sneed, 89
SPAIN, David Sneed, 90
SPAIN, David Sneed, 90
SPAIN, Delvina Jane, 89
SPAIN, Eliza Green, 89
SPAIN, Eliza Green, 89
SPAIN, Eliza Green, 90
SPAIN, Elizabeth Geneva, 89
SPAIN, Elizabeth Geneva, 90
SPAIN, George L., 89
SPAIN, John P., 90
SPAIN, John Peterson, 89
SPAIN, John Peterson, 90
SPAIN, John Peterson, 90
SPAIN, John W., 89
SPAIN, John W. (Jack), 90
SPAIN, Malissa P., 89
SPAIN, Mary A., 147
SPAIN, Mary Alice, 89
SPAIN, Mary Alice, 90
SPAIN, Mary Ann, 89
SPAIN, Mary Ann, 90
SPAIN, Mary Ann, 90
SPAIN, Mary McClaren, 90
SPAIN, Matilda C., 89
SPAIN, Matilda C., 90
SPAIN, Milly, 90
SPAIN, Nancy Edney, 89
SPAIN, Nancy Edney, 90
SPAIN, Samuel Stephen, 90
SPAIN, Sara, 90
SPAIN, Sara, 90
SPAIN, Sara (Bond), 89
SPAIN, Sarah Eleanor, 89
SPAIN, Sarah Eleanor, 90
SPAIN, Sion W., 89
SPAIN, Stephen S., 90
SPAIN, Stephen Samucl, 89
SPAIN, Thomas, 89
SPEAR, Elizabeth, 10
SPENCE, Sarah J., 16
STIMPSON, Dr., 60
STIMPSON, Rachiel, 60
STOCKIRD, Elvira A., 41
STOCKIRD, Francis J., 41
STOCKIRD, James E., 41
STOCKIRD, James E., 41
STOCKIRD, James E., 41
STOCKIRD, Lucy B., 41
STOCKIRD, Lucy B., 41
STOCKIRD, Martha C., 41
STOCKIRD, Mary Ann, 41
STOCKIRD, Mattie C., 40
STOCKIRD, Nancy F., 41
STOCKIRD, Thomas A., 41
STOCKIRD, Wm. F., 41
STODDARD, Anna, 28
STODDARD, D. M. (Rev.), 28
STONE, Suzanna, 33
STONE, ____ (m), 33
STONEMAN, Maj. Gen., 186
STONEMAN, Maj. Gen., 187
SUBLETT, Dave, 175
SUBLETT, Mr., 190
SULLIVAN, Artie, 23
SULLIVAN, John, 23
SUMPTER, Arabella Smith, 116
SUMPTER, Volney (Dr.), 116
SUTTLE, M. J., 37
SWAIN, Bluford B., 133
SWEPSON, Sarah, 86
TATUM, Alfred C. (Rev.), 93
TATUM, Alfred Carroll (Rev.), 94
TATUM, Ann Eliza N., 93
TATUM, Ann Eliza N., 94
TATUM, Edwin Alfred, 93
TATUM, Edwin Alfred, 94
TATUM, Eliza Hatton, 93
TATUM, Emma Charlotte, 93
TATUM, George Donnell, 93
TATUM, I. D., 94
TATUM, Jane Franklin, 93
TATUM, Jane Franklin, 94
TATUM, Julia Milton, 93
TATUM, Martha C., 93
TATUM, Martha Caledonia, 93
TATUM, Mary M., 93
TATUM, Mary Mason, 93
TATUM, Nuborn Mcadow?
(Rev.), 93
TATUM, Willie Hickerson, 93
TATUM, Willie Hickerson, 94
TATUM, Wm. Ivy, 93
TATUM, Wm. Ivy, 94
TAYLOR, B. B., 11
TAYLOR, B. B., 152
TAYLOR, B. B. (Mr.), 198
TAYLOR, Benjain B., 18
TAYLOR, Benjamin, 95
TAYLOR, Benjamin, 96
TAYLOR, Benjamin B., 97
TAYLOR, David A., 51
TAYLOR, Eleanor, 115
TAYLOR, Eliza, 97
TAYLOR, Eliza Branch, 152
TAYLOR, Eliza Branch, 97
TAYLOR, Eugene A. (Rev.), 134
TAYLOR, Eugene A. (Rev., D.D.), 127
TAYLOR, Fanny, 95
TAYLOR, Fanny, 95
TAYLOR, Fanny, 96
TAYLOR, Frances, 97
TAYLOR, Grizzy, 97
TAYLOR, J. T., 152
TAYLOR, James, 95
TAYLOR, James Morrow, 97
TAYLOR, John, 95
TAYLOR, John Joseph, 97
TAYLOR, July Wilmoth, 97
TAYLOR, M. A., 152
TAYLOR, Maggie Maud, 11
TAYLOR, Margaret, 95
TAYLOR, Maria Amandy, 97
TAYLOR, Martha, 95
TAYLOR, Martha, 95
TAYLOR, Martha, 96
TAYLOR, Martha, 96
TAYLOR, Martha Ann, 97
TAYLOR, Martha B., 51
TAYLOR, Mary, 95
TAYLOR, Mary A. Spain, 90
TAYLOR, Mary E. C., 51
TAYLOR, Matilda, 50
TAYLOR, Matilda, 51
TAYLOR, Matthew M., 51
TAYLOR, Minerva A., 152
TAYLOR, Minerva Ann, 18
TAYLOR, Minerva Elizabeth, 18
TAYLOR, Nora, 193
TAYLOR, Nora, 194
TAYLOR, Nora, 195
TAYLOR, Nora, 196
TAYLOR, Permelia, 95
TAYLOR, Permelia, 95
TAYLOR, R. H., 193
TAYLOR, R. H., 194
TAYLOR, R. H., 195
TAYLOR, R. H., 196
TAYLOR, Rbert, 95
TAYLOR, Robert, 152
TAYLOR, Robert, 97
TAYLOR, Robert, 97
TAYLOR, Sallie S., 40
TAYLOR, Sally S., 97
TAYLOR, Sarah, 95
TAYLOR, Sarah, 96
TAYLOR, Sarah Ann, 51

TAYLOR, Simeon, 50
TAYLOR, Simeon, 51
TAYLOR, Stacy, 121
TAYLOR, Susana, 95
TAYLOR, Thomas, 95
TAYLOR, Thomas, 97
TAYLOR, Thomas (II), 96
TAYLOR, Thos., 95
TAYLOR, Thos., 96
TAYLOR, Thos. (I), 96
TAYLOR, W. Carol, 97
TERRY, G. C. (Mrs.), 24
TEXAS, _____, 4
THOMAS, Eliza, 5
THOMAS, Gideon Wiseman, 89
THOMAS, Gideon Wiseman, 90
THOMAS, Mary Ann, 89
THOMAS, Mary Ann, 90
THOMAS, Nancy Eleanor, 89
THOMAS, Nancy Eleanor, 90
THOMAS, Wm., 4
THOMAS, Wm., 5
THOMPSON, Eva, 4
THOMPSON, Eva, 6
THOMPSON, James, 34
THOMPSON, Lee (m), 92
THOMPSON, Mary Jane, 92
THOMPSON, Sally, 191
THOMPSON, Sarah Webb, 34
THOMPSON, Wm. L. (Dr.), 122
TIPLADY, Rebecca, 33
TITTLE, Cynthia, 92
TODD, Henry W., 124
TODD, J. Wendell, 124
TODD, James, 10
TODD, Margaret F., 124
TODD, Sarah, 10
TODD, W. T. (Mrs.), 114
TOLLEY, D. H., 183
TOMPKINS, Sarah Searcy, 80
TRACY, Timothy, 96
TRAVERS, Benjamin, 91
TRAVERS, Jane C., 91
TRAVERS, John A., 91
TRAVERS, Samuel, 91
TRAVERS, Wm., 91
TRAVERS, Wm. jr., 91
TROUSDALE, Bettie, 92
TROUSDALE, Brice, 92
TROUSDALE, Brison, 92
TROUSDALE, Cynthia, 92
TROUSDALE, Elisabeth M., 92
TROUSDALE, Fannie, 92
TROUSDALE, J. K. (m), 92
TROUSDALE, John K., 92
TROUSDALE, Martha J., 92
TROUSDALE, Mary Jane, 92
TROUSDALE, Sarah H., 92
TROUSDALE, Wm. C., 92
TROUSDALE, Zona, 92
TURNER, Ann L., 12
TURNER, Annie Laurie, 114
TURNER, Joe, 114
TURNER, Laura B., 114
TURNER, R. J. (Dr.), 114
TURNER, Robert J., 12
VALENTINE, Mrs., 183
VENABLE, C. D. (Col.), 145
VENABLE, C. D. (Col.), 197
VENABLE, C. D. (Col.), 198

VENIER, Robert Cimmons, 20
VIRGINIA, _____, 4
VOORHIES, Amanda H., 39
WAIR, Eliza, 95
WAIR, Georgia Ann, 95
WAIR, Lenora Louisa, 95
WAIR, Maria Frances, 95
WAIR, Martha Ann, 95
WAIR, Permelia, 95
WAIR, Thomas Henry, 96
WAIR, Thos. H., 95
WAIR, W. K., 96
WAIR, Wm. K., 95
WAIR, Wm. Thomas, 95
WALKER, F. E. (Dr.), 28
WALKER, Hannah, 18
WALKER, Susie, 28
WALLACE, Caroline M., 50
WALTON, Bishop, 104
WALTON, Dorothy, 105
WALTON, Edward, 104
WALTON, Elizabeth, 103
WALTON, Elizabeth, 104
WALTON, Frances, 104
WALTON, Frances, 104
WALTON, George, 103
WALTON, George, 103
WALTON, George, 104
WALTON, George, 105
WALTON, George jr., 105
WALTON, Isaak, 104
WALTON, Jesse, 103
WALTON, Jesse, 104
WALTON, Jesse, 104
WALTON, John, 104
WALTON, John, 104
WALTON, John, 105
WALTON, John B., 103
WALTON, Joseph, 104
WALTON, Judith, 104
WALTON, Judith, 104
WALTON, Martha, 103
WALTON, Martha, 104
WALTON, Mary, 104
WALTON, Mary, 104
WALTON, Mizapena, 104
WALTON, Newell, 104
WALTON, Octavia, 106
WALTON, Patty, 104
WALTON, Polly, 104
WALTON, Rances, 105
WALTON, Rebecca, 104
WALTON, Robert, 103
WALTON, Robert, 104
WALTON, Robert, 105
WALTON, Robert jr., 105
WALTON, Robert sr., 103
WALTON, Robert sr., 104
WALTON, Sally, 105
WALTON, Sherwood, 104
WALTON, Sherwood, 105
WALTON, Simeon, 104
WALTON, Temperance, 103
WALTON, Thomas, 103
WALTON, Thomas, 104
WALTON, Thomas Camber, 105
WALTON, Tillman, 104
WALTON, Wm., 104
WALTON, Wm., 104
WALTON, Wm. Scott, 103

WALTON FAMILY, Original Index to the Family Record, 100
WALTON?, George, 104
WALTON?, George, 104
WALTON?, Joseph Frances, 104
WALTON?, Martha, 104
WALTON?, Robert jr., 104
WALTROP, Polly B., 9
WALTROP, Wm., 9
WARD, Andrew J., 109
WARD, Benjamin A., 107
WARD, Benjamin A., 108
WARD, Best, 50
WARD, Burrell, 107
WARD, Burrell B., 107
WARD, Burwell, 108
WARD, Burwell, 108
WARD, Burwell, 50
WARD, Charles A., 109
WARD, Elizabeth, 50
WARD, Frances C., 109
WARD, Isabella, 109
WARD, Isabella, 109
WARD, James, 108
WARD, James J., 109
WARD, James A., 109
WARD, Jane A., 2
WARD, Josephine, 109
WARD, Louisa, 109
WARD, Martha, 109
WARD, Mary B., 107
WARD, Mary B., 108
WARD, Mary B., 50
WARD, Mary C., 107
WARD, Mary C., 108
WARD, Mary E., 109
WARD, Mary J., 109
WARD, Mary J. Leath, 109
WARD, Matilda Jane, 108
WARD, Nancy E., 107
WARD, Nancy L., 108
WARD, Raiford, 107
WARD, Raiford C., 108
WARD, Robert M., 107
WARD, Robert McGulkin, 108
WARD, Sarah Ann, 108
WARD, Tennessee Texana, 107
WARD, Wm. D., 108
WARD, Wm. E., 109
WARREN, Bettie, 28
WARREN, Betty, 34
WARREN, Catherine, 153
WARREN, Elizabeth, 82
WARREN, Julia A., 37
WARREN, Wm., 153
WARRICK, E. (f), 33
WASHINGTON, Betty, 53
WASHINGTON, George, 53
WATKINS, Horace, 154
WATKINS, Robert (Col.), 105
WATKINS, Sally, 105
WEAKLEY, Josephine (Mrs.), 99
WEATHERLY, Artemesia M., 121
WEATHERLY, Jas. M., 121
WEATHERLY, Mary A., 121
WENDEL, D. D., 129
WENDEL, D. D., 131

WENDEL, David, 129
WENDEL, David, 135
WENDEL, David D., 129
WENDEL, David Deaderick, 135
WENDEL, Emma Claiborne James, 129
WENDEL, James (Dr.), 130
WENDEL, Jane Caroline, 130
WENDEL, Robert Searcy (Dr.), 129
WENDEL, S. J., 129
WENDEL, S. J., 131
WENDEL, Sally Hudson, 129
WENDEL, Sarah Jane, 130
WENDEL, Walter K., 131
WENDEL, Walter K., 133
WHEATON, Dr., 61
WHEATON, Lavinia, 61
WHEELER, E. D. (Dr.), 25
WHEELER, Margaret Angeline, 25
WHITE, Betsy, 61
WHITE, James J. B. (Col.), 61
WHITE, John, 20
WHITE, Mary, 20
WHITE, Peter, 82
WHITE, Winefred, 82
WHITUS, Julia A. F., 16
WHITUS, Robert L., 16
WILBURN, N. Y. (Mrs.), 107
WILKINSON, Lavinia Kelzer, 155
WILKINSON, Nannie L., 112
WILKINSON, W. E. (m), 155
WILKINSON, Wm. A., 112
WILLIAMS, Capt., 181
WILLIAMS, David S., 155
WILLIAMS, James B., 10
WILLIAMS, Leatha, 155
WILLIAMS, Lucy, 155
WILLIAMS, Mahala Elizabeth, 83
WILLIAMS, Nanie V., 16
WILLIAMS, Sarah V., 10
WILLIAMS, Stacy, 155
WILLIAMS, W. D. (m), 155
WILLIAMS, W. H., 139
WILLIAMS, W. M., 155
WILLIAMS, Wavie G., 155
WILLIAMS, Wm. D., 155
WILLIAMSON, Catharine Raney, 110
WILLIAMSON, Charlotte, 110
WILLIAMSON, Charlotte, 110
WILLIAMSON, John H., 110
WILLIAMSON, Martha Jane, 110
WILLIAMSON, Mary Ann, 110
WILLIAMSON, Nancy, 136
WILLIAMSON, R. W. (m), 110
WILLIAMSON, Richard T., 110
WILLIAMSON, Richard Thomas, 110
WILLIAMSON, Richard W., 110
WILLIAMSON, Richard W., 110
WILLIAMSON, Sarah, 110
WILLIAMSON, Sarah, 110
WILLIAMSON, Thos. Daniel,

WILLIAMSON, Thos., 110
WILLIAMSON, Thos. Daniel, 110
WILSON, Dock, 196
WILSON, Eliza P., 112
WILSON, John R. M.D., 112
WILSON, Sallie, 194
WILSON, Samuel, 119
WINGO, Eliza, 120
WINGO, Jno. Wm., 120
WINGO, Thos. R., 120
WINSTON, Ann, 62
WODEHOUSE, Elizabeth, 53
WOOD, Louisa Ann, 72
WOOD, Marguerite Nugent, 72
WOOD, Walter K., 72
WOOD, Walter K. (Mrs.), 72
WOOD, Walter K. (Mrs.), 73
WOOD, Wandena Nugent, 72
WOODFIN, E. W., 154
WOODFIN, Hannah, 154
WOODFIN, J. H., 154
WOODFIN, James, 154
WOODFIN, Jane, 154
WOODFIN, Mariah, 154
WOODFIN, Nicholas, 154
WOODFIN, Samuel, 154
WOODFIN, Thomas M., 154
WOODFIN, _____ (m), 154
WOODFIN CEMETERY, , 154
WOODS, John (Maj.), 134
WOODS, Susan, 96
WRATHER, Fanny Short, 82
WRAY, C. C., 138
WRIGHT, Bessie King, 57
WYNNS, Susan, 68
WYNNS, Thomas (Gen.), 68
YANDELL, Catherine M., 81
YANDELL, Wm. M. (Dr.), 81
YANSEY, Bartlet, 20
YARBROUGH, Joseph, 103
YARBROUGH, Temperance, 103
YEARGAN, C. E., 117
YEARGAN, Clinton Edwin, 18
YEARGAN, Hattie Glenn Arnold, 18
YEARGAN, Mary Annah, 18
YEARGAN, Mary Elizabeth, 18
YEARGAN, Rebecca, 6
YEARGAN, Robert Andrew, 18
YEARGEN, C. E. (Mrs.), 18
YEARGEN, Mary S., 86
YEARGEN, Rebecca, 4
YEATMAN, Mrs., 62
YOUNG, Hiram, 144
YOUNG, Judith L., 144
YOUREE, Dolly, 46
YOUREE, Dorothy, 157
YOUREE, Elizabeth, 157
YOUREE, F. H. (m), 157
YOUREE, Martha J., 46
YOUREE, Nancy S., 157
_____, Barbara, 33
_____, Jane, 33
_____, Lenora Lou, 95

www.ingramcontent.com/pod-product-compliance
Lightning Source LLC
Chambersburg PA
CBHW080920180426
43192CB00040B/2557